The Theban Plays

Sophocles

The Theban Plays

Oedipus the King
Oedipus at Colonus
Antigone

Translated, with Notes and an Introduction
by Ruth Fainlight and Robert J. Littman

The Johns Hopkins University Press
Baltimore

The Johns Hopkins University Press
2715 North Charles Street
Baltimore, Maryland 21218-4363
www.press.jhu.edu

Library of Congress Cataloging-in-Publication Data

Sophocles.
    [Selections. English. 2008]
    The Theban plays : Oedipus the king, Oedipus at Colonus, Antigone /
Sophocles; translated, with notes and an introduction, by Ruth Fainlight and
Robert J. Littman.
        p. cm.
    Includes bibliographical references.
    ISBN-13: 978-0-8018-9133-5 (hardcover : alk. paper)
    ISBN-13: 978-0-8018-9134-2 (pbk. : alk. paper)
    ISBN-10: 0-8018-9133-7 (hardcover : alk. paper)
    ISBN-10: 0-8018-9134-5 (pbk. : alk. paper)
    1. Sophocles—Translations into English. 2. Oedipus (Greek mythology)—
Drama. 3. Antigone (Greek mythology)—Drama. I. Fainlight, Ruth. II. Littman,
Robert J., 1943– III. Title.
    PA4414.A2F33 2008
    880—dc22   2008022654

A catalog record for this book is available from the British Library.

*Special discounts are available for bulk purchases of this book. For more information,
please contact Special Sales at 410-516-6936 or specialsales@press.jhu.edu.*

The Johns Hopkins University Press uses environmentally friendly book materials,
including recycled text paper that is composed of at least 30 percent post-
consumer waste, whenever possible. All of our book papers are acid-free, and our
jackets and covers are printed on paper with recycled content.

To Robert Graves

Contents

Preface

From my schooldays I have been enthralled by the stories of Oedipus and Antigone, and over the years have seen wonderful theatrical productions of Sophocles' Theban Plays; but not being able to read them in the original language meant that I certainly could not have contemplated this translation without the invaluable—indeed, essential—help of my collaborator, Robert Littman. As well as having his almost word-for-word "crib" and line-by-line notes to refer to, in order to deepen my sense of the potentialities of the text for my own work I also studied several other versions. First I would read what he had sent me, then turn to the others, from the correct and satisfying Victorian version by Jebb to the excellent but not very strict contemporary one by Fagles. Finally I would go back to Littman's, read it again, and begin. It was hard but thrilling work. Because Littman teaches at the University of Hawaii and I live in England, most of our exchanges were by e-mail. But we met a few times a year in London during the two to three years the job took, because no matter how much can be dealt with by e-mail, there is no substitute for direct discussion to arrive at agreement on every nuance of meaning. Our intention was to produce a version accurate enough to be acceptable for teaching which could also stand as a piece of literature. We hope we have succeeded.

I am grateful to Robert Littman for suggesting this project, to theater scholar Susan Solomon for arranging a very useful dramatic reading of *Oedipus the King* by a group of skilled actors, and to my husband, Alan Sillitoe.

Ruth Fainlight

The works of Sophocles, which portray a world twenty-five hundred years old, have been translated for more than two thousand years. Each generation produces translations in the idiom of its time. In earlier centuries, poets steeped in Greek and Latin wrote elegant translations that were suitable to their age. These translations are inaccessible today because of their complex and old-fashioned language. But few of today's poets know Greek, so contemporary translations of Sophocles have generally been made by Greek scholars who are not poets. As a result, while many accurate translations are available, they do not capture the beauty of Sophocles' poetry. By combining my skills as a classical scholar and the skills of a poet, Ruth Fainlight, this new translation aspires to be both a major work of poetry and an accurate translation in contemporary words. The translation is particularly useful for anyone teaching the plays because it follows the line numbers of the original Greek and stays as close as possible to the Greek text.

The Greek text used was *Sophoclis Fabulae*, edited by H. Lloyd-Jones and N. G. Wilson (Oxford: Clarendon Press, 1990), with occasional references to other editions. The line numbers of our translation coincide with the line numbers of the standard Greek text, except in the case of the choruses, where we have used block numbering. Whenever possible we have kept an equivalent number of lines to the Greek choruses, but in some cases we have a line or two more or less.

I am immensely grateful to my teachers of Greek tragedy, David Coffin, of Phillips Exeter Academy, where I first read *Oedipus the King* in Greek, and Eduard Fraenkel and Sir Maurice Bowra, at Oxford University. Many colleagues and friends deserve thanks for reading the manuscript in various stages and for their useful comments. These include Michael Hoff, Saundi Schwartz, Kathryn Hoffmann, and Susan Solomon. Brook Ellis prepared the map. Ruth and I would like to thank those at the Johns Hopkins University Press who encouraged and aided our project: the anonymous reader for the Press who provided valuable criticisms that improved the manuscript; Michael Lonegro, Humanities Editor; and copyeditor Barbara Lamb. I am grateful to my wife, Bernice Littman, for her advice and encouragement.

Robert J. Littman

Introduction

Greek culture and civilization reached new heights in science, literature, philosophy, and art in the fifth century BC. This century saw the beginnings of Greek medicine, the birth of new genres of literature such as history and tragedy, the development of philosophy, and the origin of Athenian democracy. Two of the most influential philosophers in Western civilization, Socrates and Plato, were fifth-century Athenians. Greek art advanced the notion of perspective and set the canons of sculpture that would dominate Western civilization. Architecture reached its crowning achievement in the Parthenon at Athens. The classical model shaped future Western notions of space and form. Despite their enormous cultural and intellectual achievement, like most premodern societies, the Greek city-states were a brutal place, where a large majority of the population were slaves. In the fifth century Athens labeled itself a democracy, but less than a quarter of the population had the franchise. Local city-state government functioned well, but the cities were constantly quarreling, and Greece had no political unity until Philip II and Alexander the Great of Macedon impressed it from outside in the fourth century. Our notions of the great democracy of Athens are a result of idealizations of the Greek city-state made by philosophers and intellectuals like Aristotle rather than the reality of that institution.

Greek culture spread through the eastern Mediterranean and the Near East in the fourth century BC, when Alexander the Great conquered Greece and the Persian Empire. In the western Mediterranean, Greek colonists, beginning in the eighth century, settled in southern France, Spain, and much of southern Italy and Sicily. When the Romans expanded southward through Italy and Sicily at the beginning of the third century, they conquered and absorbed a large Greek population. Finally, in 146 BC Rome made Greece a Roman province. This influx of Greeks and Greek culture led the poet Horace to say, at the end of the first century BC, "Graecia capta ferum victorem cepit et artes intulit agresti Latio" (Greece, though captured, captured its fierce captor and brought the arts to uncultured Latium) (*Epistles* 2.1.156). When the Roman Empire expanded and conquered most of southern Europe and Great Britain, the Near East, and North Africa, Greco-Roman civilization spread throughout the Mediterranean and Western Europe. North and South America were colonized from Europe by the descendants of the Romans. Today, Western civilization can be described as the heir of the Greeks and Romans.

For that reason, the classical period of Athens is of fundamental importance to the history of our culture and life. The genre of Greek tragedy developed and became the basis of our Western theater. Greek drama, read and studied since it was first written, has been a part of the school curriculum and world culture for much of the past twenty-five hundred years.

Greek Religion and Theater
Religion, Crops, and Fertility

Greek theater was closely connected to Greek religion. In turn, religion, both in its myths and in its rituals, was tied to agriculture. The fertility not only of humans but also of livestock and crops was essential to the life of the city. If human fertility failed, there would not be enough people to work the land and defend it. Since crop or livestock or population infertility brought weakness, famine, and death, fertility rites were employed in virtually all societies to ensure the birth of children and the growth of crops. Much of religion is concerned with the maintenance and increase of that fertility. For the ancient Greeks, the proper performance of rites ensured the favor of the gods and the continued prosperity of society.

Like the rest of the ancient Mediterranean, Athens raised three main crops: grain, olives, and grapes. Each of these was essential to the maintenance of life and each had a patron deity, Demeter for grain, Athena for the olive, and Dionysus for wine. Each of these three divinities had cult worship, a temple, and a major religious festival. For Athena, it was the Panathenaic Festival, for Demeter the Eleusinian Mysteries, and for Dionysus the Great Dionysia.

The center of the worship of Demeter was in Eleusis, six miles from Athens. A cult that flourished there, called the Eleusinian Mysteries, linked the annual regeneration of the land with the emergence of Demeter's daughter, Persephone, from the Underworld. Eventually, the Eleusinian Mysteries became a Panhellenic cult of immortality.

Athena was not only the goddess of the olive but also the patron goddess of Athens, after whom the city was named. Her main shrine was on the Acropolis, the temple to Athena Parthenos, the Parthenon. The Panathenaic Festival, the annual observance of Athena's birthday, consisted of a lavish procession from the northern part of the city through the agora, or marketplace, to the Parthenon, with sacrifices conducted along the route. The procession culminated in the dedication of a newly woven robe to the enormous thirty-eight-foot-high gold, silver, and ivory statue of Athena inside the Parthenon.

Dionysus, the god of wine, was especially important to the Greeks and to our understanding of Greek theater. Wine was not simply a casual intoxicant, but rather a necessity for human life. Because the water supply was often impure in Greek cities, the Greeks realized, perhaps by observation, that mixing water with wine led to fewer diseases. Hence, the Greeks rarely drank plain water, but regularly drank a mixture of wine and water, usually in a proportion of three parts water to one part wine. The fertility of the vines was therefore of primary concern for the Athenian population and was overseen by Dionysus. According to myth, satyrs—each half man and half goat with phallus erect—accompanied Dionysus in his revelries, as well as ecstatic women, known as Bacchants or maenads, who had thrown off the constraints of civilization to embrace their nonrational side. Dressed in fawn skins and each carrying a wand, called a *thyrsus,* the maenads roamed the mountains with Dionysus. In Athens the main festival to celebrate the worship of Dionysus was the Great Dionysia, which took place in late March and early April, the time of the winter harvest. In the ancient world many fertility festivals were conducted at that time of year, and many cultures, including the Babylonians, made March the beginning of the year. The feasts of Ishtar and Tammuz, Aphrodite and Adonis, and later Easter, with stories of the fertility goddess and the dying young god who was resurrected after three days, all occurred in March, as did the crucifixion and resurrection of Jesus Christ.

Myth and Ritual

All religion consists of two parts: the rituals, which are the rites that are performed; and the myths, the stories that explain those rites. As sacred histories, myths explain how the present world came into being and the relationship of the present generation to that world. These sacred histories describe a supernatural presence in the universe, the interaction between the supernatural and the natural, and between the gods and man.

Origins of Greek Tragedy

Greek tragedy originated in conjunction with the festival of the Great Dionysia and developed as an integral part of religious worship. As part of the earliest celebrations, hymns, called dithyrambs, were sung in praise of Dionysus. The next stage of development was tragedies. The word *tragedy,* or *tragoidia,* means "goat-song." We do not know why tragedy got this name. One theory is that a goat had something to do with the rituals, perhaps as a sacrifice. Another possible connection is that Greek tragedy was associated with Dionysus, and among his entourage was the half-man, half-goat satyr.

Dionysus was also worshipped at another festival, called the Lenaean (the Dionysia at Lenaea), which took place in January/February. The name

derived from *lene*, another term for maenad. Comedies rather than tragedies were usually presented there, including many of the comedies of
Aristophanes, although we do know of tragedies performed in the years
419–416.

An Athenian named Thespis, who lived at the end of the sixth century
BC, was thought to have been the originator of tragedy [Aristotle *Poetics*
4.1–6 (1449A.15) in Themistium *Orationes* 26, p. 316]. He was a singer of
dithyrambs who added an actor separate from the chorus to the performance. This actor spoke a prologue and set speeches and changed parts by
using various masks. The ancient sources record that Thespis was the first
winner of the dramatic contest at the Great Dionysia in 534 BC.

The Great Dionysia

People from the surrounding region of Attica flocked to the city for the festival, which lasted five to seven days. At the center of the worship were dramatic presentations of tragedy and comedy, as well as dithyrambs. These
performances, consecrated to the god Dionysus, were accounts of Greek
myth, the interaction of gods and men. As such, they were part of the sacred
history of the Greeks and were believed in, much in the same way that
Christian society believes in Jesus. Greek tragedy for the Greek audience
was the equivalent of the medieval Passion play in Europe, in which the life
and death of Jesus were portrayed on the stage. To the Greeks of the fifth
century, the Greek heroes and Greek gods were beings as real as their own
historical personages. Agamemnon, the leader of the Greek forces at Troy,
Heracles, who performed his twelve labors, and Pericles, the ruler of Athens, were all historical figures with the same authenticity. No one would
question the historical existence of Oedipus. For the Greeks, the gods and
goddesses existed and formed an inextricable link with humankind, with
whom they interacted; Zeus and Dionysus were real. Those who failed to
believe or differed in their beliefs could be exiled or executed.

Impiety was a capital offense in Athens. In 415, on the eve of the depar-
ture of the Athenian army to attack Sicily, throughout the city most of the
hermae—stone statues of Hermes with an erect phallus—had their phal-
luses knocked off. The impiety trials that followed found that people had
also profaned the rites of the Eleusinian Mysteries of Demeter. As a result,
numerous individuals were executed, and the general of the Sicilian expedition, Alcibiades, faced with arrest, fled into exile. The most famous person
executed for impiety was the philosopher Socrates, put to death by the
Athenians in 399. Although there were political reasons behind Socrates'
prosecution, he was convicted of impiety because he either believed in gods
other than those of the city or did not believe in the gods at all.

The Athenian tyrant Peisistratus formalized the Great Dionysia as a state religious celebration at the end of the sixth century. The festival was both a civic and a religious function, organized by the state and paid for by a form of taxation whereby a wealthy individual, called a *choregos*, was selected as the producer of the chorus for each set of plays. Three playwrights were chosen to present tragedies, and five to present comedies. Each of the three tragic authors wrote four plays, a tetralogy, consisting of a trilogy and a fourth short burlesque, called a satyr play, to be presented in a theater, equipped with wooden benches on the slopes of the Acropolis, the religious center of the city.

The Preliminary Procession

In the preliminary procession of the Great Dionysia the city's *ephebes* (eighteen- to twenty-year-old male citizens) escorted a statue of Dionysus Eleuthereus to a temple on the south side of the Acropolis, where a sacrifice was offered. The myth underlying this first part of the ritual was the tale that when Dionysus arrived at Eleutherai, the king and his daughters rejected him. In anger and retribution, he punished the males with priapism, a permanent painful erection, often associated with satyrs. On consulting the Oracle of Apollo, they were told that to be cured, they should take the statue of Dionysus to Athens and conduct a sacrifice in the sacred precincts of Dionysus. The procession, with a trumpeter at its head, was followed by maidens leading a sacrificial bull. The statue of Dionysus was placed in the theater, and the performances were conducted in front of it.

The *Proagon*

The festival began with a ritual purification of the theater and a libation of wine made by the Ten Generals of Athens, each of whom was the military leader of one of the ten tribes into which the Athenians were divided. Various citizens were honored, and the annual tribute from the Athenian empire was brought into the theater and displayed for all to see; then those involved in the productions were introduced. Judges were selected to choose the best plays, since prizes were awarded; lots were then drawn for the order of performance.

Dramatic Performances

The performances began on the first day of the festival with a contest of dithyrambs, followed by presentations of tragedies and comedies during the second, third, and fourth days. Each day, often beginning at dawn, one playwright's work was performed, consisting of a trilogy and one satyr play. In the afternoons the comedies were put on stage, a total of five, by five different authors. On the last day the judges selected the winner of the tragedy competition and awarded the author a crown of ivy, a plant sacred to Dionysus. The crown of victory conveyed enormous prestige and honor from the state, in the same way that a crown of wild olive leaves was the prize for a victor in the Olympic games. Even a hundred years later, public inscriptions still recorded the names of the winners in the tragedy contests of the Great Dionysia. An inscription from the fourth century BC on a stone known as the Marmor Parium, or Parian Marble, has preserved a list of some of the prizewinners, year by year from the early fifth century onwards.

Thirty-three Athenian tragedies of the fifth century BC have survived in their entirety. The fragments and titles of the lost plays suggest that almost all the plays were about Greek myth, the sacred religious history of the Greeks. Although based on myths, these dramas could take on moral or even political themes, rather than strictly religious ones. Only very occasionally was a nonmythological subject presented, such as the historical drama *Persians*, by Aeschylus, or the *Sack of Miletus*, by Phrynicus.

The playwright was constrained by the familiar accounts of the myths. Although he might choose variants and embellish some details, he generally would not make up his own story. On the other hand, Greek myth was not monolithic, and many alternate versions existed. For example, in some versions Helen did not go to Troy, but to Egypt. A tragedy about Oedipus would probably include Oedipus killing his father and marrying his mother. But the playwright within that mythological narrative still had great freedom to shape the material. He might concentrate on inherited curses and fate, as Aeschylus did, or, as Sophocles did with the same myth, write a tragedy about knowledge and the difficulty of knowing oneself. This left the playwright free to explore the differing relationships of man to man, man to god, and man to god's laws. Even in the literary hands of the tragedians, these tragedies were sacred histories; they explained the nature of the current world, man and his place in the world, and how man interacted with the gods.

The Production of Plays

Today, on the southern cliff face of the Acropolis in Athens, one can still see the Theater of Dionysus, where Greek tragedy originated. The present structure is the ruin of the Roman rebuilding of the theater in AD 61, which sat 17,000 spectators in sixty-four rows of seats. The Roman reconstruction, in turn, was a rebuilding and expansion of the theater erected by the Athenian statesman Lycurgus, who, in the mid fourth century BC, had replaced the original wooden theater with one of stone. The theater of the sixth and fifth centuries had wooden seats, and possibly some marble ones

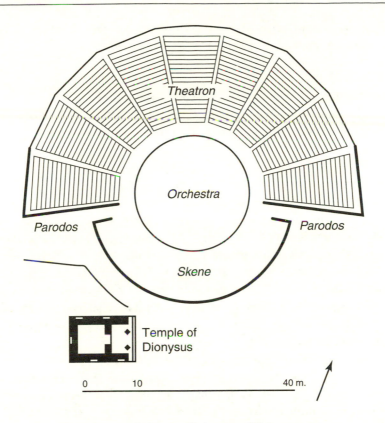

Reconstructed Theater of Dionysus, fifth century BC

in the front for important personages, which could seat perhaps 15,000 to 25,000 people.

The audience sat on cushions or wooden benches in the area known as *theatron* (viewing place), from which our word *theater* derives. In the center was the *orchestra*, or "dancing area," where the chorus performed in song and dance, interacting with the actors on the stage. Certain props, such as an altar (*thymele*), were occasionally placed in the *orchestra*, which was sixty to seventy feet across in the Theater of Dionysus.

At the end of the *orchestra* was a wooden stage, the *skene* (tent), raised two or three steps above the *orchestra*, measuring about twenty-five feet by ten feet. The *skene* acted as the set and was often decorated as a building, such as a palace or a temple, usually containing a set of doors. It had rear access, allowing gods or goddesses and various other characters to appear from a roof or from the sky.

Long ramps for entrances and exits, called *parodos* (passageway) or *eisodos* (entrance) were on either side of the *orchestra*. These could designate a direction from which someone came and went. For example, in *Oedipus at Colonus,* one side would represent the road from Thebes.

The Performance

Male Athenian citizens made up the bulk of the audience, along with resident foreigners and visitors to Athens. There is much debate on whether women other than courtesans and female slaves attended the plays.

Actors

The chorus and actors, the dancers, and all participants were males. Women's roles were played by men dressed in female masks and robes. When tragedy first developed, the performance consisted of a chorus, perhaps of twelve individuals, which was enlarged by Sophocles to fifteen. The earliest tragedies used a single actor. According to Aristotle, the tragedian Aeschylus added a second actor, and Sophocles added a third, along with scene painting. This small number of performers meant that actors had to take on more than one role. Although often more than three characters appear in a play, at no time will you find more than three speaking actors on stage at the same time, not including the chorus.

The actors, none of whom was a professional, wore masks made of linen or cork. These masks allowed ease in changing character: light skin color indicated a woman, dark a man; dark hair and a beard signified a young man; white hair an old man. The masks remained fixed, so that facial expressions were not possible. The actors also wore elaborate costumes, including thick boots and gloves. Since much of the audience was far away from the actors, exaggerated gestures were used for visibility. There were only a few stage props, such as a walking staff or a garland.

The Chorus

Every Greek tragedy had a chorus, which represented some group, such as Theban Elders in *Oedipus the King* and *Antigone,* and Elders of Colonus in *Oedipus at Colonus.* Individual members of the chorus were unnamed, anonymous individuals who were addressed either in the singular or in the plural. They often commented on the actions of the characters, and at times, especially during the last lines of the play, acted as the voice of the poet. Generally, they did not participate in the action, with some exceptions, such as in *Oedipus at Colonus.* In that play, the chorus tries to stop Creon from seizing Antigone.

Chanting in unison, the chorus presented its dialogue in the form of songs, while dancing, often to the accompaniment of a drum and a flutelike instrument called an *aulos.* Choral songs had several functions: to provide interludes between episodes, to break up long dialogue sections, and to create scene transitions. The chorus had a leader (coryphaeus) who served as its spokesman.

Greek tragedy was written in meter, consisting of rhythmical patterns of long and short syllables. In contrast, English meter consists of stressed and unstressed syllables. Unlike some English poetry, Greek verse did not use rhyme. The chorus employed a variety of complicated meters, at times unique to each choral ode. These choral odes consisted of two sets of stanzas, called the *strophe* and the *antistrophe*. Actors tended to use a meter called iambic trimeter (alternating short and long syllables). Occasionally, to indicate rapid action, anapests (two short and one long syllable) were used. The speeches of actors would be long (*rhesis*) or short (*stichomythia*) alternating lines.

Virtually no violent action took place on the stage. Jocasta hanged herself and Oedipus blinded himself off stage. A messenger would come on stage to describe to the audience what violence had transpired. Words in song, rather than action, conveyed the drama.

Tragedy as a Civic Institution

Tragedy developed as an institution in Athens at the very time Athenian democracy was emerging, at the end of the sixth century and the start of the fifth century BC. While plays began as religious dramas, throughout the fifth century they took on themes of civic issues, such as the formation of the court of the Areopagus and the relationship of bloodguilt and private vengeance to the rule of civil law, as portrayed in Aeschylus' *Oresteia*. Among other themes, *Antigone* dealt with the relationship of familial obligations to the laws of the state. Many plays dealt with the fall of a tyrannical or an aristocratic figure. Often choruses took the role of townspeople or the general populace. "The heroic figures . . . not only come to life before the eyes of the spectators, but furthermore, through their discussions with the chorus or with one another, they become the subjects of a debate. They are, in a way, under examination before the public. . . . In the new framework of tragic interplay, then the hero has ceased to be a model. He has become, both for himself and for others, a problem" (Vernant and Vidal-Naquet 1988, 24–25).

The democratic audience of fifth-century Athens viewed itself in comparison with an aristocratic, predemocratic world. That democratic world was then elucidated by the contrast with the world presented on the stage (Wiles 1997, 209). Tragedy thus allowed the Athenian audience to confront its heroic values and religious representations in comparison with developing civil law in Athens. The myths presented on the stage dealt with societies based on kinship that were completely dominated by aristocratic leaders of the kinship group, with little regard for the average citizen. Drama thus became a mirror for the developing social and civic institutions and tensions of Athens. The city's Dionysia festival gave a special license to tragedy to display images of society collapsing (Goldhill 1990). The conflicts explored in many of these tragedies mirrored those that the private individual and Athens were facing. This allowed Athenian dramatists to examine universal themes that confronted not only Athens but also societies throughout history. Consequently, many issues raised by Greek tragedy, still faced today, have contributed to the survival, adaptation, and performance of these plays even in the twenty-first century.

The festival of the Great Dionysia, where plays were presented, originated as a purely Athenian religious fertility festival. However, as Athens grew into a dominant political power in the Greek world during the fifth century BC, the festival took on greater political, economic, and civic importance. Athens started the century as a city-state that galvanized dozens of other cities to fight the Persians and organized the Delian League. By the middle of the century Athens had transformed this league into the Athenian empire. Various events marked the political and military nature of the event. Besides the libations poured by the Ten Generals of Athens, armor was presented to the sons of men killed in battle. In March all the city-states tributary to Athens and members of the Athenian empire had to bring their tribute and publicly display it in the theater during the festival. Other ceremonies, such as the awarding of golden crowns to public benefactors, further demonstrated the civic as well as religious nature of the festival.

The large crowds that gathered from all over Attica and the ships that arrived from abroad made the festival a center of trade and commerce. Thus, Greek drama was a far different institution from our modern theater. It was a cultural, religious, civic, and economic event that was at the very core of the city-state of Athens.

The Theater and Performance Space

In the past several decades, scholars have analyzed Greek tragedy through performance studies, that is, the meaning and use of space occupied by the performance (Wiles 1997, 2000; Lecoq 2001). These studies have contributed to our understanding of what drama meant to the Athenian audience and how that audience interacted with the plays.

Greek theater was a manifestation of a religious popular culture, more like today's rock concerts or football games than today's theater. The theater of Dionysus was on the slopes of the Acropolis, the religious center of the city and a sacred space. The procession of the Great Dionysia came to the ritual center of the community, where the performance took place on the area sacred to and protected by Athena, the patron goddess of Athens. Both the theater and the Temple of Dionysus were part of the precincts of Dionysus. During the performances behind the wooden stage, the audience could see the temple, a reminder of the religious importance of the play.

The Greek theater chorus functioned as narrator of the myth, as a moral guide of the actions, and as the alter ego of a specific character. In this role it was a physical extension of the audience and a link between the drama and the audience. When the actors talked to the chorus, they were also asking the audience for moral approval of their actions. The Greek chorus was not on the same level as the actors, but it had its own performance space. Through its reactions and role as intermediary, it built a link between the public and the heroes in the drama (Lecoq 2001, 132).

The theater was big compared to modern theaters, which accounts for some of the differences between modern and ancient drama. Because of the great length of the *orchestra*, which put the actors at a significant distance from the audience, all the movements of the actors had to be simple and clear. The Greek use of performance space was different from that in modern theater, since it positioned the individual in relation to the group.

Greek theater was viewed in the open, and so there was sensitivity to the environment, the sky, the natural landscape. It was part of the landscape and was constructed with a view plane, in Athens a view of the hills to the southeast and in Delphi, the mountains and sea. The open air of the Greek theater contributed to the immersion of the spectator in the present, the day of the festival. The audience participated in the same sense of space as the characters in the play. In the open air the audience shared in a relationship between them and their environment, which included the gods.

Aristotle and Greek Tragedy

Although modern interpretations of tragedy have paid less attention to the Greek philosopher Aristotle's views, nonetheless, because of his importance in the history of interpretation, his approach must be considered. Aristotle shaped the interpretation of Greek tragedy from the moment he wrote his major work on the subject, *Poetics,* in the fourth century BC. Analyzing tragedy in structural terms, he asserted that it had six components: plot, character, thought, diction, song, and spectacle. He defined tragedy as "an imitation of an action that is serious, complete, and of a certain magnitude; in language embellished with each kind of artistic ornament, the several kinds being found in separate parts of the play; in the form of action, not of narrative; through pity and fear effecting the proper purgation of these emotions" (*Poetics* 7). Aristotle saw tragedy as part of the fundamental order of the universe because it portrayed the uncertainty of what might happen, rather than what has happened. According to Aristotle, the audience developed a cathexis, or emotional connection, with the tragic hero. Then, because the audience suspected the outcome, it anticipated and feared what was going to happen to the hero. When misfortune finally struck, the audience felt pity. Through these emotions the audience came to a catharsis, or "cleansing."

Aristotle further postulated that the hero needed to be of noble birth and character and to have committed a major error, or *hamartia*. *Hamartia*, a term derived from archery, means "to miss the target." This error should arise from some circumstance or attribute of the hero caused by ignorance or human weakness, which would result in a reversal of fortune, a *peripeteia*, and in the downfall of the hero. This *hamartia* was a mistake, but not necessarily a sin or moral failing. A simple accident or an involuntary action might arouse pity, but it would not produce a catharsis for the audience. The hero would come to recognition, *anagnoresis*, or discovery of the events and situation. Often the tragic hero was guilty of *hubris*, which could be arrogance toward the gods or one's fellow men. It could consist of wanton violence against another person or the flagrant dishonoring of another. Aristotle considered Sophocles to be the best of Greek dramatists, a judgment that persists to this day.

Sophocles

Sophocles, citizen of Athens and military general, was not a professional writer; nor were any of the Athenian dramatists of the fifth century BC. With Aeschylus (525–456) and Euripides (480–406), his older and younger contemporaries, he formed a triad of the greatest dramatists of ancient Greece. Sophocles' lifetime spanned most of the fifth century. Having witnessed the Persian Wars, the building of the Parthenon, and the birth of the Athenian empire, he lived until the eve of Athens' defeat at the hands of Sparta in the Peloponnesian Wars (431–404). Born in 497/496 [Marmor Parium] or 495/494 [Apollodorus] in Colonus, a rural region of Athens, he died in 406 or 405, at the age of ninety. He was around five years old when the Athenians defeated the Persians at the Battle of Marathon (490). One ancient tradition says that after the Athenians had routed the Persians at Salamis (480), Sophocles, then a talented youth of fifteen or sixteen, led the dances celebrating victory.

We know little of his personal life except that he was born into a prosperous family. His father, Sophillus, was a wealthy armor maker. As an Athenian of letters and wealth, like so many of his class, he led an active political life. He served as *hellenotamias* (Treasurer of the Delian League) in 443–432. Along with Pericles, in 441–440, he was a general, one of the board of ten generals who led the Athenian military. He may also have served as general in the 420s with the Athenian politician Nicias. There is a tradition that in the 420s, when the cult of Asclepius, the god of healing, was introduced into Athens, Sophocles turned his house over for an altar and home for the god until a proper shrine could be built. For this service, he received the title *Dexion* (Receiver of the god). In the aftermath of the destruction of an Athenian army in Sicily in 413 he held the position of *proboulos* (special commissioner), to deal with the political fallout of that monumental defeat. In this role, during the years 412–411, when the city was thrown into upheaval by Athenian oligarchs seizing control of the democracy, Sophocles negotiated with and may have favored the oligarchs. His oligarchic sentiments are confirmed by later tradition (Aristotle *Rhetoric* 3.18.6). In contrast, however, some recent scholarship has argued that his aims and literary production are democratic in nature.

As a member of the aristocracy and governing elite, Sophocles was acquainted with all the major figures of Athens. Besides Pericles, he knew the historian Herodotus, who influenced his works, and perhaps the philosopher Archelaus, a reputed teacher of Socrates.

Many stories, most apocryphal, are found about Sophocles in short biographies written in the third and second centuries BC, long after his death. Most of these anecdotes are of questionable reliability. One account relates that he played Nausicaa in a play now lost, called the *Nausicaa*, but subsequently gave up acting because of a weak voice. Ancient sources mention that he was an accomplished lyre player and that a portrait of him playing the lyre was displayed in the Painted Stoa, a building in the agora containing battle trophies and paintings from Athenian history. Another story relates that when he heard that his younger rival Euripides had died, he dressed his chorus in mourning as a tribute. Greek comedy from the end of the fifth century and the later biographies portrayed him as handsome, pleasant, easygoing, and popular. The comic poet Phrynicus wrote, "Blessed Sophocles, who lived a long life, a happy man and a clever one. He composed many fine tragedies and died well, without enduring any misfortune."

Sophocles married a woman called Nicostratre, who bore him a son, Iophon. A story, probably made up by later biographers, relates how in his old age, Sophocles quarreled with his son, who then tried to declare him

senile in order to get control of his property. At the trial, the poet read lines
from the play he was currently working on, *Oedipus at Colonus* (lines 668–
93), in which he praised Athens. Sophocles won the case.

During his lifetime he wrote 123 plays, of which only 7 survive in their
entirety. Fragments survive of at least 18 plays, including some lines of
Progeny, discovered in 2005. His first production was in 468, and his last
for which we can fix a date was in 409 (*Philoctetes*). His final tragedy,
Oedipus at Colonus, was produced posthumously by his grandson, in 401.
He won the first prize at the Greater Dionysia eighteen times, including for
Antigone. One late source, the Suda, attributes twenty-four victories to him,
but may have included victories at the Lenaean festival. His greatest play,
Oedipus the King, only won second prize.

When he presented his first play, now lost, in 468, he defeated Aeschylus and won first prize. Of his surviving seven plays, the dates for only two
are certain: *Philoctetes* in 409 and *Oedipus at Colonus* in 401. The dates of
the others are conjectural and highly uncertain. The bulk of scholarly opinion is that *Ajax* is an early work, although some place it in the 430s and
420s; the *Women of Trachis* has been dated from the 450s to the 420s;
Antigone from the 440s to the 430s, and *Oedipus the King* to the 430s and
420s, while *Electra* was possibly written between 420 and 410.

History of the Texts

Sophocles and his plays were immensely popular during his lifetime. The
tradition of the Great Dionysia allowed a single performance of each play.
But in the fourth century his plays, along with those of Aeschylus and
Euripides, began to be performed on a regular basis. Sometime between
338 and 326, the Athenian orator Lycurgus passed a decree that an official
copy of all the plays by Aeschylus, Sophocles, and Euripides be made and
that henceforth, all productions of the plays should conform to this official
text. We next hear about the text of Sophocles in connection with the great
library at Alexandria, founded in the third century BC by Ptolemy I, the
Macedonian ruler of Egypt. One of the goals of the library was to acquire,
classify, and edit the works of Greek poets, as well as other authors. Ptolemy
III Euergetes (247–222) arranged to borrow the official copy of Aeschylus,
Sophocles, and Euripides from Athens for the ostensible purpose of copy-
ing it for the library. He left a deposit of fifteen talents, equivalent to mil-
lions of dollars in today's money. Indeed, he had the works copied, but
when it came time for him to return the originals, he sent the Athenians the
copies, telling them that they should keep the deposit and that he would
keep the originals. This official Athenian copy became the basis of the
editions prepared by Aristophanes of Byzantium (ca. 257–180 BC). Others

in Egypt continued the editing of Sophocles. Aristarchus (ca. 216–144 BC), the librarian of the library of Alexandria, wrote a commentary, and in the first century BC Didymus Chalcenterus (ca. 63 BC–AD 10) composed a comprehensive edition.

At some period, probably around the third century AD or slightly thereafter, a collection was made of seven plays of Aeschylus, seven of Sophocles, and ten of Euripides. The choice was probably based on those plays most popular at that time. The other plays gradually were no longer copied, and generally only these selections of Sophocles and Aeschylus were saved. Because of Euripides' great popularity, besides the selection of ten plays, nine others are extant. Fragments of numerous other plays have survived in quotations in other ancient authors and from papyrus fragments, mostly from Egypt. The three earliest currently existing manuscripts of Sophocles are dated from the ninth to the twelfth centuries AD. The most important is the tenth-century Laurentius (32,9), referred to with the abbreviation L, from the Laurentian Library in Florence. The printed Greek texts of Sophocles began in 1502 with the Aldine edition, printed in Venice. Modern texts are based on these medieval manuscripts, as well as on seventeen papyrus fragments, one as early as the first century BC. The standard edition of the Greek text of Sophocles is the Oxford Classical Text, *Sophoclis Fabulae*, edited by H. Lloyd-Jones and N. G. Wilson, Oxford, 1990.

The City of Thebes
Politics

The Greek city of Thebes was the setting for the story of Oedipus and his family. This Thebes should not be confused with the Egyptian city of the same name. The Greek city was the habitual enemy of Athens. During the Persian Wars, the Thebans allied with many Greek city-states to fight against an invading Persian army at the battle of Thermopylae, in 480 BC. However, shortly after the battle they changed sides and joined with the Persians to fight against Athens and Sparta.

Thebans fought side by side with Persia against most of the rest of Greece at the battle of Plataea in 479, where they were defeated. Later in the century Thebes was drawn into the struggles of Sparta against Athens for control of Greece. At one point Athens conquered and occupied Thebes (457–447). During the Peloponnesian Wars (431–404), when Athens fought a war against Sparta, enveloping the entire Greek world, Thebes found itself an ally of Sparta. When Sparta vanquished Athens in 404, Thebes pressed for the complete destruction of the city, which would have included the execution of the men and the enslavement of the women and children—the very thing Athens had done to the conquered population of the island of Melos in 416. With this political background the Athenians watched Sophocles' plays about Oedipus and Thebes.

Myths

Thebes held an important place in Greek mythology, since the mother of Dionysus came from this city. Its foundation myth centered on a brother and sister, Cadmus and Europa. Zeus, having assumed the form of a bull, abducted and raped Europa. She was not the last of Cadmus' family to fall prey to the depredations of the gods. While Cadmus was searching for Europa, he journeyed to Delphi, where the Oracle of Apollo told him to abandon his search, find a certain cow, follow it, and then found a city where the cow stopped walking. Cadmus obeyed Apollo. But when the cow stopped, and Cadmus was about to sacrifice it to Athena, a dragon appeared and disrupted the ceremony. Cadmus slew the dragon, and then, following Athena's commands, sowed the dragon's teeth in the soil. Men sprouted up from the dragon's teeth, full grown and armed for battle. Cadmus threw a stone in their midst, which precipitated a fight. Only five men survived, and they became the ancestors of the aristocracy of Thebes. Since the dragon was sacred to Ares, Cadmus was punished by a year of servitude, at the end of which he married Harmonia, the daughter of Ares and Aphrodite.

Having raped Cadmus' sister, Zeus now turned his attentions to the next generation, Cadmus' daughter Semele. She became enamored of Zeus, who soon got her with child. She begged him to come to her in his real form, but he refused. She continually cajoled him until he finally gave in. Appearing, throwing thunderbolts and lightening, he frightened her to death. To save the child, Zeus cut the fetus from Semele's womb and sewed it into his own thigh, until the baby, called Dionysus, was old enough to be born.

When Semele's nephew, Pentheus, became king of Thebes, Dionysus tried to introduce his worship into the city. He was rebuffed by everyone, and in retaliation he drove the women mad and led them into the mountains for Bacchic rites. Pentheus went to the mountains to spy on the Bacchants, but this proved to be his doom. His mother, Agave, tore off her son's head, put it on a stick, and paraded it through Thebes.

Polydorus, another child of Cadmus, succeeded to the throne of Thebes, followed in turn by his son Labdacus. Labdacus had a son, Laius, who developed a homosexual passion for Chrysippus, son of Pelops, and then raped him. Because of this crime, Pelops cursed Laius, that he not have children or, if he did, that he be killed by his own son. Laius returned to Thebes, where he married Jocasta. Afterwards he learned of the curse from the Oracle of Apollo at Delphi. Trying to forestall the Oracle, Laius avoided sex with Jocasta. However, one night, when he was drunk, his sex-starved wife seduced him. Nine months later she gave birth to a boy. Fearful of the prophecy, Laius commanded that the child be killed. He pierced the three-day-old infant's ankles and gave him to a shepherd, with orders to expose him on Mount Cithaeron, outside Thebes. Disobeying the king's command out of pity for the baby, the shepherd gave him to another herdsman on the mountain. The herdsman took the child to Corinth and gave him to King Polybus and his wife, Merope, who were childless. They named the child Oedipus, or "swollen foot," because of his pierced ankles. Oedipus grew up happily in Corinth, until one day, when he had just reached maturity, a drunken guest at a banquet questioned his paternity. When he received evasive answers from his parents, Oedipus journeyed to Delphi to inquire of the Oracle of Apollo, who responded that Oedipus was fated to kill his father and marry his mother. Horrified, Oedipus avoided returning home to Corinth, but set out in self-imposed exile. On his way toward Thebes he encountered a man who was, in fact, Laius, his father, traveling with an entourage along the road. When they ran him off the road, Oedipus killed them all in anger, except one servant who fled.

When Oedipus neared Thebes, he was accosted by the Sphinx, a monster with the head of a woman, the body of a lion, and the wings of an eagle, who had been sent by Hera to punish Thebes for Laius' crimes. Since Laius had been killed while abroad, the queen's brother, Creon, promised the vacant throne and the hand of Jocasta to whoever could rid the city of the monster. Before devouring her victims, the Sphinx gave them a chance to live, if they could answer a riddle, "What goes on four legs in the morning, two legs at noon and three legs in the evening?" When the Sphinx confronted him, Oedipus knew the answer: man. In infancy a baby crawls on all fours, in his prime a man walks upright on two legs, and in his twilight years he walks with a cane. When the riddle was answered, the Sphinx threw herself off a cliff.

A frequent theme in myths is that a hero must slay a monster that guards the virginity of a woman to win her and have sex with her. Perseus killed a sea monster to wed Andromeda. Similarly, in the Middle Ages, mythic dragons frequently guarded maidens. The hero had to kill the dragon to win her, just as Oedipus, in a variation of the virgin theme, had to kill the monster, the Sphinx, to win the woman, Jocasta.

Oedipus claimed the reward: he became king and married Jocasta. He ruled for many years in peace and prosperity, during which Jocasta bore him four children: two daughters, Antigone and Ismene, and two sons, Polyneices and Eteocles. Some versions make Polyneices the older son, and others make him the younger. Many years later, when a plague struck the city, Oedipus discovered that the gods had inflicted it because of the pollu-

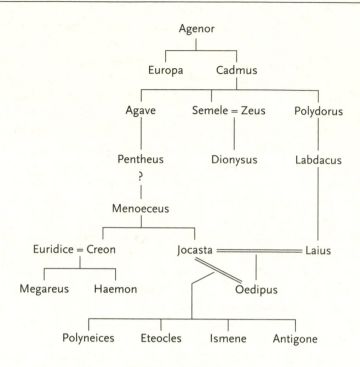

The House of Thebes

tion caused by the death of Laius. Investigating further, he came to learn his origins. When the shameful secret was about to be exposed, Jocasta hanged herself and Oedipus blinded himself, abdicating the throne to Jocasta's brother, Creon, as regent for his sons, Eteocles and Polyneices. The two heirs agreed that each would rule for one year and then alternate, Eteocles for the first year. But when it came time for Eteocles to step down in favor of Polyneices, he refused. Polyneices fled into exile to Argos, where he married the daughter of King Adrastus and enlisted his father-in-law's help to conquer Thebes.

Meanwhile, Oedipus, blind and old, accompanied by his daughter Antigone, came to Colonus, part of the city-state of Athens. Ismene soon arrived with news of the fighting at Thebes, reporting that the Delphic Oracle had foretold that the place where Oedipus was buried would be protected by the presence of his tomb. Creon arrived next, to take Oedipus back to Thebes, by force, if necessary, so that the Thebans could control his burial site. Just in time Theseus, the king of Athens, arrived to prevent this. Polyneices then begged Oedipus for help in his war against his brother, Eteocles. Oedipus not only refused but cursed his two sons. He then died, taken down to the Underworld by the gods, and his entombed corpse became a guardian of Colonus and Athens.

Polyneices and his father-in-law, Adrastus, continued their hostilities, raised an army, and marched against Thebes. This expedition was known as the Seven against Thebes. The attack failed. Polyneices met his brother in single combat at one of the gates of Thebes, where they killed each other in combat. Much of the invading force was killed, including all their leaders, the Seven against Thebes, except Adrastus, who escaped to Athens.

Creon buried Eteocles with state honors but proclaimed that under penalty of death, Polyneices' body was to be left exposed, to rot. Antigone defied the edict and spread earth on the body of her brother. When Creon's guards apprehended her, Creon ordered her to be walled up alive in a cave. Finally, after bitter argument with his son Haemon, to whom Antigone had been promised in marriage, and at the urging of the priest Teiresias, Creon was persuaded to set her free. When he arrived at the cave with Haemon, they found that Antigone, like her mother Jocasta, had hanged herself. On seeing her dead body, Haemon committed suicide. When Eurydice, Creon's wife, learned what had happened, she killed herself out of grief for her dead son. Creon had now lost all his family.

Oedipus the King

Sophocles wrote three plays about the House of Thebes, *Oedipus the King, Antigone,* and *Oedipus at Colonus,* that are extant. A fourth play, dealing with the siege of Thebes, called *Epigonoi,* was lost, but fragments of it from the Oxyrhynchus papyri were deciphered in 2005, using new multispectral imaging. *Oedipus the King* was called simply *Oedipus* by Aristotle. In later centuries the Greek title became *Oedipus Tyrannus* and in Latin, *Oedipus Rex.* A tyrant was not really a king, but rather a strong man who assumed control over a city-state. *Oedipus at Colonus* may have been given this name by Sophocles himself to distinguish it from *Oedipus the King.* Cicero (*De Senectute* 7.21), in the first century BC, called the play *Oedipus Coloneus.* The three plays were not a trilogy, but three separate plays, written at twenty- to thirty-year intervals, concerning the same theme. Sophocles was drawing on a general body of myths about Oedipus and his family, but he added his own variations and interpretations.

The Myth of Oedipus before Sophocles

Homer's *Iliad* and *Odyssey* (eighth century BC) were the earliest works of Greek literature and the earliest to mention the story of Oedipus. In *Iliad* 23.677–80 Homer reports that Oedipus was buried in Thebes after a battle involving the sons of Cadmus. This may imply that there was a hero cult to Oedipus at Thebes. The account in Homer's *Odyssey* (11.271–80) contradicts the narrative in *Oedipus at Colonus*. During his visit to the Underworld, Odysseus saw Oedipus' mother, whom Homer called Epicaste. Oedipus killed his father and married his mother, but the gods made this shame known to all mortals. Epicaste hanged herself, but Oedipus continued to rule in Thebes.

A few fragments and quotations from two epics, *Oedipodeia* and *Thebais*, composed between 800 and 550 BC, have survived. In *Oedipodeia* Oedipus takes a second wife, Euryganeia, and had children by her. In *Thebais*, Oedipus cursed his sons because they had given him an inferior cut of meat at a sacrifice and had served him wine in a cup that had belonged to Laius.

Aeschylus' trilogy, written in 467 BC, well before Sophocles' treatment of the myth, consisted of *Laius, Oedipus, Seven against Thebes*, and a satyr play, *Sphinx*. Only *Seven against Thebes* survived, but we know something about the other plays from quotations and fragments. *Laius* dealt with the curse of the house of Laius, which began with Laius' kidnapping and raping of Chrysippus, son of Pelops. As a result of the violence he suffered, Chrysippus committed suicide, and Pelops cursed Laius and his descendants. Aeschylus followed the curse from father to son to grandsons, from Laius to Oedipus to Eteocles and Polyneices. Each play dealt with one generation, with the fourth play, *Sphinx*, treating Oedipus' encounter with and defeat of the Sphinx.

Shared details of all the versions of the story were that Oedipus killed his father and married his mother. Aeschylus, like Sophocles, had Oedipus blind himself (*Seven against Thebes* 778–91), an outcome not present in earlier versions. Some scholars have argued that the lines mentioning Oedipus' blindness are a later interpolation. In his *Oedipus* Aeschylus gave prominence to the Furies, the spirits of vengeance who pursued bloodguilt, as he had in his trilogy, *Oresteia*. The theme of Aeschylus' trilogy was that the sins of the father were visited on the sons because of the curse of the house of Laius. Other fifth-century tragedians wrote about Oedipus, and we know of six plays, all of which are lost. One of these was by Euripides, Sophocles' younger contemporary, who wrote an *Oedipus*. Working with the existing body of myths, Sophocles shaped and altered them, introducing very different themes to his work.

Themes

The concept of pollution (miasma) and bloodguilt in Greek religion affects the understanding of all three Theban plays. In Greek religion the sacred and the profane intertwined. For society to function and the gods to be in harmony with mankind, pollution had to be avoided. It could come from a number of sources, from the improper exercise of rites, to the neglect of obligation to the gods. Killing an individual caused a moral pollution to the state and created bloodguilt both for the society and for the individual who had done the deed. Such pollution could be removed only through various rites of purification and the balancing of what was owed to the gods, that is, vengeance for the death, either through payment with a life or equivalent restitution. If someone died, whether that death was accidental or intentional, bloodguilt had to be assuaged. Pollution and its cure played a major role in Athenian society. In the mid fifth century BC Pericles could still be charged with being under the curse of the Alcmaeonidae for a pollution committed by his ancestor, Megacles, in the seventh century, almost two hundred years before he was born. The idea of a family curse and collective guilt would seem justified to a Greek audience, as well as to other ancient Mediterranean cultures. God says in the Hebrew Bible (Deuteronomy 5:9), "You shall not bow down to them or serve them. For I the Lord your God am an impassioned God, visiting the guilt of the parents upon the children, upon the third and upon the fourth generations of those who reject Me." A descendant several generations removed would feel himself equally guilty of a family curse as the person who had caused the pollution. Sophocles would not have seen Oedipus' inheritance of the curse of Laius as particularly unusual or tragic. Group guilt was taken for granted in ancient Greek culture. Bloodguilt, pollution, and expiation became major themes of Aeschylus' works. For Sophocles, these were secondary themes, but still an integral part of the myth of Oedipus and his portrayal of it.

Each of the plays deals with pollution. In *Oedipus the King* it is the pollution caused by the murder of Laius, in *Antigone,* the pollution caused by leaving a body unburied, and in *Oedipus at Colonus,* it is the resolution of a lifetime of pollution for Oedipus. In all three plays, the god Apollo advises the characters, through his Oracle at Delphi, what do to and how to cure the pollution. In his role as Apollo Smintheus, Apollo was associated with the bringing of plagues. But he was also a god of medicine and healing. Indeed, the prophecies of Apollo and his priests at Delphi provide the blueprint in the three plays for the healing of pollution and the return of society to its proper order.

Moral pollution brought diseases and plagues. In Homer's *Iliad* the leader of the Greeks, Agamemnon, dishonors Chryses, the priest of Apollo, and thereby dishonors Apollo, by refusing to return Chryses' captured daughter. As a consequence, Apollo sends a plague onto the Greek camp that does not cease until Agamemnon returns the girl. The plague with which *Oedipus the King* begins was caused by the physical pollution of the murder of Laius. It is uncertain whether *Oedipus the King* was written in the 430s or the 420s. If it was produced after 430, Sophocles would have composed the play and the audience would have watched the production at a time of one of the worst plagues ever to hit the ancient world. In the years 430–427 the plague of Athens struck the city and killed a quarter of the city's population, including Pericles, its general and first citizen. If the play belongs to this period, no Athenian could have watched the opening scenes, in which the populace pleads to the king for help, without them-selves fearing the plague and feeling their own loss of so many of their relatives and friends who had perished. Thucydides (*Peloponnesian Wars* 2.53.4) comments on the moral and civil chaos the plague caused: "Fear of gods or law of man there was none to restrain them. As for the first, they judged it to be just the same whether they worshipped them or not, as they saw all alike perishing; and for the last, no one expected to live to be brought to trial for his offences, but each felt that a far severer sentence had been already passed upon them all and hung ever over their heads, and before this fell it was only reasonable to enjoy life a little."

Critical interpretation of Sophocles' *Oedipus the King* began in the fourth century, when Aristotle used the play as the paradigm of Greek tragedy. He considered Oedipus to be the ideal tragic hero and *Oedipus the King* to be the finest of all tragedies. Interpretation has continued to the present day. Each age has understood the play in line with its own culture and mores.

Modern theories of literature and art have argued that any creative work, when it leaves the hands of the artist, becomes an independent entity, that the interpretation of the work belongs not to the original intent of the writer or artist but to the reader or beholder, who brings to the work the whole panoply of his or her own experience.

In one sense, this can be seen most clearly in the Bible. According to Genesis, a snake appeared in the Garden of Eden. Christianity has inter-preted the snake as the devil or the agent of the devil. The ancient Hebrews, however, did not have the concept of the devil when Genesis was written; they only began to develop it after their return from the Babylonian Cap-tivity, after 538 BC. Does the historical reality invalidate the Christian inter-pretation of the serpent? Yes and no. In the same way, we can interpret Sophocles' works as modern viewers according to our own prejudices and experiences, and we can also seek to understand the works historically, to understand what they meant to Sophocles and the Athenian audience.

Aristotle (*Poetics* 13) saw *Oedipus the King* as a tragedy driven by the character of Oedipus. Oedipus fell from his high position because of an error (*hamartia*). Aristotle probably meant by this either his *hubris* (arrogance), when he refused to yield the road to Laius and slew him and his men, or the mistakes he made about his own identity.

Throughout the centuries, many have interpreted *Oedipus the King* as a play of fate, since Oedipus could not escape the fate of killing his father and marrying his mother. Indeed, in Greek religion the concept of fate governed and bound both men and gods. Even Zeus, the ruler of Olympus, could not change fate. A story is told in Homer's *Iliad* that Zeus' son Sarpedon was fated to die at Troy, and even Zeus could not overcome fate. All he could do was bend fate to delay Sarpedon's death. The story of the life of Oedipus was about fate. Oedipus' father was fated either to have no son, or if he did, for that son to kill him and marry Jocasta, his mother. However, the play *Oedipus the King* is not about fate. No action that happens in the play was fated. All that was fated (Oedipus killing his father and marrying his mother and having children by her) happened before the play begins. Sophocles could have decided to make the play a story of fate, as Aeschylus perhaps did, but he chose not to do so.

Friedrich Nietzsche, in his *Birth of Tragedy* (sec. 9), saw this as a complex play, in which Oedipus was a "superman," one who excelled others in knowledge, and Nietzsche believed that those who excelled their fellow men always paid a price. For Oedipus, the price was incest, patricide, blindness, exile, and destruction. Through his knowledge Oedipus defeated the Sphinx, but he, himself, became the answer to the Sphinx's very riddle. For Nietzsche, Oedipus represented the guilt felt by man as a response to his domination of the natural world. The myth suggested that wisdom was an unnatural crime, that the man of knowledge brought destruction with his knowledge, that wisdom was a crime committed against nature.

Sigmund Freud was profoundly influenced by Greek thought, especially by Plato and Sophocles, and particularly by this play. He took Plato's tripartite division of man's soul—the Spirited, the Reasoning, and the Desiring—and turned them into the Ego, the Superego, and the Id. Naming the syndrome after Oedipus, Freud developed the idea of the Oedipus Complex, whereby an infant would feel lust for his mother and want to displace his father. He explained that the more than twenty-five-hundred-year fascination with *Oedipus the King* came about because the play resonated with an innate desire of men to kill their fathers and sleep with their mothers. "His destiny moves us only because it might have been ours—because the oracle laid the same curse upon us before our birth as upon him" (*Interpretation of Dreams* 296).

Freud found a paradigm for the son overthrowing the father not only in *Oedipus the King* but in other Greek myths. Cronos, the youngest born son of Gaia (Earth) and Uranus (Sky), was aided by his mother in conquering his father. In turn, Cronos was overthrown by his son Zeus, who conspired with his mother, Rhea, and grandmother, Gaia. Zeus prevented the next generation from overthrowing him by swallowing his consort, Metis, when she was pregnant with Athena. Athena was then born from the head of Zeus and was, therefore, subservient to him. Besides the paradigms of the gods, heroes such as Perseus overthrew their fathers or grandfathers.

Freud in one sense understood the dynamics of *Oedipus the King* better than most classical scholars and literary critics. He said that "the action of the play consists in nothing other than the process of revealing, with cunning delays and ever-mounting excitement—a process that can be likened to the work of psychoanalysis—that Oedipus himself is the murderer of Laius, but further that he is the son of the murdered man and of Jocasta."

Much of what Freud saw in this play was what Sophocles saw. In fact, Sophocles' view of Oedipus profoundly influenced Freud and provided the basis of Freud's theories of repression and of analysis. Because there was a problem, a plague, Oedipus searched back into the historic events to learn its cause. Only by going back to the very beginning, the circumstances of his own birth, could he discover what the problem was and how to resolve it. By blinding himself he stopped the plague. Oedipus' inquiry into the past to correct the present mirrors Freud's theory of psychoanalysis. The patient seeks the physician because of a present malady. Through analysis, that is, by going back in time to understand the cause of the problem, the patient is cured. Oedipus also became the paradigm for Freud's theory of repression. The patient represses knowledge and resists finding out the painful origin of his present condition. Thus, each time Oedipus learns a new piece of information, he represses it. Nonetheless, he persists until he can no longer repress the knowledge. Then, through blinding himself, he perpetrates the ultimate repression, never again beholding this situation or any other.

Freud believed that Greek myths reveal the fundamental processes of the human psyche. French feminists, focusing on Greek drama, have condemned Freud's neglect of the feminine and his putting all his emphasis on the father-figure Laius, while at the same time neglecting the murder and suppression of the primal mother, as illustrated in the myth of the murder of Clytemnestra by her son, for the establishment of male-dominated civil organization (Irigaray 1991).

Bernard Knox, one of the most influential writers of the twentieth century on Sophocles, analyzed both the Sophoclean hero and Oedipus as an embodiment of that hero. He argued that Sophocles depicts a heroic individual confronting his destiny alone, free to act, but taking the consequences of his actions. He is not a victim, but an active agent. Unlike the

Aeschylean hero, there is no redeeming future or larger meaning for his suffering. Sophocles' tragic hero exhibits intransigence, strength of will, stubbornness, harshness, and he is easily angered and offended. Isolated, the hero refuses to compromise, setting his own conditions for existence. Often, death is the only solution. Through the hero's loyalty to his nature humanity achieves its true greatness. The Sophoclean hero is "one who, unsupported by the gods and in the face of human opposition, made a decision that sprang from the deepest layer of his individual nature, his *physis*, and then blindly, ferociously, heroically maintained that decision even to the point of self-destruction" (*The Heroic Temper* 1964).

Knox sees Oedipus as "a paradigm of all mankind," since the essential elements of the human condition remain the same as they were in ancient Athens. Oedipus symbolizes Athens itself. The behavior of Oedipus corresponded with Athens. He demonstrates swift and courageous action based on intelligent deliberation and self-confidence, and is suspicious and easily angered, just as Athens behaves in its foreign policy and warfare. Like Athens, Oedipus got power through a response to circumstances (Oedipus to the Sphinx, Athens to the Persian Wars), rather than from ordinary political procedures. Both Athens and Oedipus were characterized by a blend of autocratic and democratic elements. The atmosphere of the play reflects the intellectual and spiritual turmoil of Athens, the contentious, litigious questioning of traditional values and the questing for anthropocentric truth. Oedipus the King is thus Athens the King. Oedipus is the embodiment of the self-destructive genius of Periclean Athens. Knox saw that Oedipus had the freedom to find out the truth about the prophecies, about the gods, and about himself. In this search he demonstrated his heroic character, intelligence, courage, and perseverance. This dedication makes the story of Oedipus a heroic example of man's dedication to the truth about himself (*Oedipus at Thebes* 1957).

The modern critic Jean-Pierre Vernant sees *Oedipus the King* in terms of the historical role of tyrants in Greece, with their excessive behavior. Plato (*Republic* 9.571) attributed incest to tyrants as part of their lawless conduct, a charge that fits Oedipus. Vernant also sees Oedipus in another role, that of the *pharmakos*, or scapegoat, who was driven out of the city after all the ills and evils of the city had been placed on him. At the end of the play, Oedipus is willing to be the sacrificial victim, by whose punishment and exile the city can be saved from its pollution of bloodguilt and the physical plague that accompanies it. Vernant also compares this expulsion of the scapegoat to the practice of ostracism at Athens, the periodic expulsion of a powerful figure whom the populace thought could be a danger to political stability (*Myth and Tragedy in Ancient Greece* 87–119).

Walter Burkert views the play as a reaffirmation of the gods. As the breakdown of Oedipus shows, "the veracity of divine prescience proves the existence of an all-comprehending intelligence that envelops this world of ours" (*Oedipus, Oracles, and Meaning* 27).

Charles Segal, in addition to the interpretations above, views Oedipus as a hero of inner visions and personal suffering, whose force of personality and integrity enabled him to confront his suffering and fate with courage, after a struggle for self-knowledge. According to Segal, this was how Sophocles created the form of the "tragic hero," which became a paradigm in Western literature (*Oedipus Tyrannus* 147). Segal sees the answer to the riddle of the Sphinx in Oedipus himself, his third foot representing him as both *homo faber* and *homo necans*, the civilizing and the destructive power of man. The staff Oedipus used to kill his father was also a sign of his kingship, and he used it as a support in his old age. Oedipus destroyed the Sphinx, a beast who ravaged the city of Thebes, and yet he himself violated the fundamental laws of civilization by committing two of the most bestial acts in human society, patricide and incest (*Tragedy and Civilization* 207–17).

A major theme of the play to Sophocles, Freud, and the modern reader is the search for knowledge and identity. Perhaps this theme of the play is best expressed by Teiresias (lines 412–19):

> But I say to you, who have taunted me in my blindness,
> that though you have sight, you cannot see your own evil
> nor the truth of where you live and whom you live with.
> Do you know your origin, know that you are the enemy
> of all your line, those below the earth and those still on it,
> and that your mother's and father's double-edged curse
> with deadly step will drive you from this land—
> like a light revealing all, before it blinds you.

Oedipus is the man of knowledge. During the play we learn that he answered the riddle of the Sphinx. In a sense, the answer to that riddle was not only "man" but also "Oedipus," for we see him in these plays as a baby with pierced ankles, as a full-grown man, and as an aged blind man with a cane. This riddle of the Sphinx resonated with the famous Delphic maxim, "Know yourself, know that you are man." Thus, inherent in the Sphinx's riddle is the idea of man's self-knowledge. Sophocles portrayed in this tragedy the theme of self-knowledge, not fate, as other tragedians had done.

Oedipus' search for knowledge begins with the very first line of the play. Because a plague had attacked the city, Oedipus has sent emissaries to the Oracle of Delphi to learn the reason. As we have seen, in many societies, including the Greek, plagues were believed to come from the gods, as punishment for man's misbehavior. The Book of Deuteronomy (28:15, 21–22) perhaps sums up a mainstream religious belief:

> But if you do not obey the Lord your God to observe faithfully all His commandments and laws which I enjoin upon you this day, all these curses shall come upon you and take effect. . . . The Lord will make pestilence cling to you, until He has put an end to you in the land that you are entering to possess. The Lord will strike you with consumption, fever, and inflammation, with scorching heat and drought, with blight and mildew; they shall hound you until you perish.

If a physical pollution strikes, the cause must be the anger of the gods because of improper human behavior. For the Greeks, any killing, even accidental, created pollution. The only way to resolve the pollution caused by the death of Laius was to kill his murderer or to send him into exile (lines 95–101):

> CREON
> I shall tell what I heard from the god.
> Lord Phoebus commands
> that to drive this plague from our land, nourished by our land,
> we must root it out, or it will be past cure.
>
> OEDIPUS
> What rite will expiate this crime?
>
> CREON
> Banishment or death for death—blood unavenged
> menaces the city like a storm.

Apollo had revealed that the death of Laius must be avenged. Oedipus questions Creon on the details, and Creon replies (lines 122–24):

> CREON
> He said it was a band of robbers
> that attacked and killed him, not one, but many hands.

Oedipus' response is revealing and sets the themes of the whole play (lines 124–25):

> OEDIPUS
> How could a single robber, unless bribed
> by some vile man from here, dare to kill him?

As Oedipus would tell the audience later (lines 800–813), when he was traveling toward Thebes, at a place where three roads cross, he encountered a man in a horse-drawn carriage, accompanied by retainers. Following an altercation, he killed them all, except one. Oedipus reveals that he subconsciously knows he is the slayer of Laius by changing the plural "robbers" to the singular "robber." He next tries to prove to himself that he is not that slayer, by cursing the murderer (lines 246–49):

> I pray that whoever did this—even if he has,
> alone or with his murderous accomplices, escaped—
> may his life always be wretched.

Teiresias then enters the stage. Teiresias is reluctant to speak, but Oedipus pushes him until he declares (line 362):

> I repeat that you yourself are the murderer you seek.

Now it is revealed to all the listeners that Oedipus was the killer of Laius. The only one who does not know is Oedipus himself. He continues to repress and deny what he knows to be true. He now tries to blame Creon and accuses Teiresias of plotting with Creon to take his throne (lines 380–403).

Despite his refusal to believe Teiresias, Oedipus relentlessly pursues the answers. He tells his wife, Jocasta, that Teiresias has accused him of being Laius' murderer. Jocasta retorts that oracles are often false, the proof being that the oracle had said that Laius would perish at the hand of their child. It could not have been the child who killed Laius, since Laius did away with the child by pinning his feet and exposing him (706–25), and later, Laius was killed by robbers, not by his son. Any man of knowledge would immediately connect his own pierced feet and the prophecy that he would kill his father with the death of Laius. But Oedipus only focuses on the fact that Laius was killed where three highways meet. He suspects that he could be Laius' killer, but he does not reach the obvious conclusion, that he is also Laius' child. Oedipus clings to the hope that it was not he who killed Laius by harping on the report that "he said that robber men had killed him. Men—not a man" (lines 842–43). Oedipus then sends for the shepherd who had survived the attack on Laius. A messenger from Corinth now enters. Oedipus learns from him that Polybus is dead and that he himself is not the son of Polybus, but came originally from the house of Laius. Jocasta immediately realizes that Oedipus is her son. She begs him to stop his inquiry. But Oedipus, the man of knowledge, is determined to seek out the truth, a truth obvious to all except him. Finally the Shepherd comes on stage and reveals that Oedipus is the child of Laius and Jocasta. Oedipus can no longer repress the truth. He now knows who he is. But unable to look upon the truth, he runs offstage, to find that Jocasta has hanged herself. Taking the brooches from her robe, he uses them to gouge out his eyes.

Major motifs that run through the play are sight and knowledge. The Greek word for "to know" is *oida*. Literally the word means "to have seen." To see is to know. Teiresias, who was blind, could see and understand. Oedipus, the man of knowledge, could see, but did not know. When he finally knew, he could not bear to see and blinded himself. There is a further play on the name of Oedipus, which means "swollen foot." The first part of the name, *"Oedi,"* in Greek sounds like the word to know *"oida."*

The events that occurred before the play begins were fated. Oedipus still has free will, and now he has fallen from a great height, as Aristotle says. But because of his refusal to know himself and who he is, he falls further, into blindness and exile.

Oedipus at Colonus

Sophocles, who came from Colonus, wrote *Oedipus at Colonus* in 406 BC, in the last year of his life, when he was close to ninety. Like Oedipus in the play, he was a very old man, near death. Sophocles did not live to see the play performed, and it was his grandson, Sophocles the Younger, who produced it at the Great Dionysia in the spring of 401.

Even more than *Antigone* and *Oedipus the King,* this play is rooted in the historical and religious experience of the people of Athens. In 406 Athens was locked in the final stages of the Peloponnesian Wars (431–404), and its defeat was looming. The year before, in 407, the Athenian cavalry had beaten a Theban force near Colonus (Xenophon *Hellenica* 1.1.33, Diodorus Siculus *Library of History* 13.72). This small victory for Athens may have influenced Sophocles in the writing of the play. Thebes, the implacable enemy of Athens, was allied with Sparta. It was almost as if Sophocles wanted to give hope to the Athenians that they would survive the onslaught of Thebes and the ravages of war, protected by the gods. By the time *Oedipus at Colonus* was produced in 401, Sparta had conquered Athens. The audience in 401 would know that the grave of Oedipus had not prevented their defeat. Yet, perhaps it did aid them from being utterly destroyed. When Athens fell in 404, the Spartans resisted the call of Thebes and Corinth for the total annihilation of Athens. The Thebans wanted to execute the men of the city and sell the women and children into slavery. The Spartans did not do this—not out of goodwill for Athens, but because they wanted Athens to act as a buffer between them and Thebes. Given this historical background, when the play was first produced it would already have struck a false note to the Athenians; the grave of Oedipus did not protect Athens.

Oedipus at Colonus is not only a drama fixed in time to the end of the fifth century BC, but it can also be seen as a modern story of suffering and reconciliation. Some later readers and critics, influenced by Christianity, read into it a story of the sinner whom God receives into His grace. Hegel pointed out this fallacy: "The reconciliation of the Christian religion, however, is an illumination of the soul, which bathed in the everlasting waters of salvation, is raised above mortal life and its deeds" (*Hegel on Tragedy* 75–76). He saw in this play the epitome of acceptance of personal responsibility for deeds done under compulsion from external forces: "The most perfect example of this in ancient drama is to be found in the very admirable *Oedipus at Colonus.*" For Hegel, Oedipus resembled Adam, losing happiness when he gained knowledge of good and evil. But after Oedipus had assumed full responsibility for his actions, his soul was purified by the Furies, and he underwent both physical and psychological reconciliation with his past deeds.

Themes

The central theme of the play is the apotheosis of Oedipus: he becomes a hero, a demigod, whose spirit will guard Athens against Thebes. There are a number of subsidiary themes, as well, including (1) pollution and the purification of that pollution; (2) the overwhelming love of Oedipus for his daughters, contrasted with the hatred he bears his sons; (3) an encomium of Athens, which glorifies the city as a protector of the oppressed; and (4) hope, that, despite all travails, the gods will protect us.

Apotheosis

At the beginning of the play Oedipus comes onto the stage, old and weak, blind, wearing rags, carrying a stick, and led by his daughter. In this scene he truly typifies Aristotle's example of *peripeteia,* or reversal, the great figure that has fallen from a high place. In *Oedipus the King* he was a great king, proud and powerful. Now he has fallen to this state. By the end of *Oedipus at Colonus,* Oedipus walks unaided, summoned by the gods for heroization and apotheosis. Through this process we watch on stage the growth of the power of Oedipus and his journey through wrath and passion, from man to hero. Sophocles dramatically portrayed the gods at work in fulfillment of divine prophecy.

The drama of this play is the process of achieving a heroic state. Oedipus knew that his fate was to be the guardian spirit in whatever land he would be buried, as Apollo had promised (*Oedipus at Colonus* 87–93). To create dramatic tension for this process of apotheosis, Sophocles fills Oedipus' last hours with drama and crisis: the kidnapping of his daughters Antigone and Ismene by Creon, who was trying to force Oedipus to return to the environs of Thebes for burial, and the appeal of his son Polyneices for him to return to Thebes.

In the final resolution the gods transform Oedipus from a blind beggar and polluted being into a hero whom they welcome as one of their own. Finally his pollution has been expiated, and he discovers that the gods did not hate him, but loved him. Throughout the play, as he comes to realize his destiny to be a demigod, a *daimon*, his strength and dignity grow. He moves from a suppliant asking for a place to sit, to a commanding figure, summoned by the gods.

As part of the heroization of Oedipus, his stature is reinforced because his tomb became a protection to Athens. The Greeks believed that the bones of dead heroes could protect a city and a land. The historian Herodotus (*Histories* 1.46) relates a story that the Spartans searched for the bones of Orestes because the Delphic Oracle had told them that they could never defeat their neighbors, the Tegeans, until they brought Orestes' bones to Sparta. Herodotus (*Histories* 8.134) and Aeschylus (*Seven against Thebes* 587–588) tell the story that Amphiaraus was buried in Thebes as a guardian hero. The body of Eurystheus in Athens would protect the city from its enemies (Euripides *Heracleides* 1032–34; Aeschylus *Eumenides* 763ff). In an account written in the first century AD, but which might go back to the fifth century BC, the biographer Plutarch (*Life of Theseus* 36) relates that the Athenians brought the bones of Theseus back to Athens. The idea of heroes being guardians would be consistent with Athenian religious beliefs. We also know of historical figures around whom hero cults developed. Brasidas, the Spartan general, became a cult hero to the city of Amphipolis, which he saved in 422 BC. These hero cults, then, were a part of Greek religious belief.

The gods, wishing to help Athens and protect the city, at the same time desired to bring some solace to Oedipus for his guiltless suffering. Oedipus wanted to help Athens and deny his protection to Thebes, which had cast him out. The Thebans wanted him back precisely because they had learned that Oedipus' body was necessary for their protection (lines 389–409). When Oedipus heard these things from Ismene, he was incensed at the Thebans. They were not acting out of honor for him, a king who had saved the city from the Sphinx, but only for the protection he might afford them in the future (lines 390–91).

The action of the play is based on the prophecy that Oedipus, after years of suffering, would find a final resting place at Colonus, where he would be a guardian hero, causing evil to those who rejected him and good to those who welcomed him (lines 88–95). Oedipus thus told Theseus that he bore a gift, and that he would be the cause of vengeance toward those who had

wronged him (lines 349–50). He knew that he would receive the offerings
of heroes and that his body would guard Athens and protect it from Thebes.

The heroization of Oedipus made partial amends for past suffering,
inflicted by the gods who are just (lines 1565–67). Not all who suffered
became heroes. Oedipus' superior powers brought him redemption. He
was a man of royal birth with great influence, the monster killer, the slayer
of the Sphinx and deliverer of Thebes. His nobility allowed him to endure
his suffering. A man of knowledge, he finally understood both himself and
man. The Greek concepts of "know thyself" and "learn by suffering" provide a background for understanding how Oedipus uniquely deserves this
reward for his suffering.

Pollution and Purification

Oedipus at Colonus relates Oedipus' reintegration into society and the gods.
This came about through purification of Oedipus' past pollution by the
Eumenides, which event was a precursor to his final apotheosis. In their
role as avengers of bloodguilt, they were called Erinyes or Furies, and as
protective deities called Eumenides or "well disposed." The Furies were
stirred up by pollution, which might arise from various causes, the most
common being the shedding of human blood and neglect of the obligation
to bury corpses. In *Oedipus the King* bloodguilt arose from the killing of
Laius; in *Antigone,* from the unburied body of Polyneices.

The Eumenides play a major role in *Oedipus at Colonus.* When these
goddesses demanded expiation of the murder of Laius in *Oedipus the King,*
Oedipus pronounced a curse on those responsible and promised to execute
or exile them. Not only did Oedipus cause pollution by killing the king of
Thebes, but the pollution was magnified because it involved parricide and
incest with his mother, compounded by the engendering of four incestuous
children. He was the epitome of a polluted individual. When he discovered
that he himself was the killer of Laius, doubly polluted by incest, and that
he was the cause of the physical pollution of the plague, he blinded himself and eventually went into exile. Bloodguilt arising from the death of
Laius had caused the plague. Only when that bloodguilt found retribution
through the punishment of Oedipus did the plague cease. Now Oedipus
had come to the Eumenides for final purification.

For the Greeks, there was a constant struggle between the gods of the
Underworld, the dark chthonic gods of emotion and passion, embodied in
the Furies, and the Olympian, gods of light, justice, and social order. Good
tended to come from the Olympians and evil and punishment from the
chthonic gods. The earth acted as both the womb and the tomb of man.

Consequently, the chthonic powers were associated with birth and death. They looked after the interests of the dead and avenged those who had died. The Erinyes, the spirits of vengeance, had punished the whole house of Laius and continued to pass the retribution from one generation to the next. When only the Erinyes ruled, blood feuds and civil war tore a society apart. The law, the just rule of Zeus and Apollo, must be observed. But that justice had to take account of the requirement for retribution. When justice was balanced by retribution, the Erinyes were satisfied and became Eumenides, guardians of the social order, who reintegrated the polluted into society. Generally, in this play, Sophocles used the name Eumenides, but in lines 1299 and 1434 Polyneices talks about the curse of the "Furies" on their house and his father's "Furies," who would pursue and destroy him.

Zeus represented justice. Cursed by his father and bearing the family curse, Polyneices appealed to Zeus (line 1267). But Oedipus also called on Zeus (line 1380) to bring justice and to join together with the chthonic gods' cries for vengeance. Zeus was the god not only of justice but also of the tribe and the patrilineal structure that defined a Greek society. Hence, as the god of the patrilineal group, he reinforced the father's curse on the son for failure in his duty to honor his father.

Innocence before the law did not prevent pollution. Innocence, however, might mitigate the expiation required. Oedipus protested his innocence three times on the grounds of having acted in ignorance in marrying his mother and self-defense in killing his father. Greek views of religion would hold him guilty of pollution, regardless of his intent. But Greek law would find mitigation. Athenian law demanded that the homicide first go into exile; when he finally returned, he could be purified (Demosthenes 23.72–73). For the Athenians, Oedipus' exile and suffering would have mitigated his pollution. Hence, Theseus did not make Oedipus' innocence a condition of accepting him as a suppliant. In one sense, the conflict between pollution and the law was similar to that faced by Antigone in *Antigone*, where the guardians of the law of the family, the Furies, demanded that she bury her brother, Polyneices, while the law of the state required that she not bury him.

Apollo was one of the Olympian gods concerned with law and justice and also with medicine and healing. He was the driving force of the events in *Oedipus the King*. Now it was Apollo who ordained Oedipus' final journey to become a divine hero at Colonus (lines 86, 102).

When all was well and there was no pollution, the Eumenides brought prosperity to the land. Since Oedipus was a polluted being, it was fitting that at the end of his life, for his final purification, he comes to the grove of the Eumenides at Colonus. Once Oedipus had appeased them for trespassing in the sacred grove through purification rites (lines 472–75), the Eumenides were invoked to be protectors of Oedipus as a suppliant. However, purification by the Eumenides should not be considered the same as redemption. Violation of the sacred and of bloodguilt must be balanced by expiation and ritual purification. Guilt or innocence was not at issue, only that the pollution must be rectified.

Coupled with notions of pollution were the importance and sanctity of proper burial. Burial was a requirement for all members of Greek society, and the responsibility for burial fell on the family of the deceased. If there was no immediate family, the obligation passed to the wider kinship group and ultimately to the tribes that composed the state. Oedipus had been driven out of Thebes, but in the play, Creon came to Colonus to persuade Oedipus to return to Thebes for burial, thus becoming a hero protecting his native land. However, because Oedipus remained a polluted being, Thebes would not allow him to be buried within the precincts of the city (lines 399–400), but just outside the gates. This would serve the purpose of Thebes, but it would not give Oedipus full cleansing from his pollution. In Athens, on the other hand, he could receive full burial rites because his deeds had not been done in Athens but in Thebes. Therefore, the pollution that was caused in Thebes would not stain Athenian soil. Oedipus rejected the proposal to be buried in Thebes, opting to take vengeance on Thebes by an Athenian burial.

Pollution caused Oedipus to be virtually a man without a country. Greek society was patrilineal and patrilocal, and a person's kinship network gave him a place of security and a support system. Ancestral land was of great importance, both as a place of identity and as a place of livelihood and burial. Expelled at birth from his native Thebes because of a curse, Oedipus was adopted by Polybus, the ruler of Corinth. On reaching manhood and learning of the curse on him, he left what he considered to be his native land to avoid it. He traveled to Thebes, where he encountered the curse again. He married and became a part of the country. But the curse reasserted itself, and he was expelled as a blind beggar. Finally, at the end of his life, he came to Colonus and Athens for burial. Thebes now wanted him back, not for a proper burial, but for burial outside the city. This final request was not made on behalf of him and his final purification, but because his soon-to-be-hero status would serve as a protection for Thebes. The Eumenides, however, who dealt with pollution and bloodguilt, deemed that Oedipus had become purified and was worthy of burial in their precincts. Oedipus in death became a purified citizen of Athens.

Loyalty of Children

During the play Oedipus is transformed from powerless beggar to powerful hero. He reveals the extremes of his nature, extremes of hatred for his sons and love for his daughters. Great emotion is displayed through the love between father and daughters. Antigone serves as his eyes as well as his guide and nurse. Both daughters made great sacrifices to help their father in exile. That is what their culture expected of them. But these daughters went beyond this expectation and, according to Sophocles, acted as if they were sons in their protection of their father—a duty that Oedipus' sons, Polyneices and Eteocles, failed to carry out (lines 337–45):

> OEDIPUS
> Those two—it seems they follow Egyptian customs
> in their style of life!
> There, the men spend all day at home,
> working the loom, while the wives
> go out to earn the daily bread.
> Oh children—those two should be doing these things,
> but they keep to the house like unmarried girls
> and you, instead, must bear the burden
> of your wretched father.

Antigone and Ismene thus went well beyond the filial requirements of Greek society. In return, Oedipus had a great love for his daughters (lines 1365–69):

> if I had not engendered these daughters
> to care for me, I would not be alive.
> These girls saved me, they were my nurses,
> they have been like men, not women, in their labor for me.
> You two are not my sons, but from some other stock.

In the poignant farewell scene, Oedipus expressed his profound love for them (lines 1615–21):

> "I know it was very hard. But one simple word,
> I hope, will recompense all your pain and toil.
> Never will you be loved
> more than I have loved you—of that,
> you will indeed be deprived for the rest of your lives."
> Clinging to each other, the three of them,
> father and daughters, wept.

When she lost her father, Ismene expressed her immense grief (lines 1689–92):

> Why ask me? Oh, let murderous Hades
> take me now, to join my aged father!
> My future is wretched—
> a life not worth living.

Their love for him transcended his death. Antigone lamented (lines 1700–1704):

> Oh dear father, dearest one, now
> cloaked in the earth's eternal darkness,
> not even there are you unloved—
> we shall always love you, she and I.

This intensity of love for his daughters was mirrored by the depth of anger and even hatred he felt for his sons, Polyneices and Eteocles. In the end, he cursed them. Having assumed power in Thebes, they had expelled him from the city. They had violated the obligation of sons to fathers, so important in all patrilineal societies that fathers could legally execute rebellious children. In Athens, under a law attributed to the Athenian statesman Solon in the sixth century BC, a son convicted of mistreating his parents and not providing housing for them lost his citizenship rights. Plato, who thought this law too mild for his ideal city, advocated banishment and flogging (*Laws* 11.932d).

Polyneices came to Colonus to beg Oedipus to return. But even before his arrival, Oedipus was angry at his sons for their failure to help him when he had been driven out of Thebes, preferring power to their father (lines 447–49). When Oedipus found that Polyneices had come for his help, he immediately realized that his son's only motive was to further his own position in his struggle against his brother, Eteocles, not filial piety. Thus, his previous anger intensified and he laid a curse upon him (lines 1383–90):

> So go—I spit on you and deny I am your father,
> you foulest of beings. Take these curses
> I heap upon you: that you will not defeat
> your native land by force of arms nor ever return
> to the valley of Argos, but will die by a kindred hand
> and slay the one who drove you out.
> Thus I curse you—to dwell in the hateful
> paternal darkness of Tartarus,

Polyneices had offended not only the morals and laws of Greek kinship but the laws of the gods as well. Oedipus claimed that his curse was justified by Zeus (lines 1381–82). Plato (*Laws* 9.881d) would have agreed. He said that sons who maltreated their parents would be cursed by Zeus, the guardian of kinship ties. A Greek audience would applaud Oedipus' curses of his sons and their fate. Despite this, Antigone asked her father to be mindful of his own parents and to give up his anger against Polyneices (lines 1195–98). But to no avail. The Athenian audience might have identified with Antigone's plea for her brother, equally as much as with Oedipus and his curses.

Oedipus thus acted favorably toward his daughters, who loved and cared for him, and cursed his sons, who rejected him. In the same way, he acted with favor to Theseus and to Athens, which sheltered him, and with hostility to Creon and Thebes.

Encomium of Athens

Sophocles presented a portrait of the glory of Athens and at the same time attempted to console and instill hope. Theseus was the hero of Athens—the mythical king of Athens who unified the territory called Attica under Athenian rule. He represented Athens and its civilization and its reputation for equality and justice. He and Athens welcomed Oedipus as a suppliant, not because of the benefit Oedipus would confer, but because they were protectors of suppliants and of justice. Throughout the play there are praises of Athens and its greatness (lines 707–14):

> And we give further praise
> to this, our mother city,
> whose proud boast
> and gift from the great god
> is the glory of its colts and horses
> and the waters of its sea. It was you,
> son of Cronos, our lord Poseidon,
> who raised the city to this proud height,

and lines 913–14:

> This city believes in justice
> and decides nothing without the law.

The words of Sophocles' friend Pericles, delivered in the Funeral Oration at the end of the first year of the Peloponnesian War in 430, might well have still echoed in the minds of the Athenians when he said, "We alone do good to our neighbors, not upon a calculation of interest, but in the confidence of freedom and in a frank and fearless sprit."

The play was also an attempt at consolation of the Athenian people, near the end of a twenty-seven-year war and a plague that had killed a quarter of the population. When the play was written, in 406, defeat was close at hand for the war-weary Athenians. The presence of a heroic figure, Oedipus, who had suffered terribly in his lifetime but who had, in the end, been forgiven, showed the power of the gods and showed that suffering could be ameliorated. When the play was produced in 401, Athens was on the road to a rocky recovery. It had been soundly beaten in 404, but in 403 the Spartans allowed Athens to regain its independence and restore the Athenian democracy.

A Play of Hope

This is a play of hope, with the message that in the end the gods are just and will protect Athens, despite all travails. The gods showed that they could be just by compensating Oedipus for a lifetime of suffering, caused not by his own actions but by the curse on his house. While on a personal level Oedipus might not have been guilty, the Greek notion of guilt and pollution by association with ancestors would have been a normal one. The sins of the fathers would be visited on the sons, regardless of the character of the sons. But this recompense for a life of suffering may have been granted because Oedipus was a mighty figure, a hero who conquered the Sphinx and saved Thebes. A lifetime of suffering ended in peace and power. The gods have the power to inflict suffering and to exalt. There is hope for redemption and for balancing the scales of fate.

For a Greek audience, this play would have had a satisfactory ending: purification has been achieved, and a hero will protect Athens against Thebes. The curse of the house of Laius seems to be reaching its end in the apotheosis of Oedipus. However, more misery lay ahead for Oedipus' children. At the end of the play Antigone asks Theseus to send her and Ismene back to Thebes to try to prevent the fratricide that would occur. But the ultimate fate of Polyneices and Eteocles was sealed by the curse of Oedipus. Antigone was heading for her death, caught not by fate, but by the inevitability of actions driven by her culture and her character.

Oedipus at Colonus reflects the Greek view of the relationship of the gods toward man and the interaction of the divine and natural worlds, wherein the gods, through the agency of Oedipus as a guardian spirit, ultimately protected Athens, whose glory would prevail.

Antigone

While Aristotle held *Oedipus the King* to be the best of all Greek tragedies, in the nineteenth century European poets, philosophers, and scholars considered *Antigone* to be the finest tragedy and a work closer to perfection than any other produced at any time. Kant, Shelley, Mathew Arnold, and Nietzsche, among many others, shared this view. Hegel called it "that supreme and absolute example of tragedy." For him, Antigone was the embodiment of absolute right, the representative of ethical consciousness in opposition to the state.

Antigone has so appealed to modern audiences because it has been interpreted as the clash between religion and law, the divine and the secular, the resistance to unjust laws. However, the play clearly says that Creon had the right to impose order and laws on the state and that everyone was subject to those laws, however unjust.

This ambiguity of who was in the right, Antigone or Creon, is illustrated by the response to the version of *Antigone* by Jean Anouilh. First performed in wartime Paris on February 6, 1944, the play ran for more than five hundred performances. Both Frenchmen and Nazis were in the audience. Both warmly applauded the play. The French saw Antigone as a spirit of the French Resistance, as the spirit of Freedom, and Creon as the Vichy government. The Nazis saw in the play the destruction of those who irrationally resisted the law.

Antigone was the earliest of Sophocles' Theban plays to be produced, perhaps some time in the 440s or 430s. A story, dated to the late third century BC, attributed to Aristophanes of Byzantium, the head of the library of Alexandria, related that Sophocles had been appointed general in the Samian War (441/440) because of the success of *Antigone*. Since Euripides, not Sophocles, won the first prize at the Festival of Dionysus in the year preceding Sophocles' election as general, the story is clearly wrong in some aspects. Based on this anecdote, modern scholars have suggested various dates, ranging from 444/443 to 438. All the dates have some problems. The only thing certain is that slightly more than two hundred years after Sophocles wrote, it was thought that *Antigone* had been written around 441/440.

In writing the play, Sophocles could have chosen the common account of the story. In that version of the civil war between Eteocles, on one side, and Polyneices and his Argive allies, on the other, Creon left the bodies of the entire defeated Argive army unburied. Only after the intervention of Theseus, king of Athens, and an Athenian army did Creon back down and allow the burial of the enemy dead. Instead, Sophocles focused on Creon's refusal to allow the burial only of Polyneices.

Themes

Tragedy involves conflict. Melodrama represents a struggle of good against evil, whereas tragedy represents the battle of right against right. *Antigone* embodied the struggle of two rights: on one side, divine law, which obliged kin to bury their dead relatives, no matter what the situation; on the other side, Creon, who represented civil law and government. Each side had legitimate claims to defend its action. While modern audiences might tend to side with Antigone, who willingly died in her resistance to what she considered an unjust law, the Greek audience, as well as many audiences throughout history, would have found Creon's position preferable, sympathetic, and defensible. The city of Thebes had just gone through a devastating civil war. One brother, Eteocles, sat on the throne. The other brother, Polyneices, led foreign forces in an effort to conquer Thebes and put himself on the throne. Creon sided with Eteocles against the foreign invaders. The invasion was fought off and public order was restored. In the fighting, both Eteocles and Polyneices were killed. This left Creon to inherit the throne from his sister's son. Once on the throne, he buried Eteocles with honors but forbade the burial of Polyneices, a traitor to the city. Creon was uneasy in his rule, both by temperament and because his claim to the throne was weak. Not a descendant of King Laius, he ruled because his sister had been queen. Needing to act decisively to stabilize the state, he decided to make an example of traitors.

The importance of the relationship of the individual to the state, the subordination of the individual to the laws of the state, and the relationship of morality to law have been basic questions since humans first formed societies. Because *Antigone* addresses these fundamental issues, the play has resonated with audiences for the past two and a half millennia. The issues raised in this play confront us today, as they will a thousand years from now.

While today we may see these issues as major themes, to understand the play we must also see it in its historical context. At the end of the sixth century and during the fifth century BC, Athens was moving from being a tribal collection of kinship groups, to being a city governed by the rule of law. This was not an easy path. Greek societies were based on an organizing principal of patrilineal kinship. Membership in the group was determined by descent through the male line from a common male ancestor. Athens itself was divided into larger and smaller kinship groups, some of which had a formal structure and others a de facto organization. On the largest level was the tribe. All citizens in Athens belonged to one of four tribes, as well as to a smaller kinship group called the *phratry*. The smallest kinship group was the *oikos*, or household. Since the society was patrilocal as well as patrilineal, kinship groups formed military and political alliances. Members of a kinship group had reciprocal obligations, which included self-defense, support, inheritance, marriage, and burial of dead kinsmen.

We can see in Aeschylus' *Oresteia* trilogy some of the conflicts in Athens caused by the gradual transference of obligations of the kin groups to the state. Kin were required to take vengeance for the death of a member of the group. Murder brought bloodguilt to the perpetrator, but it also caused bloodguilt to the surviving relatives if they failed to take vengeance. *Oresteia* dealt with the murder of Agamemnon by his wife Clytemnestra and, in turn, the killing of Clytemnestra by their son, Orestes. The trilogy ends with the establishment of the court of the Areopagus, instituted in Athens to deal with bloodguilt. In that play the jury was deadlocked, six for conviction and upholding the spirits of vengeance, the Furies, and six for acquittal. Athena cast the deciding vote and Orestes was freed. Both the Furies and Orestes had their conflict governed by a court of law. The message of the play is clear: kinship groups must surrender their rights of vengeance to the state, and in turn the state must recognize, but not be ruled by, the moral imperatives of kinship groups.

The conflict between Antigone and Creon in *Antigone* has some similarities to *Oresteia*. In the latter, the laws of vengeance and bloodguilt are in the hands of the Furies, as opposed to the civil laws, which are in the hands of Apollo. The conflict is not only of the chthonic gods against the Olympian but also of female against male. The chthonic gods tended to be female, the Olympian, male. So in Sophocles' play, Antigone, a female, is like the Furies, advocating the interests of the chthonic gods against the male, the advocate of the law of the state. In both *Oresteia* and *Antigone* a just state would take cognizance of both the claims of the female chthonic gods and those of the male civil law. For Aeschylus and Sophocles, a well-ordered state embodied the idea of the social contract, expressed by the French philosopher Rousseau—the surrender of private and religious rights to the state in return for its protection and guardianship of rights.

Although the tragedies at the Great Dionysia portrayed mythological themes, they could reflect contemporary fifth-century issues and situations, and at times might deal with current events. However, since the dating of most Greek tragedies is at best uncertain, contemporary-theme analysis is highly conjectural, except in the case of those few plays that can be accurately dated. *Antigone* has usually been dated just before the Samian War in the late 440s. But Tyrrell and Bennett (1998), following a conjectural date of 438, have tried to tie the issues of burial in *Antigone* to Pericles' abuse of the rebel Samians in the Samian War and Pericles' eulogy for those killed in that war (Plutarch *Life of Pericles* 28, 4–7). For several decades before this Athens had adopted the practice of bringing home for burial, at public expense, the bodies of soldiers killed in foreign wars. At the same time, the state was regulating private displays of wealth at funerals. So whether *Antig-*

one belongs to the 440s or 430s, the tension between private and public control of burial underlies the struggle of Antigone and Creon in Sophocles' drama and would have been in the minds of the Athenian audience.

Given the process of the building of civic institutions under way in Athens, *Antigone* represented a further step in their development. In *Antigone* a relative insists on performing the rites required by the obligation of kin, rites ordained by the gods, rites that, if omitted, would bring bloodguilt down on the head of the relative and the land. The play then grapples with the question of the extent of the power of the state over the kinship groups and their rites. Sophocles' answer was very clear: The individual is governed by the laws of the state, regardless of whether these laws are just and in harmony with divine law. Antigone believes the law forbidding the burial of her brother Polyneices to be unjust and contrary to the laws of the gods (lines 450–60):

> Zeus did not command these things,
> nor did Justice, who dwells with the gods below,
> ordain such laws for men.
> Neither do I believe that your decrees,
> or those of any other mortal, are strong enough to overrule
> the ancient, unwritten, immutable laws of the gods,
> which are not for the present alone, but have always
> been—and no one knows when they began.
> I would not risk the punishment of the gods
> in fear of any man.

Antigone chose to disobey the laws of the state, and not for one moment did she expect to do this with impunity (lines 459–70):

> I already knew I was going to die—how could it be otherwise,
> even if you do not command it?
> And if I die before my time—to me that seems a gain.
> Whoever lives as I do, amid so many evils,
> how can that person not welcome death?
> I do not fear that fate: it is the common lot, no special woe.
> But if I should allow the corpse of my brother,
> my mother's son, to lie unburied,
> that would grieve me—nothing else.
> And if it seems to you that what I do is foolish,
> Well—perhaps it is a fool who thinks so.

Sophocles then upheld the right and duty of Creon to make the laws of the state and the obligation of Antigone to obey those laws.

But Sophocles did not see Creon as blameless or his power as absolute. Again, this must be viewed in the light of fifth-century politics and society. During the last decade of the sixth century Athens developed a democracy, the rule of all its citizens. In the early part of the fifth century, Athenians fought resolutely against the Persians, whose intent was to destroy and enslave them. Greeks were divided in their loyalties, and Thebes, among others, fought on the Persian side. After the defeat of Persia, the Athenian democracy was faced by a hostile ideology—oligarchy—with Sparta as its greatest proponent. Greece had suffered at the hands of tyrants in the sixth century, and Athens had overthrown its own tyrants, Hippias and Hipparchus. In fact, a statue of Harmodius and Aristogeiton, the assassins of Hipparchus, stood in the agora at Athens. Hippias was killed in 490, fighting on the Persian side against Athens, at the battle of Marathon, where the Greeks defeated the Persians.

Sophocles was no lover of tyrants, who ruled with arrogance. But the problem with Creon was not that he was a tyrant but that he exercised his power inappropriately, an error to which tyrants were prone. Although Sophocles believed that Creon had the power to enact any law he chose, nonetheless he did not see Creon's behavior as correct, for with power comes responsibility. While the individual had an obligation to the state, the state also owed an obligation to allow the kin groups to uphold their religious and moral duties. Creon had the authority, but he abused it by going too far. While he had the legal right to order Polyneices to remain unburied, by doing so he brought religious and moral pollution on the land.

It was perfectly in keeping with Athenian law to forbid the burial of traitors. We have the case of the Athenian politician and war hero, Themistocles, who was exiled from Athens through ostracism. When he died abroad, his family wanted to bring his body back to Athens for burial, but they were refused. An unburied corpse caused pollution on the land. Just as in *Oresteia*, where Athena told the Furies that the people of Athens must have regard for them, so Sophocles and the people of Athens realized that the power of a tyrant or the power of the state did confer absolute authority on them. Creon could have had the body of Polyneices carried outside the land of Thebes and left there. This would have denied a traitor burial in the precincts of Thebes, while permitting the kin to bury him outside the city. In fact, in Aeschylus' *Seven against Thebes* and in Euripides' *Phoenician Women*, this was the punishment for Polyneices' corpse.

Unsure in his power, Creon was struggling to reestablish order after a civil war. As a result of his weakness and insecurity, he adopted a rigid position and made laws too severe, without good judgment. He had decreed that anyone who buried Polyneices would be put to death. Although it is not stated in the play, the audience would have recognized that Creon had a possible alternative of casting the body outside the land. Creon's decree was extreme in a culture in which the gods required that a corpse be buried. When Antigone is apprehended, in order to avoid the pollution of killing her outright, Creon entombs her alive with a small amount of food, to let her die from starvation. However, he does not succeed in avoiding pollution. The priest Teiresias, who, as in *Oedipus the King*, represents the reasoned position and the wisdom of the gods, tells Creon that he has polluted the state and upset the natural order of the universe by burying a living person and leaving a dead person unburied (lines 1064–76):

> And you should know as well, that you will not live
> through many more swift circuits of the sun
> before you yourself will give, in exchange for corpses,
> a child of your loins, a corpse of your own flesh and blood.
> For you have thrust below one who belongs above,
> blasphemously entombed a living person,
> and at the same time have kept above ground
> a corpse belonging to the chthonic gods—
> unburied, unmourned, unholy.
> Neither you nor the heavenly powers should have a part in this,
> but your violence has forced it. Now, sent by those gods,
> the foul avenging Furies, hunters of Hell,
> lie in wait to inflict the same evils on you.

Teiresias finally persuades Creon to change his mind, but it is too late to avert disaster. Creon hurries to the cave where he buried Antigone only to find that she has hanged herself. Upon finding the dead Antigone, Haemon, Creon's son and fiancé of Antigone, commits suicide. Creon's wife, Eurydice, kills herself on learning of the death of her son.

The tragic conflict is finally resolved by the death of Antigone and the destruction of the family of Creon. Sophocles' message to his audience was that the rites and obligations of the family must be subsumed under the rule of law. However, those who made the rules must take cognizance of the laws of the gods, thereby creating a harmony between divine laws and civil laws. Failure to do so results in death, destruction, pollution, and tragedy. The chorus, at the end of *Antigone*, perhaps best summarizes this (lines 1348–53):

> Reason is the greatest part of happiness,
> and knowing not to sin against the gods,
> but honor and revere them.

The mighty boasts of haughty men
bring down the punishment of mighty blows—
from which at last, in old age, wisdom comes.

Aristotle (*Poetics* 13) had almost nothing to say about *Antigone*, except to criticize the way Sophocles handled Haemon's suicide. However, Aristotelian precepts of tragedy have often been applied to the play by twentieth-century critics. Creon, not Antigone, better fits the definition of tragic hero. Creon, a person of high status, commits an error (*hamartia*), that is, his *hubris* or arrogance makes him think that he has the power to override the laws of the gods. He undergoes recognition (*anagnoresis*) when he finally changes his mind about Antigone. His fate, the loss of his child and wife, creates pity through fear and suffering and a catharsis for the audience. Antigone commits no error (*hamartia*), except perhaps her extreme stubbornness and devotion to the obligation of burying her brother. But she acts in keeping with the dictates of the gods. Her deeds and character allow no catharsis. She is a hero, but she does not fit Aristotle's definition nearly as well as Creon.

Antigone and Women in Greek Tragedy

In recent years scholars have analyzed Greek tragedy and literature increasingly through attention to gender. Feminist critics have been revising Freud's masculine theories and shifting from male to female heroes as paradigms. Some of these feminist critics have, in part, been influenced by the French feminist Luce Irigaray (*The Irigaray Reader* 1991). Irigaray's view is that women and mothers are the unacknowledged foundation of the social order and that Western culture is not founded on patricide as Freud suggested in *Totem and Taboo*, but on matricide. In one sense, Antigone represents for Irigaray the killing of the woman for the preservation of the social order. Among the more important works on gender in Greek tragedy have been Zeitlin's *Playing the Other: Gender and Society in Classical Greek Literature* (1995), Foley's *Female Acts in Greek Tragedy* (2001), and Butler's *Antigone's Claim: Kinship between Life and Death* (2000).

Greek society was completely dominated by men; women were practically invisible in the civic life of Athens. They could not vote, serve on juries, testify in court, or own property. They spent their entire lives under the guardianship of men, first their fathers, then their husbands or other male relatives. Aristotle (*Politics* 1259a) says that a husband rules his wife like a master his slave.

Greek myth portrays the followers of Dionysus as maenads and satyrs. Yet, paradoxically, women were virtually absent from the religious rites of worship of Dionysus at the Great Dionysia.

Despite these attitudes toward women, many Greek tragedies portray women in major dramatic roles, as in *Antigone*. The major religious and ethical obligation that drives *Antigone* is the need to bury the dead. In Greek society males and females had certain prescribed roles in dealing with the dead. Ritual mourning for the dead belonged to the realm of women; they would pour libations and lament, but only under male supervision. The burial ceremony and interment of the body were the duty of the male. The system ensured that some male relative was always available for this task. If there was no one in the immediate family to bury the dead, the obligation would pass to the males of a kindred group known as the *anchisteia*, patrilineal and matrilineal relatives to the degree of second cousin. If still no one was available, then the larger kinship group of the phratry would have the responsibility. In Athenian law it would be highly unusual for the obligation of burial to fall to a female. Athens from the sixth century aimed increasingly to control women's participation in death rituals and in public displays of emotion. To the Athenian audience, it would have been almost unthinkable for a woman to step forward to perform a burial.

The person most responsible for the burial of Polyneices would have been Creon, as a maternal uncle and nearest living male relative. However, it is precisely Creon who violates this obligation toward family, by refusing to bury his nephew and forbidding anyone else to do so. Not only does Creon prevent the burial of his nephew by a male but he also prevents the female relatives from mourning by taking their part in the rites, lamentations, and libations. Antigone has been denied her role as a woman who mourns the dead. To regain that prerogative, she thus takes on both aspects, the male role of burying and the female role of mourning. That Sophocles had a woman fulfill the kinship obligations of men would be particularly startling to the Greek audience and would emphasize a world turned upside down. In Greek religion the female spiritually guarded blood ties. It was the Furies, the spirits of vengeance, chthonic female goddesses, who pursued those who had spilled kindred blood. Antigone acts as a reminder of these Furies.

Foley (2001) argues that the gendering of ethical positions permits exploration of the moral complexities and conflicting demands enunciated in the play. Antigone takes on the role of sacrificial virgin, sacrificing marriage for the greater cause of burying her brother and serving unwritten laws. By leaving Polyneices unburied, Creon prevents the marriage of his son to his niece. Creon and Antigone face ethical moral and legal choices. Antigone's motive is her personal responsibility to bury blood relatives and honor the gods of the Underworld. She believes her sister, Ismene, has the same assumptions about burial and therefore does not try to persuade her of the rightness of the act but only seeks to stir her into action. When Ismene refuses to help, Antigone justifies her own position by saying that her act would be a holy crime (lines 69–75) and would not dishonor what was due to the gods below (line 77).

Both Antigone and Ismene assert the general principle that women should not act against men and the city. Ismene abides by that principle; Antigone defies it. As the last surviving member of her family who is willing to act, she defies men and the state to bury her brother. She adopts goals normally appropriate for men, such as pursuit of honor—and the citizens of Thebes praise her actions.

Antigone ignores the claims of the city in favor of familial bonds and abandons her marital bonds. As her guardian, Creon has the duty to arrange and complete Antigone's marriage, but instead he chooses civil obligations over familial ties. Creon argues to his son Haemon that sons should obey fathers and that wives are easily replaced. But Haemon's response to Creon is that kinship bonds play a critical role in public policy. Justice cannot be detached from the person or the family.

Gender can be a critical factor in defining moral action in Greek literature. Greek culture did not permit adult moral autonomy in women. Antigone considers that the unwritten laws require her to bury her kin. She tries to explain her behavior to three audiences: to Ismene, with arguments of family bonds; to Creon, with the argument of general principles of religion; and to the chorus, to whom she says that she has sacrificed marriage and children to follow a greater obligation toward kin. For Creon, interests of state are paramount and blood and marital obligations secondary to his obligation to the state.

Thus, Antigone is used in the play to represent significant moral alternatives. Tragedy creates extreme situations and unusually difficult choices. Moral authority is articulated in relation to gender in this play. The female expresses particular principles, while the male generalizes the principles of the state. The play examines cultural clichés about women and gender as a way to highlight and explicate contemporary Athenian social and political issues.

Johnson (1997) argues that Antigone manifests an Electra complex of the classic Freudian type in all three Theban plays of Sophocles. She is fixated on her father and unable or unwilling to transfer emotional attachment to an exogamous male replacement. First, Antigone goes into exile with blinded Oedipus, just after *Oedipus the King* ends; then, in *Oedipus at Colonus,* she escorts him in his wanderings until his death at Colonus; and in *Antigone,* she transfers her fixation onto Oedipus' son, her brother. It is modern psychoanalytic theory that gives these patterns of Antigone's be-

lviii   INTRODUCTION

havior a name. Johnson observes that Antigone claims to be acting only for her brother, not for all her relatives. In all three plays Antigone shows no interest in "normal" exogamous relations and is willing to give up all in a "marriage to death." Since this fixation may be part of incestuous desires in her pattern of devotion to father and brother, she is truly part of the perverted family of Oedipus, her father's daughter and sister.

Butler (2000) reinterprets Antigone as a model for feminism that resists and redefines the state. Most interpretations have been from a male perspective, one that sees Antigone in terms of the state she opposes, as a sign of the limits of the state. Butler compares the actions of Antigone to the acts of those who differ from the norm in our society, saying that a culture of normative heterosexuality obstructs the understanding of freedom from prescribed gender roles. She sees Antigone as a boundary figure between family and state, and between life and death, and she tries to reconceptualize her as a symbol greater than just an icon of defiance, whose form of defiance leads to her death. Sophocles' Antigone shows that the constraints of normative kinship, established by males, unjustly decide a woman's life and fate.

Sophocles' tragedy *Antigone* is a "possession for all time," since it encapsulates a basic struggle of all societies, as to whether the rule of law or the rule of morality and religion should take precedence. Creon has his defenders and Antigone hers. We see them in the many adaptations and versions of Sophocles' play throughout the millennia. One of the most recent is Mikis Theodorakis' opera *Antigone* (1999). When a military junta seized control of Greece in 1967 it first banned Theodorakis' music and then arrested and imprisoned him. The junta then outlawed the performance of various Greek tragedies but left Sophocles' *Antigone* alone. The play, which became a rallying cry against the junta, was performed as a protest almost weekly in Athens. When faced with an international outcry about the three-year-long detention of Theodorakis, the junta freed him on condition that he go into exile. In his opera, written decades after the junta's fall, he associates the junta with Creon. For him Antigone is the epitome of good, and Creon of evil. He writes about the opera:

> Antigone is a complete closed circle of a repeated human tragedy. It symbolizes eternal Evil, the repeated drama that accompanies the human race like a curse. It changes form and expression, adapting to the conditions of place and time. But its essence remains the same. The same applies to the principal players in the drama. On one side are the persecutors, on the other, the victims. . . . Out of the ashes and smoke of utter catastrophe, above the blackness, rise two pure white figures

like doves against a background of the darkness of death: Antigone and Haemon are no more than the obligatory innocent victims who will be sacrificed on the altar of ritual sacrifice, destined to propitiate the Shades of Evil, defiant and triumphant as ever. . . . The stance and the words of Antigone will be recorded as the impossible hope of all those who need to believe that the Good is not dead and that one day the basic instinct of evil will be defeated by the weapons of Love, the source of life, and Justice, its beauty.

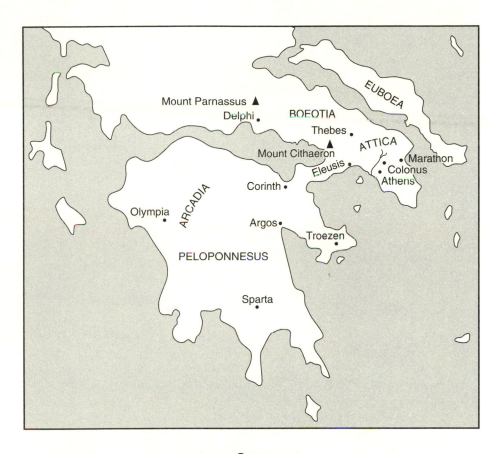

Greece

Time Line

Eighth century BC	*The Iliad* and *The Odyssey*, by Homer
540–527	Peisistratus, tyrant of Athens, founds festival of the Greater Dionysia
534	Thespis presents first tragedy in Athens and wins the first prize at the Great Dionysia
525	Aeschylus born
500	First satyr play, in Athens
497/96	Sophocles born
490	Battle of Marathon, invasion of Persia; beginning of Persian Wars
484	Aeschylus' first victory at the Great Dionysia
480/79	Euripides born. Battle of Thermopylae and Persian victory; battles of Salamis and Plataea and defeat of Persians
468	First play of Sophocles presented in Athens; Sophocles defeats Aeschylus at the Great Dionysia
467	Aeschylus writes trilogy about Oedipus
462/61	Pericles emerges as dominant leader of Athens
456	Aeschylus dies
449	Peace of Callias and end of Persian Wars
447	Parthenon, the temple of Athena, begun on the Acropolis of Athens
444–441?	*Antigone* produced
431	Beginning of Peloponnesian Wars, Sparta against Athens
431–425?	Herodotus writes *Histories*, describing the Persian Wars
429	Pericles dies

430–420?	*Oedipus the King* produced
409	Sophocles' *Philoctetes* produced
406	Sophocles dies; Euripides dies
404	End of Peloponnesian Wars; Athens defeated by Sparta and Thebes
401	*Oedipus of Colonus* produced by Sophocles' grandson
399	Trial and execution of Socrates
380s	Plato, in *Republic*, discusses Greek tragedy
330s	Aristotle, in *Poetics*, describes Greek tragedy and comedy
338–326	The Athenian orator Lycurgus' decree to make official copies of Aeschylus, Sophocles, and Euripides
ca. 200	Aristophanes of Byzantium (ca. 257–180) writes edition of Sophocles' works
ca. 180	Aristarchus (ca. 216–144) writes commentary on Sophocles
End of first century BC	Didymus Chalcenterus (ca. 63 BC–AD 10) composes comprehensive edition of Sophocles

Oedipus the King

Cast of Characters in Order of Appearance
OEDIPUS, King of Thebes, son of Jocasta and King Laius
PRIEST of Zeus
CREON, brother of Jocasta
CHORUS of fifteen Theban elders
TEIRESIAS, a blind prophet
JOCASTA, wife and mother of Oedipus
CORINTHIAN MESSENGER, old man of Corinth, servant of King
Polybus
SHEPHERD, slave of the royal house of Thebes
SECOND MESSENGER, servant within the house

Nonspeaking Parts
ANTIGONE, daughter of Oedipus and Jocasta
ISMENE, daughter of Oedipus and Jocasta
GUARDS and ATTENDANTS
YOUNG BOY who leads Teiresias

SCENE: *In front of the palace of Thebes. Double doors on the stage are the entrance to the palace, and an altar of the god Apollo is in the middle of the orchestra. One entrance, on the left side of the stage, represents the road to Corinth and Delphi. The entrance on the right side of the stage is the direction of the city of Thebes.*

TIME: *Two generations before the Trojan War. Oedipus has been king for many years since solving the riddle of the Sphinx. A plague has struck the city.*

(A procession of citizens and priests, carrying the signs of suppliants, enters. The double doors open and OEDIPUS *comes forward.)*

OEDIPUS

My children, new stock of old Cadmus,	1
why are you seated here before me	
crowned by suppliants' wreaths,	
and the air of the city dense with incense,	
groans, paeans, and prayers?	5
It is not enough to learn such things	
from others, and so I come myself.	
I, Oedipus, whose fame is known to all.	

Tell me, old man, you are the one	
who should speak for the people—why are you here,	10
what do you want, and fear? I will help	
however I can. It would be heartless	
not to pity such desperate pleas.	

PRIEST

O Oedipus, ruler of our country,	
you see us gathered at the altar—	15
some not yet strong enough to fly the nest,	
others crippled by age. I am a priest of Zeus.	
The best of our youth stand here with me.	
All your people, garlanded, wait in the marketplace	
at the double shrines of Pallas Athena,	20
the mantic fire on the banks of Ismenus.	

You can see that the city is in turmoil,	
everything in confusion. Bloody plague	
crashes over our heads like a tide of death,	
blighting the fruits of the earth,	25

blighting the wombs of cattle and women.
A fiery fever god stalks among us,
the city is emptied, the house of Cadmus
is mortally weakened, and black
Hades fattens on groans and tears.   30
No man can be the equal of the gods.
We do not compare you to them. But,
as first among men, tempered by life,
you know how to deal with whatever the gods bring.
You came to Cadmus' city and freed us   35
from the tribute payment the Sphinx demanded—
that cruel singer! We could not tell you what
to do or how to do it—but we are sure
that the gods must have helped you to save our lives.

O Oedipus, most powerful of all,   40
as humble suppliants we beg for help.
Strengthen us now—either
through the inspiration of a god or
by human wisdom. I know that
the man who has lived most gives the best advice.   45
Come, noblest of men, rescue our city.
Come—act—because the whole country calls you
its hero since you first saved us.
Let your reign not be remembered
as starting in triumph but ending in disaster.   50
Save us again and rescue our city.
You brought good luck then and good omens—
bring equal fortune now.
You have power over this land—surely
it is better to rule living men.   55
An abandoned ship or the broken walls and towers
of an empty city are nothing.

OEDIPUS
Pitiful children, you come to me
wanting answers I cannot always give.
I already know how sick you are—but you   60
must know that I am stricken most of all.
The misery of each is for himself alone, none other.
But my soul groans for the whole city,

for each of you as well as for myself.
Do not think you woke me from sleep. 65
Sleepless I pace and weep and my mind
wanders all the roads of thought
in search of remedy. The only one I found
was this: to send my kinsman Creon,
Menoeceus' son, my wife Jocasta's brother, 70
to the Pythia at the shrine of Phoebus Apollo,
to ask the god what I could do or say to save my city.
But too much time has passed, and now
I wonder, what is he doing?—
he has been away so long. 75
Whatever message he brings,
I shall obey the god's command.

PRIEST
These are gracious and timely words—and look,
your servants wave and call that he approaches.

OEDIPUS
O lord Apollo, let it be your favored blessing on us 80
that shines from his eyes.

PRIEST
And all seems well—why else would his head
be garlanded with full-berried bay leaves?

OEDIPUS
Soon we shall know. He is close enough to hear.
Creon, welcome, my kinsman, son of Menoeceus. 85
What word do you bring from the shrine of Apollo?

(Enter CREON *from direction of Delphi.)*
CREON
Good news, I say, because if it ends well,
even what seems the worst would be good fortune.

OEDIPUS
What do you mean? As yet
I do not know whether to hope or fear. 90

CREON
Do you want these others to hear,
or should we go inside?

OEDIPUS
Speak to us all. I bear the pain
of everyone, not merely my own.

CREON
I shall tell what I heard from the god.   95
Lord Phoebus commands
that to drive this plague from our land, nourished by our land,
we must root it out, or it will be past cure.

OEDIPUS
What rite will expiate this crime?

CREON
Banishment or death for death—blood unavenged   100
menaces the city like a storm.

OEDIPUS
Does Apollo reveal the man who was killed?

CREON
Laius, O lord, was the ruler
of this city, before you saved it.

OEDIPUS
I have heard about him. But I never saw him.   105

CREON
He was killed, and the god clearly commands
vengeance upon his murderers.

OEDIPUS
Where can they be? Where
can we find the traces of this ancient crime?

CREON
He says it lies in this land. What is sought   110
is found; the ignored will disappear.

OEDIPUS
Was it in another place, or here
in his own house or fields, that Laius died?

CREON
He was traveling abroad, so he said, on pilgrimage to Delphi,
but never returned home.   115

OEDIPUS
Did no one survive, was there no one else on the road
who saw what happened and could tell us something?

CREON
Everyone died, except one, who fled in fear
and could remember only one thing—

OEDIPUS
What did he say? From one clue   120
much can be deduced. This gives me hope.

CREON
He said it was a band of robbers
that attacked and killed him, not one, but many hands.

OEDIPUS
How could a single robber, unless bribed
by some vile man from here, dare to kill him?   125

CREON
That was thought of then. But with Laius' death,
we had no defender against the many evils.

OEDIPUS
The king overthrown,
what evil was enough to stop the search?

CREON
The Sphinx's riddling demands   130
kept our thoughts on what was at our feet.

OEDIPUS
I shall go back to the start of it all—
I know the god's and your concern
for the one who has died.
You will see me as a true ally   135
avenging this land and Phoebus Apollo.
Not only for old friends but also for myself
must I drive away this defilement.
Whoever killed Laius now might choose
to murder me. To solve that crime   140
is to protect myself.
Come, children, hasten
from the altar steps, and raise your olive wreaths.
Let someone call the people of Cadmus
to join us. I vow to do all that I can.   145
With the god's help, either we triumph or fail.

PRIEST
Rise to your feet.
We have heard what we want: Oedipus agrees.
And may the sacred power of Phoebus Apollo,
and the oracles he sent, defeat this plague.   150

(The PRIEST *and suppliants leave through the right side, toward Thebes.*
OEDIPUS *exits through the double doors.* CREON *exits on the right.)*

(The CHORUS *of fifteen elders of Thebes enters the orchestra from the right*
and sings the opening ode, the parodos.*)*

CHORAL ENTRY SONG *(parodos)*
CHORUS   Strophe A (151–57)
Is that the sweet-sounding voice of Zeus
from the gold-decked Pythian shrine
come to glorious Thebes?
My mind shudders with fear.
In awe we invoke you, healer-god of Delos.
What price will you exact, now or in the future,

for what we ask?
Speak, immortal child of golden Hope,
we crave your words.

Antistrophe A (158–67)

First we call on you, daughter of Zeus,
deathless Athena, and your sister Artemis,
queen of our earth, on her throne in the marketplace,
and on Phoebus the far-shooting archer—
O you three, with your threefold power
to defend us now from death, appear!
As you have saved us before from destruction
racing toward our city,
save us again from these new flames of woe.
Come to us here.

Strophe B (168–78)

Alas, our troubles are endless.
All the people are sick—
no one knows how we can defend ourselves,
even the hardest thought cannot forge spear or sword.
Our richest fields are sterile now.
Our women labor in stillbirth.
Wherever you look, like winged birds
or forest fire, crowds flee toward
the darkening west, to Hades' land.

Antistrophe B (179–89)

The city dies through these unnumbered deaths.
Its unmourned children rot on the plain
in pitiless contagion,
its wives and faded mothers wander
from one altar to another
groaning their woes and prayers.
The voices blend with the flutes in a paean to you,
O bright-faced, golden daughter of Zeus.
Send us your aid.

Strophe C (190–202)

We hear no clash of brazen arms,
but Ares' threats and war cries ring through the city,
torment us night and day.
Oh, drive him from the borders of our fatherland
out to the furthest reaches of the western sea
and Amphitrite's chamber,

or toward the rocky northern shores of Thrace
beyond the Hellespont,
for what night leaves unfinished, day completes—
you who wield the power of lightning stroke
to blast, and thunderbolt to crush him,
Great Father Zeus.

Antistrophe C (203–15)

And you, shining wolf-god Apollo,
let the adamantine shafts, our defenders,
fly from your plaited golden bowstring
like Artemis' fiery torches
when she hunts on the Lycian hills.
Let the gold-crowned god
named for this land, wine-faced Bacchus,
come with his troop of maenads
brandishing their pitchy torches
and crying *Euoi!*
to drive off Ares our enemy—
that god despised by every other god.

(OEDIPUS *enters through the double doors.*)
OEDIPUS
I hear what you ask. And if you heed my words,
and tend the plague, much might be done
to overcome these evils.
I speak as a stranger to the story
and commission of this crime, with no idea   220
where to hunt for clues and signs.
But now I am one of you, a citizen
of Thebes—and announce to all Cadmeans
that whoever knows the name of the killer
of Laius, son of Labdacus,   225
I command him to reveal it to me.
Even if he must confess the crime
*   *   *   *   *   *
himself, he has nothing to fear but banishment.
Unharmed he may depart this land.
If someone knows the murderer,   230
be he citizen or stranger, he should speak now.
He will be rewarded and thanked.
But if no one will speak, and shielding a friend

or himself, ignores my words,
let him hear the punishment.   235

This man, whoever he is, will be forbidden
in any part of my realm,
nor may anyone give him aid
or shelter or greeting,
nor with him share the rites, libations,   240
and sacrifice to the gods, but should
thrust him from their house—being one accursed—
as the Pythian Oracle revealed to me.
Thus I honor my duty to the god
and to the dead man.   245
I pray that whoever did this—even if he has,
alone or with his murderous accomplices, escaped—
may his life always be wretched.
And I pray that if he should be one of my household—
and I know it—then let me suffer   250
every punishment I call down on others.
I ask you to make sure these things are done—
not only for my sake and for the sake of the god
but for our barren, god-forsaken land.
Even if it were not god-urged,   255
it would be wrong to allow this foulness to survive.
A noble man, a king, has died.
We must seek out the cause and avenge it.
Now that I rule with the same power he held,
become his kin, his wife and bed now mine—   260
and if he had been blessed with children as I have,
their birth from the same mother
would have bound us even closer.
But evil fortune came to that man.
Now, as if he were my own father,   265
I shall do everything I can to find the murderer
of the son of Labdacus, son of Polydorus,
of Cadmus before him, and ancient Agenor.
And whoever does not help me, I pray the gods
may blight their land and the wombs   270
of their wives, that their fate will be
to die an even worse death than his.
But for all loyal Cadmeans,

may their ally Justice,
and all the gods, be gracious and kind.   275

CHORUS *(The coryphaeus, the leader of the* CHORUS, *speaks.)*
Because of your curse, my lord, I must speak,
for I did not kill him nor can I say who did.
Phoebus set the task—it is for the god to tell
who did the deed.

OEDIPUS
You are right. But no one can force   280
the gods to speak if they do not wish.

CHORUS
The second thing I'll say—

OEDIPUS
And if you have one, give me your third reason also!

CHORUS
I know that the seer Teiresias sees most like Phoebus.
If you can know what he sees,   285
you will come closest to the truth.

OEDIPUS
But I have not been idle and done nothing.
After hearing Creon talk of him, I sent two messengers,
and it is strange that he is not yet here.

CHORUS
All those old reports are dull and stale—   290

OEDIPUS
What reports? Is there something I have not looked into?

CHORUS
They say he was attacked by a gang of thieves and killed on the road.

OEDIPUS
That's what I heard. But no one saw who did it.

CHORUS
If he knows what fear is, that man,
he will not linger, after your curses.   295

OEDIPUS
If he did not fear murder, he will not fear curses.

CHORUS
But here comes the one to find him—
Teiresias. They lead him in, the divine seer—he who,
alone among men, always knows the truth.

(*Enter* TEIRESIAS, *a blind seer, led by a* YOUNG BOY, *from the direction
of Thebes.*)
OEDIPUS
O Teiresias, you who know and teach   300
Olympian secrets and mysteries here on the earth!
Though sightless, you perceive everything.
You know what sickness gnaws at the city.
Like a soldier in the front row of the phalanx
who takes the first onslaught, you alone can save us.   305
You must already know Phoebus' message—
that the end to this plague will only come
when we track down Laius' murderers
and kill them, or drive them from this land.
Whatever method you have to read the future—   310
from the flight of birds, or other ways of augury—
use it now to save yourself, your city, and me
from the pollution of unavenged murder.
We are all in your hands. For a man to use
his gifts to help others is the most noble labor.   315

TEIRESIAS
Alas, how awful it is to have wisdom, when such knowledge
is useless. I knew this already, but ignored it—
or else I would have known better than to come.

OEDIPUS
How is it that you are so reluctant?

TEIRESIAS
Let me go home. It will be better.   320
We shall each bear our fate easier if you obey me.

OEDIPUS
It is neither right nor kind to the city that bred you
if you deny it your prophetic powers.

TEIRESIAS
I see your words fall wide of the mark and miss their aim.
I don't want mine to do the same.   325

OEDIPUS
With the knowledge you have from the gods,
we bow at your feet and implore you to speak, not turn away.

TEIRESIAS
You cannot imagine what evil I know already—
though I will not reveal it.

OEDIPUS
Do I hear right—that you will not tell what you know?   330
Do you want to betray us and destroy the city?

TEIRESIAS
I do not want to harm you—or myself.
Do not interrogate me. I will say nothing.

OEDIPUS
O wicked, heartless man—you would madden
even a stone. Why will you not speak out   335
but insolent, stay stubbornly mute?

TEIRESIAS
You attack my anger and blame me,
unconscious of your own.

OEDIPUS
Who would not be angry, hearing how
you deny me and dishonor our city?   340

TEIRESIAS
These things will come, though I muffle them in silence.

OEDIPUS
What will come? You must tell me!

TEIRESIAS
I shall say nothing else, but stay silent,
no matter how you rage and storm.

OEDIPUS
And I shall not hold back what I know, my anger   345
will not allow it. Know that I think you
were part of the plot, and even, I say,
that you alone would have done the evil deed
with your own hands, if you were not a blind man.

TEIRESIAS
Is this so? Let me tell you—   350
you must abide by your own decree.
From this day forth, you must not speak to me or any man.
You yourself are the sacrilegious curse of this land.

OEDIPUS
Shameless to say such things!
Where do you think to escape now?   355

TEIRESIAS
No need to escape. My words are true.

OEDIPUS
Who taught you this? Not your prophetic skill!

TEIRESIAS
It was you; and made me speak against my will.

OEDIPUS
What did I say? Tell me once more, so I can try to take it in.

TEIRESIAS
Have you not yet understood? Do you want to test me?   360

OEDIPUS
Perhaps I did not comprehend—explain it again.

TEIRESIAS
I repeat that you yourself are the murderer you seek.

OEDIPUS
You will be sorry if you say that again—

TEIRESIAS
I'll tell you something else, which will anger you even more.

OEDIPUS
Spew out whatever you like—it will mean nothing to me.   365

TEIRESIAS
All unaware, you have done shameless things with
your closest and dearest, and do not yet see the full horror of your
    deeds.

OEDIPUS
Do you think you can say that and go unpunished?

TEIRESIAS
There is strength in truth.

OEDIPUS
In truth, yes. But this is not truth,   370
but the ravings of a deaf, witless, blind man—blind in all his senses.

TEIRESIAS
And you, poor wretch, will soon be the butt
of every insult you now direct at me.

OEDIPUS
You are a creature of night, and cannot
harm me, nor any other who can see the light.   375

TEIRESIAS
It is not I who has made your fate.
That was Apollo's task—that is his care.

OEDIPUS
Is it Creon, or another, who set you to this?

TEIRESIAS
Creon is not your enemy—it is yourself.

OEDIPUS
Power and wealth, kingship and skill   380
surpassing skill in every art of life—
how they all produce only envy!
And is it because of this power—which the city
granted of its own free will, unasked for—
that Creon, whom I trusted as a friend,   385
now tries to undermine and depose me
by sending this trickster, this wizard
who can see nothing but his own gain,
being blind in his supposed art?
Give me an example of your vision.   390
How is it that when the dog-haunched singer squatted here
you said nothing to save the city and its people?
The riddle should not have waited for a stranger
to solve it. There was need of a prophet—
but neither from birds nor gods did you learn   395
the answer. It was I, Oedipus,
the ignorant, who stopped her, who triumphed
through my own intelligence, not the help of gods or birds—
I, whom you call the curse, and think to depose, hoping
it will bring you closer to power in Creon's court.   400
Believe me, the two of you, your plotting
will end in tears. If you were not so old
I would punish you for such disloyal thoughts.

CHORUS
It seems to us that the words of both—his
and yours—are spoken in anger. Oedipus,   405
this is pointless, and will get us no further
toward obeying the words of the oracle.

TEIRESIAS
Even though you are the king, I am your equal
in this—the right to reply.

I am no man's slave. I serve Loxias.   410
Creon has no power over me.
But I say to you, who have taunted me in my blindness,
that though you have sight, you cannot see your own evil
nor the truth of where you live and whom you live with.
Do you know your origin, know that you are the enemy   415
of all your line, those below the earth and those still on it,
and that your mother's and father's double-edged curse
with deadly step will drive you from this land—
like a light revealing all, before it blinds you.

Every cave and shelter in Cithaeron will echo   420
with your cries, when you realize
the full meaning of the marriage
you thought would be your safe harbor.
You cannot yet see the throng of other evils
which will reduce you to the level of your children.   425
Say the worst that you can about me and about Creon—
pelt us with mud—but there is no mortal
who will be more befouled than you.

OEDIPUS
I will not suffer this! I refuse to listen!
Damn you—get out—   430
why have you not gone, why are you still here?

TEIRESIAS
I would not have come if you had not summoned me.

OEDIPUS
If I had known you would say such foolish things
I would not have ordered you here.

TEIRESIAS
I might seem a fool to you—   435
but your parents thought me wise.

OEDIPUS
My parents? Wait—you knew those who bore me?

TEIRESIAS
This day bears your birth and destruction.

OEDIPUS
Riddling again!

TEIRESIAS
You are good at riddles.   440

OEDIPUS
You mock my talent.

TEIRESIAS
The same talent has destroyed you.

OEDIPUS
But if I saved the city—that is all I care about.

TEIRESIAS
Good. I shall go. You, boy, lead me away.

OEDIPUS
Yes, let him lead you away. Your presence disturbs me.   445
I shall be glad when you have gone.

TEIRESIAS
When I have said what I came to say, then I shall leave—
not because I fear you. You cannot do me harm.
I tell you—the man you have sought for so long,
threatened, and denounced as the murderer   450
of Laius—that man is here.
Now he is called a stranger, an alien, but soon
will be known as a native-born Theban—
which will bring him no joy.
A beggar not a rich man, blind who now has eyes,   455
hesitantly tapping his staff through a foreign land,
he will be exposed as brother and father
to his own children, son and husband
to the woman who bore him, sharer of the marriage bed
with the father he murdered.   460

You go inside, but think on this. If I have seen wrong,
then call me blind—a false prophet.

(*Exit* TEIRESIAS, *led by the* BOY, *toward Thebes, stage right.* OEDIPUS
exits through the double doors into the palace. The CHORUS *sings the first*
stasimon.)

FIRST *STASIMON*

CHORUS   Strophe A (463–72)
Who is this man the oracular rocks of Delphi curse
for unspeakable deeds
too terrible to describe?
Whose blood-drenched hands have done such work?
The hour has come for him to flee
like a horse before the storm
from the wrath of leaping Apollo,
armed like his father Zeus with fire and lightning bolt,
and from the implacable Keres,
goddesses of death, who snap at his heels.

                                        Antistrophe A (473–82)

See how the signal flashes
from snow-capped Parnassus
for all to hunt the fugitive
through the tangled forest
and the deepest caverns
where he lurks between boulders
like a mountain bull with a crippled foot,
wretched and solitary, desperate to hide
from the oracles of the Omphalos
who flutter and squeak around his head.

                                        Strophe B (483–97)

What this wise old prophet reads
from the auguries, agitates me, agitates me.
I am torn, and cannot decide
if I should believe what he says, or deny it—
waver between hope and fear,
uncertain where to seek the truth.

Tell me, what was the quarrel
between the house of Labdacus
and Polybus' son?

I have never heard talk of one,
now or in the past,
which might serve as proof; without it
how can I go against the good name of Oedipus—
I who am defender of the house of Labdacus—
and blame him for this obscure death?

Antistrophe B (498–512)

Zeus and Apollo are wise,
see deep into the hearts of men.
But even the most famous seer
is only a man, in the end—
need be no wiser than me.
Until I am convinced
that what the auger says is true,
I shall not believe those who blame the king.
When he bested the Sphinx, the Winged Maiden,
and saved our city
everyone loved him—
that will be my touchstone.
Until his guilt is proved,
for me he will be innocent.

(Enter CREON *from the direction of Thebes, stage right.)*
CREON
Citizens, I am told
that King Oedipus makes vile accusations against me.
It is unbearable!   515
If in his present misfortunes
he thinks he has suffered at my hands,
his troubles caused by anything I've done
by word or deed, I would not want to live.
Such slander is not a simple thing to bear   520
but the worst of all—it taints me doubly
as an evil, both to my city and to my friends.

CHORUS *(The coryphaeus speaks.)*
He says it, yes—but perhaps
he speaks without thinking, in anger.

CREON
Does he claim that I persuaded the seer   525
to make these accusations and say these lying words?

CHORUS
That is what he said, but I do not know the reason.

CREON
Were his eyes clear, did he seem calm
when he laid this charge against me?

CHORUS
I cannot tell you, I am not witness of my master's acts.   530
But he himself now comes out of the house.

(Enter OEDIPUS *through the double doors of the palace.)*
OEDIPUS
You—wretch—how dare you show your face? Or
are you so shameless that you come to my house
openly, as an acknowledged murderer,
who schemes to rob me of my kingdom?   535
By the gods—do you regard me
as such a fool and coward that you can do these things,
or think I would not guess your most secret
plans and then protect myself?
And what a stupid plan—without   540
the backing of party and fortune and friends—
to think that you could track and seize the crown.

CREON
Do you have a better idea? Listen to me,
I will speak calmly, and you can judge.

OEDIPUS
You are good at making excuses, but I am bad   545
at believing them. To me, they sound like threats.

CREON
At least, hear what I have to say.

OEDIPUS
As long as you do not claim you are not evil.

CREON
If you think this mindless bluster
is something to be proud of, you think wrong.   550

OEDIPUS
And if you think you can do evil against your kinsman
and not be punished, you think wrong.

CREON
I admit your words are just. But tell me,
what harm have I done you?

OEDIPUS
Did you, or did you not, insist I must   555
send for that man, that famous prophet?

CREON
And I would still give the same advice—

OEDIPUS
And how long is it since Laius—

CREON
Since Laius did what? What do you mean?

OEDIPUS
Vanished. Was murdered.   560

CREON
It was a very long time ago.

OEDIPUS
And was this seer as famous then?

CREON
Yes, and just as honored.

OEDIPUS
Did he mention my name then?

CREON
Not as far as I know.   565

OEDIPUS
But you searched for the killer?

CREON
Of course we did. But we discovered nothing.

OEDIPUS
And if he was so wise, why could he not find out these things?

CREON
I do not know, and so can give no answer.

OEDIPUS
You know very well—so say what you know.   570

CREON
What do I know? I would speak if I had something to say.

OEDIPUS
Because—if he were not in league with you,
he would never have said I killed Laius!

CREON
If he does say that, then you know why—
I am learning as much from you as you from me.   575

OEDIPUS
Learn then that I will not be named a murderer.

CREON
Yet, did you not take my sister for wife?

OEDIPUS
How can I deny it?

CREON
And rule with equal power, you and she, over this land?

OEDIPUS
She has an equal share in everything. 580

CREON
And therefore am I not also equal to you both, one third of three?

OEDIPUS
Now you show your true thoughts—treacherous friend!

CREON
Not if you think about it coolly, as I have.
Consider this first: would anyone
choose to rule with all the fear that brings, rather 585
than sleep in peace, yet with the same power?
It is not in my nature to crave
the name of king—I'd rather do what a king does,
like anyone with good judgment.

Now, I have everything—except the fear. 590
If I were king, I would be forced into actions I hated.
How much sweeter to have the power
but not the grief of being king.
I am not such a fool that I need
more than the privilege and profit. 595

Now, I greet everyone equally, and they all praise me.
Now, whoever wants a favor from you, shows favor to me,
hoping it will help them gain what they wish.
Why would I give up all this?
A man who sees the world clearly does not plot treason. 600
No, I would never think like that,
nor fraternize with those who did.
And for proof, to test my words, go to the Pythia at Delphi,
question the oracle whether what I say is true.
If you should catch me out, plotting 605
with the seer, then sentence and slay me, not only
with your one vote, but with two—both mine and yours.

But if you are not sure, do not accuse me.
It is not justice to believe without proof
in the virtue of bad men, or that good men are evil.   610
To reject a true friend
is like casting away your own life.
In time you will understand such things,
for time alone reveals the just man—
but the evil-doer is recognized at once.   615

CHORUS
What he says makes sense—safer to heed it
than to act in haste, stumble, and fall.

OEDIPUS
If he plots swift and secret
I must be as quick.
Otherwise, he will act while I wait   620
and all my aims miss their targets.

CREON
What do you want? To banish me?

OEDIPUS
Exile is not enough. I want your death.
*   *   *   *   *   *   *

CREON
That's what envy leads to!
*   *   *   *   *

OEDIPUS
Stubborn wretch! Why don't you believe me?   625

CREON: Because it's clear your mind is in chaos.
    OEDIPUS: —about myself?

CREON: Certainly about me.
    OEDIPUS: You are treacherous!

CREON: And you understand nothing—
    OEDIPUS: Except that I am king, and rule.

CREON: —rule badly.
　　OEDIPUS: O city, my city!

CREON
My city also, not only yours!　　　　　　　　　　　630

CHORUS
Stop, lords! Here, just in time
I see Jocasta come from the house.
She will make peace between you.

(*Enter* JOCASTA, *through the double doors.*)
JOCASTA
You foolish men, why have you begun
to quarrel? Aren't you ashamed,　　　　　　　　　635
the whole land sick, to flaunt your petty discontents?
Go home, the two of you. You—and you also, Creon.
You are making much of nothing.

CREON
Sister, your husband thinks he can do
what he likes to me—either drive me　　　　　　640
out of my home and land, or kill me.

OEDIPUS
Yes wife, it's true, exactly that—for I caught him
plotting evil against me.

CREON
May I never prosper and let me die accursed
if I have done any of this!　　　　　　　　　　　645

JOCASTA
If he swears by the gods it is true,
then by the gods, trust him, Oedipus—
do this for me, and all these others.

FIRST *KOMMOS*

CHORUS　　　　　　　　　　　Strophe (649–78)
Think carefully, then yield,
I beg you, my lord.

OEDIPUS
What exactly do you want me to do?

CHORUS
Accept his word. He is no fool,
and swears before the gods.

OEDIPUS
Do you know what you are asking?

CHORUS *(The coryphaeus speaks):* I know—   655
        OEDIPUS: Say it again—make it absolutely clear.

CHORUS
That you should not believe an unproved charge
against a friend who swears his innocence.

OEDIPUS
Can you not understand that what you ask
signifies my banishment and destruction?

CHORUS
Never! not even by the greatest of the gods,   660
Helios. Let me die godless,
friendless and desperate,
before I think such things.
My grief is the fate of this blighted land,   665
and my heart will be torn in two
if to this evil is added
such hatred between you both.

OEDIPUS
Let him go, then—even if it means I must die,
or be forced into exile, dishonored.   670
It is not his words that move me, but yours.
Wherever he is, I shall always hate him.

CREON
How hard it is for you to yield!
The weight of your own nature
is heavier for you to bear than any other.   675

OEDIPUS
Get away from me—leave me alone!

CREON
I am going. You are vicious—
but these others have saved me.

(Exit CREON *toward Thebes, stage right.)*

CHORUS   Antistrophe (679–96)
Why so slow, O wife of Oedipus,
to lead this man into the house?   680

JOCASTA
When I know what's happened—

CHORUS
Unjust suspicions, ignorant accusations
gnaw at the heart.

JOCASTA
From each of them?

CHORUS: Yes.   685
     JOCASTA: But what was said?

CHORUS
Already we suffer enough through our land's misfortunes.
We need no other cause of grief.

OEDIPUS
Good man that you are—yet
you see what it leads to, your effort to soothe my anger.

CHORUS
Dear lord, I say it again—   690
that I would be quite mad, an idiot,
to turn from you now, you
who carried our land to safety,
like a ship before a fair wind,

from its time of woes.   695
Now once again may you be our good pilot.

JOCASTA
By the gods, tell me the truth,
my lord—what it was
that caused such anger?

OEDIPUS
Wife whom I respect more than these men,   700
I say it is Creon who has plotted against me.

JOCASTA
But can you tell me clearly the cause of the quarrel?

OEDIPUS
He dares to say that it was I who murdered Laius.

JOCASTA
Is this his own accusation, or is he repeating another's?

OEDIPUS
He sent his charlatan-wizard to speak for him,   705
so he is free of blame.

JOCASTA
My dear, forget all that.
Listen to what I have to say, and learn
that no mortal can prophesy the future—
and I can prove it.   710
Long ago, an oracle came here to Laius—
I will not claim from Phoebus himself, but one of his priests—
who told him it was his fate to die by the hand
of any child born to me and him.
But you know the story—it was foreign robbers   715
who killed him at the crossroad where three roads meet.
And three days after the birth of our boy
Laius pinned the infant's feet together
and gave the order to expose him on the pathless mountainside.
So Apollo's prophecy was not accomplished: 720
that child could never murder his father,

nor Laius suffer the fate he feared.
Such predictions can be ignored;
they mean nothing. Whatever a god wants,
he can tell us himself. 725

OEDIPUS
What agitation grips my mind and spirit
as I hear you, wife.

JOCASTA
But why does this make you so anxious?

OEDIPUS
I seemed to hear you say that Laius
was butchered where three roads meet. 730

JOCASTA
That was the story then, and still is now.

OEDIPUS
Where did this awful thing happen?

JOCASTA
Phocis the place is called,
where the roads from Daulis and Delphi join.

OEDIPUS
And how long ago was it? 735

JOCASTA
It was just before you appeared and took power in this land,
that the news came to the city.

OEDIPUS
O Zeus, what are your plans for me?

JOCASTA
Tell me what troubles your heart, Oedipus.

OEDIPUS
Don't ask yet. Just say—what did he look like,   740
how old was Laius then?

JOCASTA
Tall enough, and beginning to go grey.
Very much as you look now.

OEDIPUS
Woe is me! How wretched I am, self-cursed
through my own ignorance.   745

JOCASTA
I don't want to understand what you mean.

OEDIPUS
I dread that seer saw right.
But you will help me most if you can tell me one more thing.

JOCASTA
I shrink with dread also, but if I can, I'll answer your question.

OEDIPUS
Was he alone, or did he have armed men with him,   750
the proper escort of a leader?

JOCASTA
There were five of them, including a herald,
and Laius rode in the carriage.

OEDIPUS
Alas, it all comes clear. Who was it
who told this to you, wife?   755

JOCASTA
A servant who returned alone, the only survivor.

OEDIPUS
Is he still here in the house now?

JOCASTA
No. Because when he arrived from that place and saw
that you were lord now Laius had perished,
he knelt, taking my hand, and begged me   760
to send him away to the fields to be my shepherd,
far from all sight of this city.
And I agreed. He was the sort, though a slave,
who deserved even greater favor.

OEDIPUS
Can he be brought here, quickly?   765

JOCASTA
Yes, it can be done. But why do you ask?

OEDIPUS
I am afraid, Jocasta. I have said too much already.
That is why I must see him.

JOCASTA
Then he will come. But surely I deserve to be told
what is tormenting you, lord.   770

OEDIPUS
I shall not hold back from telling you
my worst fears. Who else is dearer to me, or better
to share these things than you?

My father was Polybus of Corinth,
my mother, Merope, a Dorian. And I   775
was thought the first among our citizens
until, one night, something unexpected happened—
which I would have done better to ignore.
A drunken guest at a banquet called out
that I was a bastard, not my father's son.   780
I managed to hold my tongue then, but it rankled,
and the next day went to my parents, repeated
what he had said and demanded the truth.
They were furious and denied it absolutely.
I believed them, but was still angry.   785
And the story spread—the way they always do.

Not saying a word to my parents,
I presented myself to the Pythian oracle,
but Phoebus refused my question—
instead, made terrible forecasts   790
that I was doomed to sleep with my mother
and engender a monstrous brood; become
the murderer of my own father.
Hearing such awful things, I fled,
using the stars as guides to make sure   795
I always moved away from Corinth,
so the evil oracle would never be accomplished,
and at last arrived at the place
where you say your old king died.

Wife, to you I can tell the truth.   800
As I came near to where the three roads join
I met a herald, and a horse-drawn carriage
like those you describe—
and the herald, and the man in the carriage,
forced me off the road.   805
It was the driver, as he tried to turn me aside,
I struck out at first in my anger.
Then, as I pushed past, the old man
jabbed from above at my head with his double goad.
But he paid for this—for now,   810
with the staff in my hand, I tumbled him out of the cart
and onto his back in the road
and slaughtered them all. If that stranger
had any connection with Laius,
what man is more wretched than I?   815
Who could be more hated by the gods than he
whom no stranger or citizen must allow into their house
nor speak to, but must cast out
and turn away—and it is I alone
who laid these curses on myself!   820
The very bed of the murdered man
is polluted by the same hands that killed him.
O awful! Totally evil, I must seek even further
exile, to make sure I'll never meet one of my own kin
nor tread the soil of my birth, or else I am doomed   825
to mate with my own mother and slay Polybus,

the father who begot and raised me.
How could someone, judging such a fate,
not think me the plaything of a savage god?
No, let me vanish and die first,   830
before my name is stained forever by such shame.
Never, never, believe me, shall I allow
such things to happen, or commit such acts.

CHORUS
We shrink from such knowledge, O lord,
but until he has spoken, you can have hope.   835

OEDIPUS
Indeed, this is my only hope—
to wait for the shepherd.

JOCASTA
And when he comes, what is it you want to hear?

OEDIPUS
I shall tell you. If his story confirms yours,
my suffering will be over.   840

JOCASTA
What did I say that seemed so important?

OEDIPUS
You insisted he said that robber men
had killed him. Men—not a man. If he still
says that, I could not have done it,
because one is not the same as many.   845
But if he is sure it was one man alone,
then the scales of justice tilt and make me guilty.

JOCASTA
That is what he said at first
and he cannot deny it.
Everyone heard, not only me.   850
And even if he should say something different now
it still will prove nothing
about the murder of Laius, whom Loxias said

would be killed by my son.
That wretched child could never   855
have done it—he was already dead.
I pay no heed to prophecies—look neither
to right nor left, but on the road ahead.

OEDIPUS
That may be so. Still, do not neglect
to send someone to bring that man here.   860

JOCASTA
It shall be done at once. Now come into the house.
I wish only to please you.

(*Exit* OEDIPUS *and* JOCASTA *into the palace, through the double doors.*)

Second *STASIMON*

CHORUS   Strophe A (863–72)
Let me fulfill my fate
through the holy purity
of all my words and deeds
and follow the heavenly laws,
engendered in the bright ether
by their father Olympus,
laws we humans could not have framed;
they will never be forgotten
nor blotted out by sleep—the god lives
in them, eternal and mighty.

                                          Antistrophe A (873–82)

Pride breeds tyrants, arrogant,
glutted on folly.
Pride blindly mounts the heights
then tumbles down the precipice
to the utmost depths,
losing its footing.
I pray the god will not revoke the need
for that healthy rivalry
which strengthens the city,
that he will always be our champion.

Strophe B (883–896)

The man who struts through life
vicious and arrogant in word and act,
who does not fear Justice
nor honors the gods—
may evil befall him
for such insolent impiety.
But if he profits fairly, shuns all outrage
nor lays profaning hands on holy things,
and still is punished,
then how can any mortal man evade
the angry arrows aimed from Olympus,
or the threat of heavenly vengeance?
If evil deeds like his are honored,
who would dance before god's altar?

Antistrophe B (897–910)

No longer shall I go
in reverence to Delphi,
Omphalos of Earth.
I shall not visit the oracle at Abae
nor that of Olympia
because their words
no longer ring true,
though every mortal still wants to believe them.
O Zeus, as you are indeed called, ruler of all,
do not be unaware of this.
For the old prophecies about Laius
are already dismissed, and Apollo's glory dimmed;
the gods grow weak and feeble.   910

(Enter JOCASTA *from the palace, through the double doors. She is carrying
wreaths and incense.)*

JOCASTA
Lords of the land, I have decided to go
on pilgrimage to the temples,
bearing wreathes and incense-offerings to the gods,
for Oedipus torments himself with fear of the future
as much as dread of the past.   915
Whatever he's told he believes.
He pays no heed to what I say.
I can do no more, but turn to you,

(JOCASTA *makes an offering at the altar.*)
shining wolf-god Apollo, closest and dearest of all gods,
entreating your aid with these prayers—   920
that you release us from this curse.
For now we are all dismayed, to see
the pilot of our vessel himself disoriented.

(*Enter* CORINTHIAN MESSENGER *from the direction of Corinth, stage
left. He is elderly.*)
CORINTHIAN MESSENGER
Strangers, can you tell me where
Is the house of King Oedipus?   925
Better still—tell me if you know where he is?

CHORUS
Here is his house, stranger, and he himself inside,
and this his fruitful wife, mother of his children.

CORINTHIAN MESSENGER
May she be blessed, and all her kind—
the legitimate wife.   930

JOCASTA
And blessings on you, stranger. You deserve them,
for your good words. But tell me,
why have you come, what news do you bring?

CORINTHIAN MESSENGER
Good news for your house and your husband, woman.

JOCASTA
What is it—and who sent you?   935

CORINTHIAN MESSENGER
I come from Corinth, and what I have to say
will surely give you pleasure—how not?—yet will grieve you as much.

JOCASTA
Tell me—how can it have this double power?

CORINTHIAN MESSENGER
The people of Isthmian Corinth
want him for king—that is what they say.   940

JOCASTA
Why? Isn't old Polybus still king?

CORINTHIAN MESSENGER
No—not since Death took him to his kingdom.

JOCASTA
You say that Oedipus' father is dead?

CORINTHIAN MESSENGER
May I die, if I'm not telling the truth.

JOCASTA
Maid, hurry, go to your master, and tell him   945
at once. So much for prophecies!

(Maid exits through the double doors into the palace.)
Where are they now? How many years is it
since Oedipus fled his land, fearing he must kill his father—
who now has died quite naturally, not by a son's hand!

(Enter OEDIPUS *from the palace, through the double doors.)*
OEDIPUS
Jocasta, my dearest,   950
why did you send for me to come from the house?

JOCASTA
Hear what this man says—then tell me
where they have gone, those prophecies of the gods?

OEDIPUS
Who is he, and what does he have to tell me?

JOCASTA
He's from Corinth, come to inform you   955
that your father Polybus has died.

OEDIPUS
What! Stranger, let me hear it from you.

CORINTHIAN MESSENGER
If you want to hear it clearly again,
then know that he is dead and gone.

OEDIPUS
How did he die? Was it treachery? Sickness?   960

CORINTHIAN MESSENGER
The least tilt of the scales puts an old man to rest—

OEDIPUS
Poor man, to die of sickness.

CORINTHIAN MESSENGER
—and the many years he'd lived.

OEDIPUS
Ah, wife, why would anyone go
to the shrine of the Pythian seer, or look for auguries   965
from the screeching birds above, who prophesied
that I would kill my father. Now he is dead,
rests beneath the earth, and I am here, innocent,
with sword untouched—unless you could say
that it was longing for me that killed him.   970
Those useless oracles now rot in Hades,
taken there by Polybus.

JOCASTA
Isn't that just what I always said?

OEDIPUS
Yes, but I was frightened and did not believe you.

JOCASTA
Now you know not to take any of it to heart.   975

OEDIPUS
But surely I must still fear the bed of my mother—

JOCASTA
Why be afraid?
Chance rules us all.
No one can foresee the future.
Best to live in the present, making no plans.   980
And why should you fear the bed of your mother?
Many a man has slept with his mother in dreams.
He who dismisses such thoughts lives easiest.

OEDIPUS
All that you say might be true,
if she who bore me were not still alive. But she is,   985
and so I have every reason to fear.

JOCASTA
Yet your father's funeral is a cause to rejoice.

OEDIPUS
Yes—but she is still alive.

CORINTHIAN MESSENGER
Who is this woman you fear?

OEDIPUS
Merope, old man—who lived with Polybus.   990

CORINTHIAN MESSENGER
Why be frightened of her?

OEDIPUS
A dreadful prophecy from a god.

CORINTHIAN MESSENGER
Can you tell it to me, or is that forbidden?

OEDIPUS
It was Loxias who said
I was doomed to couple with my mother   995
and kill my father with my own hands.
Because of this dreadful prophecy, many years ago

I quit Corinth. Since then, my life has been fortunate—yet
to look into the eyes of one's parents is the greatest joy.

CORINTHIAN MESSENGER
And this is the reason you fled the city?   1000

OEDIPUS
I had no wish to be my father's murderer!

CORINTHIAN MESSENGER
I can so easily free you of these fears, my lord,
since I am well-disposed toward you.

OEDIPUS
What a favor you would grant me!

CORINTHIAN MESSENGER
And I came especially for this—   1005
to bring you home, and reap the benefit.

OEDIPUS
I can never go near there.

CORINTHIAN MESSENGER
My child, you don't know what you are doing.

OEDIPUS
How, old man? For the gods' sake, tell me!

CORINTHIAN MESSENGER
So you won't go back because of this story?   1010

OEDIPUS
I dread that Phoebus' curse will come true.

CORINTHIAN MESSENGER
Or that pollution would come from your parents?

OEDIPUS
Exactly that is what most terrifies me.

CORINTHIAN MESSENGER
Well, you can be sure that you have nothing to fear.

OEDIPUS
How could that be, if they begot me?   1015

CORINTHIAN MESSENGER
There is no kinship of blood between you and Polybus.

OEDIPUS
What do you say? Polybus not my father?

CORINTHIAN MESSENGER
No more than I am. In that we were equal.

OEDIPUS
A nothing like you the equal of he who sired me!

CORINTHIAN MESSENGER
He did not sire you, neither he nor I.   1020

OEDIPUS
Then why did he name me his child?

CORINTHIAN MESSENGER
I gave you to him as a gift—he received you from my hands.

OEDIPUS
Yet strange, that from another's hands, he loved me dearly.

CORINTHIAN MESSENGER
It was the years of childlessness won him over.

OEDIPUS
Had you bought me somewhere, or did you find me?   1025

CORINTHIAN MESSENGER
I found you on the wooded slopes of Cithaeron.

OEDIPUS
Did you have some reason to be there?

CORINTHIAN MESSENGER
It was on that mountain I kept my flocks.

OEDIPUS
Ah—a wandering shepherd—

CORINTHIAN MESSENGER
—and your savior, then.   1030

OEDIPUS
Was I crying, when you took me up?

CORINTHIAN MESSENGER
Crying with pain—your ankles still bear witness.

OEDIPUS
Why must I be reminded of that old story?

CORINTHIAN MESSENGER
Your feet were pierced and pinned together, and I freed them.

OEDIPUS
This fearful scar I've borne since my cradle.   1035

CORINTHIAN MESSENGER
And so you are called "swollen foot."

OEDIPUS
But tell me, for the gods' sake, was this done by my mother or my
    father?

CORINTHIAN MESSENGER
That I cannot. The one who gave you to me knows better than I.

OEDIPUS
So you did not find me yourself?

CORINTHIAN MESSENGER
No, another shepherd handed you over.   1040

OEDIPUS
But who was he? Can you tell me?

CORINTHIAN MESSENGER
They said he was one of Laius' men.

OEDIPUS
You mean the old king of this land?

CORINTHIAN MESSENGER
Yes, a shepherd of Laius.

OEDIPUS
And is he still alive? Can I see him?   1045

CORINTHIAN MESSENGER
Your local people can answer that best.

OEDIPUS *(addressing the* CHORUS*)*
Do any of you know if he is still alive,
the shepherd of whom he speaks,
or has seen him out in the fields or here in the city?
Speak at once!—the time has come to learn these things.   1050

CHORUS *(The coryphaeus speaks.)*
I think he must be the countryman
you wanted to see. But here's Jocasta—
she can tell you better than I.

OEDIPUS
Wife, do you know if the man we sent for
is the same person this shepherd mentions?   1055

JOCASTA
Why even try to find out? Pay no attention
to all that nonsense.

OEDIPUS
Having come so far, do you think I can hold myself back
from trying to learn the truth of my birth?

JOCASTA
Stop, in the name of the gods—if you value your life—   1060
from going further. I have been plagued enough!

OEDIPUS
Be brave, woman! Even if I am proved three times a slave,
from three generations of slaves, that will not make you base-born.

JOCASTA
I beg you to heed me. Do not do this.

OEDIPUS
You cannot stop me from learning the truth.   1065

JOCASTA
Believe me, I only want the best for you.

OEDIPUS
Your "best," it seems, is what can grieve me most.

JOCASTA
Unlucky man, may you never learn who you are.

OEDIPUS
Someone go—bring her shepherd to me—
And leave her to gloat over her own noble birth!   1070

JOCASTA
Oh, poor doomed man! That is all I can say—
my final words.

(JOCASTA *rushes off stage through the double doors.*)

CHORUS
Why has she fled, your wife,
in such wild pain? Oedipus, I fear this silence
will be torn apart by evil.   1075

OEDIPUS
Whatever may come, let it burst forth! Even
if I spring from lowly stock, I must know.

Being a woman, she might have grand ideas
and feel ashamed of my base birth.
But I am a child of Fortune—   1080
who has treated me well—and cannot be dishonored.
She is my mother, and the months, my brothers,
have marked me out to wax and wane like them from slave to king.
Such is my nature, I have no wish
to change it—nor not seek out the truth of my birth.   1085

(OEDIPUS *and* CORINTHIAN MESSENGER *remain on stage.*)

THIRD STASIMON

CHORUS   Strophe A (1086–97)

If I am a seer,
gifted by Olympus to speak the truth,
I prophesy, Mount Cithaeron, that you will know,
at tomorrow's full moon,
how Oedipus exalts you as his native land,
his nurse and mother.
And we shall praise you
with wild cries, song and dance,
because you honor our king,
and make him glad.
Phoebus Apollo,
may these things please you!

                                        Antistrophe A (1098–1109)

Oedipus, who was your mother?
Was she a long-lived nymph,
consort of goat-legged father Pan,
roamer of mountains,
or some mistress of Loxias,
who loves the empty pastures?
Maybe the Lord of Cyllene, or Bacchus himself,
god of the stormy peaks,
found you—a present left there
by one of his favorite playmates,
those almost-immortal
Helicon girls!

(Enter elderly SHEPHERD *with* OEDIPUS' *men from Thebes, stage right.)*

OEDIPUS
Though I have never met him,   1110
yet, Elders, I can guess this is the shepherd
we have looked for—he is old enough
to be that man.
I also recognize the ones who lead him as servants of mine.
But having seen the shepherd before,   1115
you must know better than I.

CHORUS
I know him well—he was Laius' man,
one of his trusty shepherds.

OEDIPUS
Tell me, Corinthian stranger,
is this the one you mean?   1120

CORINTHIAN MESSENGER
The very man before your eyes.

OEDIPUS *(addressing the* SHEPHERD)
You there, old fellow—look at me, answer
my questions. Were you one of Laius' men?

SHEPHERD
Yes, a slave—not bought though, but born into the household.

OEDIPUS
What sort of work did you do?

SHEPHERD
I followed the flocks for most of my life.   1125

OEDIPUS
Where did you usually camp when you were out with the flocks?

SHEPHERD
Sometimes in Cithaeron, or else nearby.

OEDIPUS
Then you must know this man—maybe you met him there?

SHEPHERD
What has he done—who do you mean?

OEDIPUS
This man here. Have you ever had anything to do with him?   1130

SHEPHERD
I can't remember just like that!

CORINTHIAN MESSENGER
And no wonder, my master! But
I'll jog his memory—then I'm sure
he'll remember when we both were at Cithaeron.
He with his two flocks, I with my one,   1135
*   *   *   *   *   *   *
three seasons we stayed together up there,
the six months from spring to the rising of Arcturus.
When winter came, I would drive
my herd to its fold, and he went back to Laius' barns.
He can't deny that all this happened.   1140

SHEPHERD
It's true—though it was long ago.

CORINTHIAN MESSENGER
And do you remember that child you gave me
to rear as my own?

SHEPHERD
What's it to you—why do you talk of it?

CORINTHIAN MESSENGER
And here, my friend, is the one who was that child.   1145

SHEPHERD
May you be cursed! Why won't you be quiet?

OEDIPUS
Do not attack him, old man. It is you
who should be punished.

SHEPHERD
What have I done wrong, O best of masters?

OEDIPUS
You would not describe the child he asks about.   1150

SHEPHERD
He doesn't know what he's saying—he wastes his breath.

OEDIPUS
If you won't speak willingly, I'll make you talk.

SHEPHERD
For the gods' sake, don't put an old man to the torture.

OEDIPUS
Quickly, someone, twist back his arms.

(OEDIPUS' *men grab the* SHEPHERD *and twist back his arms.*)

SHEPHERD
Wretched me! What do you want to know?   1155

OEDIPUS
Did you give the child he asks about to this very man?

SHEPHERD
I did. I wish I had died on that day.

OEDIPUS
You'll come to it now, if you don't speak the truth.

SHEPHERD
It will be worse for me, if I do speak.

OEDIPUS
This man, it seems, is determined to waste my time.   1160

SHEPHERD
No, no, I've already said I gave him the child.

OEDIPUS
Where did he come from? Your own house, or somewhere else?

SHEPHERD
Not mine. Someone gave him to me.

OEDIPUS
Which of the citizens here—which house?

SHEPHERD
For the gods' sake, do not ask me more, master!   1165

OEDIPUS
You're dead already if I have to ask again.

SHEPHERD
Then—if I must speak—it was someone from the house of Laius.

OEDIPUS
Slave—or kin?

SHEPHERD
Now it comes—the terrible thing I must say—

OEDIPUS
—and I to hear. Whatever must be heard.   1170

SHEPHERD
They said the child was his. She—she, the one inside—
your wife—she can best tell it all.

OEDIPUS: It was she who gave the child to you?
    SHEPHERD: Yes, master.

OEDIPUS: Why?
    SHEPHERD: So I would kill it.

OEDIPUS The poor woman—her own child. Why? Why?   1175
    SHEPHERD Because of the evil prophecies.

OEDIPUS: What prophecies?
    SHEPHERD: That he would kill his parents.

OEDIPUS
Then why did you not obey—but give him to this man?

SHEPHERD
I felt so sorry for him, master, and thought
he would take the child away to his own land.
But instead, he saved him for an awful fate.   1180
For if you are who he says you are, you were doomed from birth.

OEDIPUS
Alas, alas, it all comes clear!
O light of day, this is the last time I see you!
I am exposed as cursed—in my birth
and my marriage bed, and by those I should never have slain.   1185

(OEDIPUS *rushes off through the double doors.* SHEPHERD *and*
ATTENDANTS *exit toward Thebes, stage right, and the* CORINTHIAN
MESSENGER *toward Corinth, stage left.*)

FOURTH *STASIMON*

CHORUS   Strophe A (1186–96)
O mortal generations,
lives passing so quickly and
equaling nothing. Show me
a man who thinks he is happy
and I will show you a man deluded—
his life means nothing.
Your fate, O wretched Oedipus,
is the example I take,
to prove the gods bless nothing.

                                  Antistrophe A (1197–1203)
You it was who drew back your bow
beyond mortal limit, and gained the blessing of wealth.
By Zeus, it was you who destroyed the Sphinx,
the oracle singer, with her crooked-taloned claws,

and stood like a tower
against the death that threatened our land.
Since then, we have called you our king
and crowned you with grand honors,
ruler of mighty Thebes.

Strophe B (1204–12)

And now, whose story is more wretched?
Who has suffered a worse agony or more painful
fate than you, your life in chaos.
O famous Oedipus, how could the same deep harbor
serve for son and father,
sharing the same marriage bed and chamber;
how could the furrows your father ploughed first
be strong enough to bear you in silence?

Antistrophe B (1213–22)

Against your will, all-seeing Time has found you out
and judged your marriage an abomination
of begetting and begotten,
parent and child as one.
O son of Laius,
would I never had seen you.
Lamentations pour from my mouth.
I must say this—for it was you
who gave me the courage to live,
but now bring darkness down into my eyes.

(Enter SECOND MESSENGER *from the palace, through the double
doors.)*

SECOND MESSENGER
Honored nobles of this land
what dreadful thing you are about to hear, and see
with your minds' eye; what great woe will overcome you,   1225
if you feel kinship to the house of Labdacus!
Not even the mighty rivers, not Ister nor Phasis,
could scour this house clean from pollution.
So much hidden evil exposed,
will it or no. The worst woes   1230
seem those we bring upon ourselves.

CHORUS
What we know already
is bad enough. What more will you say?

SECOND MESSENGER
The shortest tale to tell and to hear—
our royal lady, Jocasta, is dead.   1235

CHORUS
Poor wretched woman—how?

SECOND MESSENGER
By her own hand.
    But you are spared the worst—you did not see it all.
I'll tell you, though, what I can drag from my mind—
where it's already buried—of her pitiful end.

Frantic, she rushed into her rooms,   1240
to the marriage chamber, slammed the door behind her,
and threw herself onto the bed,
tearing her hair with desperate fingers
and calling on Laius as if he were not dead
to remember the night they lay together   1245
and made the one who would kill him—
and then left her to be a mother to polluted children.
Weeping, she cursed her evil double fate:
to bear a husband from a husband,
and children from her own son.   1250

I cannot tell you more about her death,
for then, Oedipus, roaring with grief,
burst into the hall and I could only watch him,
raging around the walls, begging one after another
to give him a sword—and tell him where   1255
to find it, that double-ploughed field:
his wife not a wife, his mother the mother to his children.
One of the gods must have shown him the way—
it was none of us who were near—we were too frightened,
because shouting in frenzy, he threw himself   1260
at the great double doors,
tore the hinges from their sockets, and fell into her room—

and we saw, O horrid spectacle, the woman hanging,
her neck entangled in a noose of coiled rope.

Then, with what a ghastly roar he leapt   1265
to loosen the cord and lay her gently on the ground.
Poor suffering man—and the horror,
to watch him tear away the beaten golden brooches
from each shoulder of her robe, lift them high
and plunge them into the sockets of his eyes,   1270
crying out that they should never see him again,
nor what he suffered nor the evil he did,
nor look on those they should not—
but only darkness, forever.
Like a dirge, over and over he chanted,   1275
lifting the pins, striking through his eyelids
until bloody matter spurted down his cheeks and beard—
not drops, but a gush like black rain
or hail drenching him.

All this was their doom,   1280
husband and wife—evils doubled between them.
The old happiness was finished,
but it had been real. Now,
anguish and despair, madness, dishonor and death—
every evil assailed them; no curse forgotten.   1285

CHORUS
And has he no relief from this agony?

SECOND MESSENGER
Hear how he shouts for someone to swing back the doors
and let all the people of Cadmus see the father-killer,
the mother–. . . ;—no, I will not speak that sinful word!—
that he will banish himself from his house and land,   1290
the curse invoked by his own mouth.
But he is feeble now, and needs a guide.
The shock and pain are more than he can bear.
Look—he is showing us—the gates are opening.
Soon you will see such a sight   1295
that would move to pity even those who hate him.
(*Exit* SECOND MESSENGER *toward Thebes, stage right.*)

*(Enter O E D I P U S from the palace, through the double doors, wearing a
mask that shows he is blind.)*

CHORUS
Terrible, to witness how men suffer.
I have never seen worse suffering.
What frenzy possessed you,
O ill-fated one? What god, leaping   1300
from the furthest peaks, forced you
to the depths of ill-fortune?
Poor wretch!
I can hardly bear to watch you, though
there is so much I want to ask,   1305
so many things I want to learn and understand—
but even the sight of you makes me shudder.

OEDIPUS
Woe, woe, wretched I am indeed.
To what place am I being driven?
Where is my voice flying, carried before me?   1310
O fates, where are you rushing?

CHORUS
To a terrible place—silent, invisible.

SECOND *KOMMOS*

OEDIPUS   Strophe A (1313–20)
A cloud of darkness
overwhelms me—nameless
it conquers, driven
by a resistless wind.
Ah woe is me—the gadfly-goads
of memory torment me cruelly!

CHORUS
Who can wonder that you suffer doubly
these present evils and remembered ones.

OEDIPUS   Antistrophe A (1321–28)
Friends—
you are still here for me,
stay to take care of me

though I am blind—still loyal.
I sense you there and recognize your voices
though I am in darkness.

CHORUS
How could you dare such a dreadful thing—
to blind yourself? Which god drove you to it?

OEDIPUS   Strophe B (1329–49)
Apollo, my friends, it was Apollo
who made me do these acts which caused such suffering.
But it was my own hands, no one else's, that blinded me.
What need for eyes
when there was nothing I could see that gave me joy?

CHORUS
That is what happened—just as you say.

OEDIPUS
There was nothing worth seeing
or loving or hearing. Friends,
are there still joyful sounds to hear?
Take me away from this place
as fast as you can.
O friends, lead away this evil,
murderous man,
the most accursed,
the most hated of mortals—
even to the gods.

CHORUS
Equally wretched in your thoughts and fate—
better never to have known you!

OEDIPUS   Antistrophe B (1349–69)
Let him die, whoever he was, the one
who cut the fetters from my ankles
and saved me from death.
That was no favor.
If I had died then,

how much pain would have been kept
from my dear ones, and me.

CHORUS
If only it had been that way!

OEDIPUS
Then I would not have become the murderer
of my father nor be called
the defiler of the mother who bore me.
Now I am rejected by the gods—an unholy child—
the one who shared the bed of his engenderer.
If there are worse things yet
to be said or done,
be sure they are the lot of Oedipus.

CHORUS
You have not planned this well—better,
it seems to me, to be a dead man than a blind one.

OEDIPUS
Do not tell me how things are best done nor try to give
      me advice.   1370
What sort of eyes would I need, to look
at my father when I meet him in Hades,
and at my poor mother? What I have done
to the two of them deserves worse than hanging.
And the sight of my children, conceived   1375
as they were, should I want to see them?
Far better not to have eyes.
And the city with its high towers, sacred statues, and temples
of the gods, from all of this—
Thebes, the city that nourished me—   1380
I, wretched creature, have banished myself, I myself insisting
that the impious one should be thrust out. Now, I am
the one revealed by the gods as defiled—of Laius' lineage.
My sinfulness exposed,
how could I face the people with open eyes?   1385
Never. And if it were possible
to block the stream of sound from entering my ears,
I would not have held back from sealing off my wretched body,

not only blind but able to hear nothing.
It would be good to be beyond the reach of dreadful thoughts. 1390

O Cithaeron, why did you accept me—why
did you not kill me at once, so that I could never
reveal my origins to any human?
O Polybus, and Corinth—my so-called
ancestor and home, what sort of creature,   1395
beautiful to see but foul underneath, you nurtured.
Now evil I am revealed, evil from birth.

Those three roads, the deep valley
and woods, the narrow place where they crossed
which drank my father's blood   1400
spilled by my hands—how can I forget,
having done this, how I arrived here, and what I did next?
Oh, marriages, marriages,
one after another: first to give me life
and then for me to sow my own seed in the same field   1405
and bring forth confusion of fathers, brothers, sons,
sisters, daughters, mothers, and wives—every
atrocious thing a human can do, I have done.

But it is wrong to talk of wrongful acts.
Quickly, for the gods' sake, hide me somewhere   1410
far from this land; kill me or throw me
into the sea so you will never have to look at me again.
Come, don't be frightened to touch such a wretched creature.
Don't flinch away—my sins are not contagious.
No mortal can bear them but me.   1415

CHORUS
For that which you ask, Creon is here
and will do whatever is necessary.
He alone remains to be the guardian of this land.

OEDIPUS
What can I say to him?
How can he trust me? Everything   1420
I've said and done to him was wrong.

(Enter CREON *from Thebes, stage right.)*

CREON

I do not come to mock you, Oedipus,
nor to reproach you for past crimes.
And you—*(he turns to* CHORUS *and* ATTENDANTS*)*
    —if you have no regard
for human feelings, still you should respect   1425
the sun, Lord Helios, whose fire feeds all life, and not display
such an ill-fated being, which neither the earth,
the rain, nor the light of day can bear to see,
but hurry him into the house.
Only the closest kin should witness   1430
the shame of one of their own.

OEDIPUS

This is not what I expected, that you, the best of men,
would be so generous to the worst of men; so with the gods' help,
let me persuade you, for your sake more than mine—

CREON

What is it you wish to persuade me to do?   1435

OEDIPUS

Expel me from this land, as soon as you can, to some place
far from the sight of man, where I cannot hear another human voice.

CREON

I would already have done it—but first
I must learn if that is the god's will.

OEDIPUS

Everything cries out in his voice   1440
that I, the parricide and sinner, must die!

CREON

So it is said. Nevertheless, when unsure,
better to ask for a clear message.

OEDIPUS

You would consult the god for such a miserable creature?

CREON
And you must trust what he says. 1445

OEDIPUS
I charge you, I implore you,
to arrange her burial—she inside the house—
however you think fit. It is your right as her kin.
And as for me—never let this city
of my fathers be cursed by my presence again. 1450
I'll go to the peak of Cithaeron—
that is the name of the place my mother
and father chose for me to die—
so that I can fulfill their wish at last.
Yet I am sure that nothing can destroy me, neither sickness 1455
nor anything else. I have been saved for another fate—
strange and terrible.
I must let what is destined happen.
As for my sons, Creon,
no need to worry about them. They are grown men, 1460
and can look after themselves, wherever they go.
But my two daughters—pity the poor young creatures
who always were close to me, ate at my table,
shared all that I touched.
Take care of them—even let me 1465
touch them with these hands
and for a moment break the evil spell.
Please, my lord,
noble one—if I could feel them with my hands,
it would be as it was before, when I could see. 1470

(ANTIGONE and ISMENE, weeping, enter with ATTENDANT from the
palace, through the double doors.)
What am I saying?
By the gods—can I really hear my two darlings
weeping; has Creon, taking pity,
sent for my two dear children?
Am I right? 1475

CREON
You are right—I did arrange it, remembering
the joy they gave you in the past.

OEDIPUS
I wish you all good fortune—that a god
will guard you and guide you along a better road than mine.
Children, where are you? Come,   1480
come to these brotherly hands
which destroyed the shining eyes
of one who never saw nor learned nor understood
that he fathered you, O sister-children,
in the same furrow where he himself was sown.   1485
All I can do is weep for you both—I cannot bear to contemplate
the bitterness of the rest of your lives
and all you will suffer at the hands of men.
If you ever should dare to join the people's celebrations
you will go back home in tears   1490
long before seeing the festival's ending.
When the time for marriage comes,
what sort of man would risk
the scorn and reproaches, the insults
and hints about your lineage,   1495
yours and mine alike.
Such an evil heritage: your father his father's killer,
who ploughed where he was sown—the mother of his children—
and you two come from the same place.
Taunted with this, who would marry you?   1500
No one, dear children—it is clear
you must die virgin and barren.

O son of Menoeceus, you are the only father
left to them—their natural parents
no longer exist. Now, their only kin,   1505
do not let them wander like beggars,
husbandless, punished for my evils.
Have pity on them, so young
and vulnerable except for your protection.
Noble Creon, I'll know you'll do it, by the touch of your hand. 1510
And daughters, if you were old enough to understand
I would give you much advice. But promise me this,
wherever your future—to live a better life
than the father who sired you.

CREON
Enough of weeping. Go now into the house.   1515

OEDIPUS: Though it's hard, I shall obey.
    CREON: What must be done, in time will seem good.

OEDIPUS: You know my terms?
    CREON: State them and I shall hear and know.

OEDIPUS: That you banish me from Thebes into exile.
    CREON: You ask of me what only the gods can give.

OEDIPUS: But the gods hate me.
    CREON: Then your wish will soon be granted.

OEDIPUS: Does that mean you consent?   1520
    CREON: I don't equivocate, I only say what I mean.

OEDIPUS: I am ready, lead me inside.
    CREON: The time has come—let go of the children.

OEDIPUS: Oh no, no—do not take them from me as well!
    CREON: You cannot control everything.
All your former power is ended.

(*Exit* CREON, ANTIGONE, *and* ISMENE *to the palace, through the
double doors. Exit* OEDIPUS *through the double doors into the palace.*)

CHORUS
Fellow Thebans, look on Oedipus—
he who solved the famous riddles, the man of power   1525
whom every citizen envied. See
what a wave of terrible misfortune has submerged him.

Before that final day when one can say
his life has reached its end with no distress or grief,
no man should be called happy.   1530
(*Exit* CHORUS *toward Thebes, stage right.*)

Oedipus at Colonus

Cast of Characters in order of appearance
OEDIPUS, former king of Thebes
ANTIGONE, daughter and incestuous half-sister of Oedipus
COUNTRYMAN, a native of Colonus
CHORUS of fifteen elders of Colonus
ISMENE, daughter and incestuous half-sister of Oedipus
THESEUS, king of Athens
CREON, king of Thebes, uncle and guardian of Antigone and Ismene,
and brother-in-law of Oedipus
POLYNEICES, son and incestuous half-brother of Oedipus
MESSENGER

Nonspeaking Parts
ATTENDANT to Ismene
GUARDS to Creon
ATTENDANTS to Theseus

SCENE: *The Sacred Grove of the Eumenides at Colonus, part of the territory of Athens, a mile and a half northwest of the city proper. A rock is visible in the middle of the stage. On stage is a statue of the cult hero Colonus. The entrance, stage right, leads to Athens. The entrance at stage left leads to Thebes.*

TIME: *Many years have passed since Oedipus blinded himself when he learned that he had killed his father and married his mother, Jocasta, and she had committed suicide.*

(Enter from direction of Thebes, stage left, OEDIPUS, blind and dressed as a beggar, led by his daughter ANTIGONE. He carries a staff and a beggar's pouch.)

OEDIPUS

Antigone, child of a blind old man,
tell me where we are and who lives in this land,
who will take us in today
and offer alms to wandering Oedipus—
I who ask for little and get less—   5
though whatever it is will be enough.
Time, the fate I have suffered, and lastly, noble birth,
my companions for years, have taught me to accept whatever comes.

Child, can you see somewhere to sit,
either a public place or a grove of the gods?   10
Seat me there and we can ask where we are.
We come as friendly strangers
to learn from the citizens the right thing to do.

ANTIGONE

My poor suffering father, as far as I can see
the city's towers are still some distance.   15
This place though is sacred, I'm sure, flourishing
with laurel, olive, and vine, every branch
thick with sweet-singing nightingales.
Here, bend your knees and rest on this rough rock.
It has been a long journey for an old man.   20

OEDIPUS

Yes, help me sit down—look after the blind man.

ANTIGONE
No need to tell me, after so long.

(ANTIGONE *helps* OEDIPUS *to sit on the rock in the middle of the stage.*)
OEDIPUS
Do you know where we have stopped?

ANTIGONE
It is Athens, I'm sure of that, but not of this exact place.

OEDIPUS
Everyone we pass on the road says that it is.   25

ANTIGONE
I could go and try to find out.

OEDIPUS
Yes—if there are people about.

ANTIGONE
There are, and no need for me to go—
I see a man nearby.

(*Enter* COUNTRYMAN, *an inhabitant of Colonus, stage right.*)
OEDIPUS
Is he coming toward us?   30

ANTIGONE
Yes indeed. Ask him what you want to know,
because here he is.

OEDIPUS
Stranger, I hear from this girl, my eyes as well as her own,
that you come like an auspicious messenger
to tell us what we're in the dark about.   35

COUNTRYMAN
Before you ask anything else, get up from that seat.
This is holy ground, not to be trodden.

OEDIPUS
To which god does the place belong?

COUNTRYMAN
It is forbidden land. The fearful goddesses,
daughters of Earth and Darkness, claim it.   40

OEDIPUS
What name should I use, to pray to them?

COUNTRYMAN
The people here call them the all-seeing Eumenides.
But others give them other names.

OEDIPUS
May they receive this suppliant with kindness,
for I shall never leave this seat.   45

COUNTRYMAN: What do you mean?
        OEDIPUS: It is the confirmation of my destiny.

COUNTRYMAN
I dare not send you away
without the city's approval—I must report your actions.

OEDIPUS
By the gods, stranger, do not disdain me, though I look a beggar,
but tell me what I beg to know.   50

COUNTRYMAN
Ask, then—I shall respect you.

OEDIPUS
What is the nature of this place we have come to?

COUNTRYMAN
Everything I know, I'll tell.
The whole place is sacred to Lord Poseidon
and the fire-bearing Titan Prometheus.   55
Just where you tread is called
the Bronze-mouthed Threshold of this land,

mainstay of Athens. Those near fields
proudly claim this horseman Colonus as their first lord,
(COUNTRYMAN *indicates a statue of Colonus*)
and all who tend them still bear his name.   60
That is how it is here, old man—
traditions honored not so much in words
as by the way we live.

OEDIPUS
So there are people who live here?

COUNTRYMAN
Certainly there are—and named for this hero.   65

OEDIPUS
Do they have a ruler, or do the people decide?

COUNTRYMAN
There is a king in the city, he rules us.

OEDIPUS
Who is this man, who commands by strength and speech?

COUNTRYMAN
His name is Theseus, son of Aegeus, our previous king.

OEDIPUS
Is there a messenger nearby who could go to him?   70

COUNTRYMAN
For what reason? To tell him you are here, or ask a favor?

OEDIPUS
With a small favor he would gain much.

COUNTRYMAN
What can a blind man do for him?

OEDIPUS
My words will be all-seeing.

COUNTRYMAN
Take my advice, friend, and be careful.   75
I can tell you are nobly born, even though
down on your luck. You stay here, and I'll go
and talk to the local people—not those in the city.
They will decide whether you can stay
or must move on.   80

(*Exit* COUNTRYMAN *toward Colonus and Athens, stage right.*)

OEDIPUS
My child, has the stranger gone?

ANTIGONE
Yes, father, so now you can say whatever you like—
I am the only one here.

(OEDIPUS *raises his hands to pray to the Eumenides.*)

OEDIPUS
You fierce-eyed queens, since this sacred seat
was the first place in your country where I stopped to rest,   85
do not be harsh to Phoebus or to me.
When he prophesied the many ills I'd meet,
he also promised that I would find at last
a welcome in the furthest land I'd reach,
at the holy shrine of Awesome Goddesses,   90
there to run the last lap of my suffering life—
bringing gains to those who'd take me in,
but doom to those who cast me out and drove me away.
The foretold signs of what would come
were earthquake, thunder, or a lightning-bolt from Zeus.   95

Now I am sure it must have been some sign,
some omen from you which led me
along this road and to this grove. How else,
having traveled so far, so soberly,
would I have met you, who do not drink wine,   100
or found your unhewn rocky throne? Goddesses,
do what Phoebus Apollo foretold and grant me
a final closure and consummation to my life—

unless you think me too lowly, always
in thrall to the worst misery a man can know.   105

Come, daughters of ancient Darkness,
come, Athens, city of great Pallas,
most honored city of all,
pity this wretched simulacrum of what was Oedipus—
whose form and look were once completely different.   110

ANTIGONE
Quiet! Some aged men approach,
hoping to find you seated here.

OEDIPUS
I shall stay silent, and you hide me in the grove
away from the road, where I can listen
and hear what they have to say—   115
once I learn that, we'll know what to do.

(OEDIPUS and ANTIGONE move out of sight in the grove.)

(Enter CHORUS of fifteen elders of Colonus, stage right.)

PARODOS

CHORUS   Strophe A
Who is he? Seek him—where is he hiding?
Where has he hurried
out of the way,
like the most shameless.   120
Seek for him everywhere
and ask everyone. That old man
must be a stranger,
not someone from here—
who would have known better   125
than to come to the sacred grove
of the irresistible Maidens
whose name we dare not pronounce—
nor dare to glance at
as we pass, not speaking   130
that name, but silently

moving our lips in prayer.
And now we hear
that a stranger has come—oh, impious!
But I cannot see him   135
here in the sacred precinct,
nor tell where he hides.

(OEDIPUS *and* ANTIGONE *show themselves.*)

OEDIPUS
I am the man you seek. I see through sound,
as they say of the blind.

CHORUS
Ah! ah!—   140
he is as terrible to see as to hear.

OEDIPUS
I entreat you not to think of me as a criminal.

CHORUS
O Zeus, Protector, who is this old man?

OEDIPUS
One you could hardly call fortunate,
as you can see, ye guardians of the land.   145
Otherwise, why would I
be using the eyes of another
to steer my way, dragging my anchor
behind this lighter vessel?

CHORUS   Antistrophe A
Ah, your blind eyes!   150
Poor man, was it so from birth?
A long life of pain?
It will not be with my help
that another curse
is added to your misfortune.   155
Yet you go too far—
you must not tread
in this silent grassy glade

where a brimming bowl
overflows with honeyed offerings.   160
Stranger, beware,
walk away from where you are.
Put distance between it and yourself.
Hear me, suffering wanderer,
and if you would appeal to us,   165
leave that forbidden place
and come closer—here,
where it is lawful to speak—
but until then, hold your peace.

OEDIPUS
Daughter, what is your opinion of this?   170

ANTIGONE
That we should follow their customs, father dear—
listen carefully and do what they say.

OEDIPUS: Take my hand in yours—
    ANTIGONE: Here, you can feel it.

OEDIPUS
Strangers, can I trust that I will come to no harm
if I move from this refuge?   175

CHORUS   Strophe B
No one will ever force you, old man,
to leave this place of the goddesses' seats against your will.

(Guided by ANTIGONE, OEDIPUS hesitantly moves forward.)

OEDIPUS
Further forward?

CHORUS
Yes, still a little further.

OEDIPUS: Even more?   180
    CHORUS: Lead him, maiden, further forward—
you can see the way.

ANTIGONE
Come, dear father—
follow with your sightless step.

OEDIPUS
*   *   *   *   *

ANTIGONE
*   *   *   *   *
*   *   *   *   *
OEDIPUS
*   *   *   *   *

CHORUS
Be brave, long-suffering stranger
here in this strange land—   185
and learn to hate what the city hates
and love and honor all it loves.

OEDIPUS
Then take me, child,
to a permitted place
where we may talk   190
yet not affront the laws.

(ANTIGONE *leads* OEDIPUS *to a rock ledge that bounds the grove.*)

CHORUS   Antistrophe B
No need to come further
than that rocky ledge.

OEDIPUS
Just here?

CHORUS
You heard right—you're close enough.   195

OEDIPUS
Shall I sit down?

CHORUS
Yes, turn and stoop to sit
on the low edge of that stone.

ANTIGONE
Father, I'll help you—gently,
lean your tired body on my arm   200
and step where I step.

OEDIPUS
Ah, woe is me—
my sad fate!

(OEDIPUS *sits on the ledge.*)

CHORUS
Poor wretched man—now that you can rest,
tell us who you are and of whom born.   205
Why do you suffer thus? What
was your fatherland?

OEDIPUS
Strangers, I have no city. But do not ask—

                                        EPODE
CHORUS
What do you mean, old man,
what do you forbid?

OEDIPUS
Do not ask who I am, I insist,   210
nor make any attempt to discover it.

CHORUS: But why?
        OEDIPUS: Dreadful was my birth—
                CHORUS: Speak—

OEDIPUS: Wretched I am—
        CHORUS: Speak!

OEDIPUS
Tell me, child, what shall I say?

CHORUS
What is your lineage, stranger,
who was your father?   215

OEDIPUS
Child, what must I suffer yet?

CHORUS
Tell us, speak—you are almost there!

OEDIPUS
I shall—I can't conceal it any longer.

CHORUS
But you're still holding back—get on with it!

OEDIPUS: Have you heard of a certain Laius—?   220
    CHORUS: Oh no! No!

OEDIPUS: —and the family of the Labdacids?
    CHORUS: Good god! O Zeus!

OEDIPUS: —and the miserable Oedipus?
    CHORUS: Can you be that man?

OEDIPUS: I beg you not to fear what I say.
    CHORUS: Oh! Oh!

OEDIPUS: How wretched I am!
    CHORUS: Oh! Oh!

OEDIPUS
Daughter dear, what will they do now?   225

CHORUS
Go away from here—go far from our land!

OEDIPUS
But your promise! How will you keep your promise to me?

CHORUS
Fate will not punish
the man who avenges
the affront he has suffered.   230
One deception leads to another,
treachery brings pain, not pleasure.
You two—get away
from this place of shelter—
far away, before you bring   235
more ill fortune to our city.

ANTIGONE
Strangers, be compassionate to suppliants.
If you cannot tolerate my aged father
for what you have heard of his deeds—
though unknowingly done—   240
nevertheless, I beg you, O strangers,
to take pity on me
and heed a daughter's pleas for her father.
My eyes implore you—eyes not blind—
that look into yours and ask,   245
as one of your own blood might,
that you respect this man of sorrows.
We are at your mercy, as if you were gods.
Come, grant this extraordinary favor,
be merciful, I beseech you, by all you hold dear: 250
child, wife, home, or god.
You will never find a mortal man who,
if the gods will it so, can escape his fate.

CHORUS
Believe us, child of Oedipus, we pity you both
for your misfortunes. But we fear   255
what the gods might do—and lack the strength
to change or add to what we said already.

OEDIPUS
What use is a fine reputation or glory,
once it flows away like water?
Athens, they say, is the most sacred city   260
which alone can give a stranger shelter,
save and protect him. But what use to me,
when you make me rise from this seat,
then drive me away, frightened by my name?
It cannot be my appearance or actions you fear.   265
Listen—it is the effect of others' actions,
rather than my own, which I have suffered.
No need to mention my mother and father—
I well know it is that story which frightens you.
Yet how does it show me as evil-natured   270
if, when attacked, I retaliate? Even if I had known
what I was about to do, would that make me evil?
But I knew nothing. Unaware, I went where my path led.
It was the others who knowingly destroyed me.

And so I beg you, strangers, in the name of the gods   275
that just as you made me move from where I was
to obey the gods, now protect me
and do not deny them their due. You should not forget
that they judge men by their piety
as well as their transgressions—never yet   280
has an impious man escaped their justice.
With their help, do not sully the good name
of Athens with unholy actions but,
having given this suppliant your protection,
guard me well. Although my countenance   285
is frightening, do not dishonor me.
I come like a sacred being, with the power granted by piety
to bring blessings for the people. And when
your leader comes, you will hear what I say
and understand it all. Until then, let us wait together   290
without malice or evil thoughts.

CHORUS
Your words fill me with awe, old man—
you state your thoughts so forcefully.
To me it seems that we must wait
for the lord of our land to judge what to do.   295

OEDIPUS
And where is your ruler now?

CHORUS
In his ancestral home, his father's town.
The messenger who brought me here has gone to get him.

OEDIPUS
And do you think he will have any thought or care
for a blind man, and come here in person?   300

CHORUS
He surely will, when he hears your name.

OEDIPUS
And who will tell him that?

CHORUS
The road is long and crowded with travelers—
news spreads fast. When he learns who you are,
you can be sure he will come. Your name is known   305
everywhere. Even if he is asleep
he will rouse himself and come here quickly.

OEDIPUS
Then he will bring good luck to his city and to me.
What man who does good is not also his own friend?

ANTIGONE
O Zeus, what shall I say? What shall I think, father?   310

OEDIPUS: What is it, Antigone my child?
    ANTIGONE: I see a woman,
approaching, mounted on a colt
from Aetna, and with a leather

Thessalian hat shading her face.
Oh—what shall I say—   315
is it, or is it not? Am I out of my mind?
First yes, then no, then I'm not sure—
I'm at a loss—but no,
it can be no one else! See how her eyes sparkle
as she comes closer and calls out to me.   320
There's no doubt that she is Ismene.

OEDIPUS: What did you say?
    ANTIGONE: That I see your daughter,
my sister. I recognize her voice at once.

(Enter ISMENE *from direction of Thebes, stage left.)*
ISMENE
Father—sister—the two sweetest names to me.
It has been so hard to find you—   325
and now it is hard to see you through my tears.

OEDIPUS: Child, you have come—?
    ISMENE: I can barely look at such unfortunates.

OEDIPUS: You are really here?
    ISMENE: It was hard—

OEDIPUS: Touch me, my child!
    ISMENE: I embrace you both.

OEDIPUS: O my daughters—sisters—   330
    ISMENE: in such a wretched state

OEDIPUS: —of she and I?
    ISMENE: and I as well, the third.

OEDIPUS: Child, why have you come?
    ISMENE: To find out how you were—

OEDIPUS: Did you miss me?
    ISMENE: —and with the only servant I can trust,
to bring the news myself.

OEDIPUS
And what of your brothers? What are they doing?   335

ISMENE
They are where they are—it is a dark time for them.

OEDIPUS
Those two—it seems they follow Egyptian customs
in their style of life!
There, the men spend all day at home,
working the loom, while the wives   340
go out to earn the daily bread.
Oh, children—those two should be doing these things,
but they keep to the house like unmarried girls
and you, instead, must bear the burden
of your wretched father. Antigone,   345
as soon as she left childhood behind
and gained a woman's strength, became my helper
and guide, wandering with me, ill-fated one,
through trackless woods, hungry and barefoot,
through drenching storm and burning heat,   350
enduring everything—never thinking
of her own comfort, but only her father's.
And you, my Ismene, I remember how you came before
to bring to your father—unknown to the Cadmeans—
every oracle foretold about him. You remained there   355
as my trusted witness when I was driven from the land.
Now you come again. What news
this time for your father, what mission from home?
You do not come empty-handed, that is clear.
But should I fear the news you bring?   360

ISMENE
What I went through, father,
trying to find you, I will pass over in silence.
It was bad enough at the time,
without having to live it all again.
But the evils now assailing your two ill-fated sons,   365
this is what I have come to tell you.

At first they agreed that Creon should rule,
to save the city from defilement
by the ancient curse which almost destroyed
our family and home. But now,   370
as if from the gods, or their own sinful minds,
strife rises up between this thrice-wretched pair
as they struggle for rule and power.
The younger one robbed his brother,
first-born Polyneices, of the throne   375
and drove him from their fatherland.
And he, they say, has fled into exile
to the valley of Argos, made a new marriage
and gathered an army of friends and allies
either to conquer the Cadmean plain   380
or to die there with honor.
Father, these are not empty words I speak
but reports of terrible acts. When, I ask, will the gods
at last show mercy and lessen your pain?

OEDIPUS
Do you have some hope then, that they might relent   385
and I one day shall be saved?

ISMENE
Yes father, according to the latest oracles.

OEDIPUS
What sort of oracles, my child? What do they say?

ISMENE
That men from there—from Thebes—will seek you out,
whether living or dead, for their own sake.   390

OEDIPUS
What good could such a man as I do?

ISMENE
They say you hold their power in your hands.

OEDIPUS
From being nothing—I then become a man?

ISMENE
Now the gods raise you up, though they did what they could to destroy
you, before.

OEDIPUS
It is easy to raise an old man, whose youth was ruined.   395

ISMENE
Let me tell you that it is because of these things
that Creon will soon arrive.

OEDIPUS
To do what, daughter? Explain it to me.

ISMENE
To take you near Cadmean land and have power over you,
but not let you cross the border.   400

OEDIPUS
What use will I be, outside their gates?

ISMENE
If your tomb is neglected, that will bring them bad fortune.

OEDIPUS
That's common knowledge, without help from a god.

ISMENE
This is why they want to move you nearby,
where they will have power over you.   405

OEDIPUS
And will they bury me in Theban soil?

ISMENE
Alas, father, the shedding of kindred blood does not allow it.

OEDIPUS
Then they will never get me in their power.

ISMENE
This will mean bad luck for the Cadmeans.

OEDIPUS
But what combination of events will bring it about, my child?   410

ISMENE
The force of your anger, when they stand at your tomb.

OEDIPUS
Who told you this?

ISMENE
Men who consulted the Oracle at Delphi.

OEDIPUS
And did Apollo really say these things about me?

ISMENE
So they said—the men who came to Thebes.   415

OEDIPUS
And did my sons hear it?

ISMENE
Both of them—and clearly.

OEDIPUS
Those villains! When they learned this,
they preferred the throne to their father's return.

ISMENE
That is what I heard, and it pains me to tell you.   420

OEDIPUS
Then may the gods never quench their strife,
and may the outcome for them both
depend only on me—this battle
in which they're locked, spear to spear.
Let neither he who holds the scepter and throne   425
remain in place, nor the one he banished

ever return. For when I, their father,
was brutally and dishonorably thrust from my homeland,
driven away and proclaimed an exile,
they did not defend me.   430

You might say the city was granting
my dearest wish: what I had claimed to want.
But no, because on that first day
when I was in turmoil and longed for death—
pleading to be stoned to death— no one would help me.   435
Then later, when my anguish had weakened
and I realized I had been too hard on myself,
that my acts did not deserve such punishment,
only then, after so much time had passed,
did the city decide to force me out from my own land—   440
and they, the sons who could have helped, did nothing,
did not speak the one word which would have saved me,
but left me to wander, a beggar and exile.
It is these two sweet maidens, as far
as they could, who between them have sustained me,   445
found my daily food and shelter, done all that kin
can provide, while the others, my two sons, chose,
above and rather than their own father,
the throne and scepter, and kingship of the land.
Therefore I shall never support the cause of either,   450
nor shall any benefit come to them
from Cadmean rule. I'm sure of this,
both from what Ismene tells, and remembering
the ancient prophecies of Phoebus Apollo.

So I say, let them send Creon, and whoever else   455
has power in Thebes, to seek me.
For if you, strangers, and your Awesome Goddesses,
guardians of all, are willing to protect me,
then this city will have a savior,
and my enemies be confounded and destroyed.   460

CHORUS
You deserve our pity, Oedipus,
you and your daughters. And since you claim
you can be savior of this land,
let me give you the best advice I can.

OEDIPUS
You are my dear protectors, I shall do whatever you tell me.   465

CHORUS
First you should perform the rites of purification
to those goddesses on whose holy ground you trod.

OEDIPUS
What must I do? I pray you, teach me.

CHORUS
First, with unpolluted hands,
bring drink-offerings from the ever-flowing fountains.   470

OEDIPUS
And when I have that holy water?—

CHORUS
There are bowls there, made by a master craftsman.
Wreathe their rims and handles—

OEDIPUS
—with olive sprays and finely woven cloths?

CHORUS
Use the fresh-shorn fleece of a young lamb.   475

OEDIPUS
That I shall do. And then, what next?

CHORUS
Facing east, toward the dawn, pour the libation.

OEDIPUS
From the bowls you mentioned?

CHORUS
Yes, in three streams. Empty the last one completely.

OEDIPUS
Should I fill it again? Tell me with what—   480

CHORUS
With water and honey—but do not add wine.

OEDIPUS
And when the shaded earth has drunk my offering?

CHORUS
With both hands, carefully, lay three times nine
twigs of olive there, and pray to the goddesses.

OEDIPUS
This is the most important part—I want to hear everything.   485

CHORUS
We call them the Eumenides, the Kindly Ones,
so pray they take you to their kindly breasts and
receive you with kindness. Or better still, let someone else,
soft-voiced, almost silent, beg on your behalf
for their protection. Then move away and do not look back.   490
I'll stand beside you, friend, if you do this.
Otherwise, I dread what might happen.

OEDIPUS
Children, do you hear what they say, these local people?

ANTIGONE
We heard—now tell us what we should do.

OEDIPUS
I cannot manage these things—I am weighed down   495
by two evils, old age and blindness.
One of you girls go to perform these rites,
for I believe that one soul will suffice
for ten thousand, if done in the right spirit.
Act quickly—but do not leave me   500

alone, my body is too feeble
to creep and stumble on unguided.

ISMENE
I will fulfill this task. But
tell me where I must go to do it.

CHORUS *(to* ISMENE*)*
There, on the far side of the grove, stranger.   505
If you need help, the one who lives there will explain.

ISMENE
I will do this, Antigone, and you stay
to look after our father. Whatever there is
to do for parents must be done.

(Exit ISMENE, *stage right.)*

CHORUS   Strophe A
It is cruel to bring to life a sorrow   510
which was laid to rest—and yet I yearn to know—

OEDIPUS
What—what?

CHORUS
How you survived the dreadful pain
of all that happened.

OEDIPUS
In the guise of kindness to a guest,   515
do not expose my shameful sufferings.

CHORUS
But the story is still so widely known,
I need to have the facts clear in my head.
    OEDIPUS: O woe!

CHORUS: Be calm, I beg you.
    OEDIPUS: Alas! alas!

CHORUS
I granted your wish—now satisfy mine.   520

OEDIPUS   Antistrophe A
I suffered the worst evils, strangers, and suffered against my will.
Let the gods be my witness.
None of it was my choosing.

CHORUS
But why did it happen?

OEDIPUS
All unknowing, the city bound me   525
in an unhallowed marriage and bed.

CHORUS
And is it true what I hear,
that you were bedded with your own mother?

OEDIPUS
It makes me want to die, to hear these things, strangers—
because these two girls were conceived there.   530

CHORUS
What do you say?

OEDIPUS: Two children—a double curse.
    CHORUS: O Zeus!

OEDIPUS
Born from the womb of the same mother.

CHORUS
So they are your daughters and—

OEDIPUS   Strophe B
Yes—my sisters—sisters of their own father.   535

CHORUS
Oh!

OEDIPUS
Oh, and again oh! The repetition of countless woes!

CHORUS: You suffered—
    OEDIPUS: suffered horribly.

CHORUS: The things you did—
    OEDIPUS: I did nothing!
        CHORUS: —and then?

OEDIPUS
I received the reward for saving the city—   540
oh, if only I had not accepted it!

CHORUS   Antistrophe B
And then, unhappy man, did you shed blood in murder?

OEDIPUS
What do you mean? What do you want to know?

CHORUS: Was it your father?
    OEDIPUS: Ah—a second blow—anguish after anguish.

CHORUS: You killed—   545
    OEDIPUS:I killed—but I have—

CHORUS: What do you say?
    OEDIPUS: —a just defense.
      CHORUS: What?
        OEDIPUS:I will tell you.
Caught by madness, I slew him—
but I am innocent by law. I acted in ignorance.

(Enter THESEUS *from Athens, stage right.)*
CHORUS
But here is our lord, son of Aegeus.
Theseus, at your request, is now present.   550

THESEUS
For many years already I've known the story
of how you bloodily destroyed your own eyes,

and now, seeing you here by the road,
I recognize you, son of Laius.
Your ragged clothes and tragic face   555
make clear who you are, and with compassion
I ask, ill-fated Oedipus, that you explain
what you want of me and of Athens, what we can do
for you and the unfortunate girl who stands by your side.
Tell me—it would have to be something truly monstrous   560
to make me turn away.

I remember being brought up like you,
an exile alone in a strange land,
forced to defend myself from many dangers—
and therefore I would never refuse to protect a stranger,   565
such as you are now. I am well aware that
I am only a man—with no more control
of the future than anyone else.

OEDIPUS
Theseus, in those few words, your nobility
is proved, and there is little need to add more.   570
You have said who I am, from what family
and land I have come, and where I was born.
There is nothing left for me to say
than what I hope—and then my tale is told.

THESEUS
Tell me just that—your wish is what I want to learn.   575

OEDIPUS
My wretched body is all I have to offer—
a gift that seems of little worth. But
what you will gain is greater than its appearance.

THESEUS
What good do you claim it will bring me?

OEDIPUS
That you will know in time, but not yet.   580

THESEUS
How long before your bounty is made clear?

OEDIPUS
When I have died, and you are the one who buries me.

THESEUS
You talk of life's end—but what comes before
either you have forgotten or disdain.

OEDIPUS
If I am granted the one, I gain both.   585

THESEUS
This favor you ask seems small.

OEDIPUS
Do not believe that—the struggle will not be small.

THESEUS
Is it one of your children you mean, or someone else?

OEDIPUS
They will try to force me back to Thebes.

THESEUS
But if you are willing—? It is not good to be an exile.   590

OEDIPUS
When that was my dearest wish, they refused me.

THESEUS
O foolish man, it is useless to be angry with misfortune.

OEDIPUS
When you hear my story you can advise me, but spare me now.

THESEUS
Tell me, then. I cannot blame you before I know more.

OEDIPUS
I have suffered, Theseus, such wrongs—evil upon evil.   595

THESEUS
You mean the ancient family curse?

OEDIPUS
No, not that—all Greece cries that old story from the housetops!

THESEUS
What worse could happen, beyond the lot of all mankind?

OEDIPUS
These are the facts: I was banished from my land
by my own children, and I can never go back—   600
it is forbidden to a parricide.

THESEUS
Then why take you there—yet leave you outside?

OEDIPUS
It is a god's voice that compels them.

THESEUS
And what do the oracles threaten?

OEDIPUS
That they will be defeated here in this land.   605

THESEUS
But how should bitterness arise between them and me?

OEDIPUS
Dearest son of Aegeus, it is the gods alone
who do not have to age and die.
Everything else is overcome by the power of time.
The earth decays, the body wastes away,   610
trust dies while bad faith flourishes
and friendship withers between
the closest comrades and neighboring cities.
For some it happens soon, for others later

that pleasure fades and then again is sweet—   615
and if now all is well between you and the Thebans
yet still, in the passage of time, many months
and years of harmony and friendship
can be destroyed for the most trivial reason
by a single spear-thrust.   620
When that happens, my sleeping, buried corpse,
cold in death, will lap hot blood—
if Zeus is still Zeus and Zeus' son Apollo's words are true.

But I should not speak of this.
Let me stop where I began and add no more except   625
that, if you honor your pledge, you will never need to say
Oedipus was useless to you and your kingdom—
unless I am deceived by the gods.

CHORUS
My lord, since he first arrived this man has promised
to do such things for our land.   630

THESEUS
Who would reject the kindness
of such a man? First of all, he is an ally
to whom our hearth is always open, and next,
because he comes as a suppliant to our gods
and to give his favor to the land and to me.   635
Honoring this, I'll never cast him out,
but make him a citizen of our country.
(addressing the CHORUS)
If it pleases him to stay here, I will set you to protect him—
or he can come with me. Whichever
you prefer, Oedipus, you may choose,   640
and I shall agree to your choice.

OEDIPUS
O Zeus, may you bless such men as these!

THESEUS
What then do you wish? Will you come to my house?

OEDIPUS
If it were allowed—But this is the place—

THESEUS
Where you will do what? I shall not stand in your way.   645

OEDIPUS
Where I shall conquer those who cast me out.

THESEUS
The gift of your presence will be our strength.

OEDIPUS
If you keep to your pledge and do all you said.

THESEUS
Have confidence in me—I shall not betray you.

OEDIPUS
I do not ask you to swear on oath, like a base man.   650

THESEUS
You would receive no more than by my simple word.

OEDIPUS: What will you do then?
    THESEUS: What do you most fear?

OEDIPUS: Men will come—
    THESEUS: These men here will deal with them.

OEDIPUS: Be careful when you leave—
    THESEUS: Do not teach me what I must do!

OEDIPUS: Fear can make one reluctant—   655
    THESEUS: My heart does not fear.

OEDIPUS: You do not know the threats they make.
    THESEUS: But I know this—
no man can take you from here against my will.
Many make threats, blustering empty words,
but when their minds have calmed and

reason prevails, the threats soon fade.   660
It is easy to swear they will fetch you away,
yet I suspect that the threatened hardship
of a long journey will take the wind out of their sails.
Heed my advice and have courage
and faith in yourself, because Phoebus guided you here.   665
I am confident that even without my presence,
my name will be your shield.

(Exit THESEUS *toward Athens, stage right.)*

FIRST *STASIMON*
CHORUS   Strophe A
Stranger, you have come to the best shelter,
pale-earthed Colonus,
country of noble horses,   670
where the clear tones of nightingales
sound from shady groves and
trees are wreathed by wine-dark ivy,
leaves heaped beneath their boughs
on ground sacred to the god   675
where others may not step;
trees that are fruitful always,
untouched by sun or storm,
where Dionysus and his divine
attendants revel and tread.   680
                                                     Antistrophe A

There, fed by the heavenly dew
and always in bloom, grow clusters
of lovely narcissi, flowery crown
of the two great goddesses,
and the gold-gleaming crocus.   685
There the springs never fail,
but daily and nightly flow
into Cephisus' streams,
spreading their undefiled waters
across the earth's broad bosom   690
and over the verdant plain.
The choruses of the Muses love this place,
and Aphrodite, mistress of the golden reins.

Strophe B

And something grows there
unknown in Asian lands   695
or on the Dorian island of Pelops,
an ancient tree,
a terror to the enemy,
unconquerable and self-renewing,
which here does flourish mightily—   700
the sacred, grey-leaved, nurturing
olive. And neither young
nor aged man can do it harm,
because the sleepless gaze of Zeus Morios,
and Athena of the bright grey eyes,   705
keep guard upon it.

Antistrophe B

And we give further praise
to this, our mother city,
whose proud boast
and gift from the great god   710
is the glory of its colts and horses
and the waters of its sea. It was you,
son of Cronos, our lord Poseidon,
who raised the city to this proud height,
you who first tamed a horse with bit and bridle   715
here in these very streets,
and formed the smooth oar blade
to race through the waves along the shoreline
where the Nereids on their hundred feet go dancing past.

ANTIGONE
O land most eulogized by praise—   720
now you must prove by action that these words are true.

OEDIPUS
What now, my child?

ANTIGONE
Creon is here—with an escort of his men.

OEDIPUS
O kindly elders—now show me
that you will indeed protect me.   725

CHORUS
Be brave—though we are past our prime,
the strength of this land has not grown old.

(*Enter* CREON *with* ATTENDANTS *from direction of Thebes, stage left.*)
CREON
Noble people of this land,
I see the apprehension in your eyes
at my arrival. Do not shrink   730
away or curse me unkindly,
for I have not come with hostile plans.
I am too old for that—and know well
that this city is strong, perhaps the strongest in Greece.
But I have been sent, in spite of my age, to try to persuade   735
this man to follow me back to the land of Cadmus—
a summons not only from me, but all our citizens
although, because we are kin, the greatest regret
for your suffering is felt by me.
Unhappy Oedipus, heed me and come home!   740
Every Cadmean implores your return,
myself most of all; unless I am the basest
of men, I mourn your ills as no one else,
seeing you in such straits, always
a stranger and wanderer, in such poverty,   745
with only this poor girl to attend you.
Wretch that I am, I never imagined
she would fall into such a state,
worse than a slave, as she cares for you,
living like a beggar, unmarried,   750
and prey to any evil-minded passerby.
These are harsh words, I know, that I cast
at you—and at myself and all our kin.
But one cannot deny the obvious,
so let me persuade you, in the name of our paternal gods,   755
to come back to your city and the home
of your fathers, and take leave of Athens.
This city of friends is worthy, but your native place

should have first claim on your love and reverence—
the same that you would feel for your childhood nurse.   760

OEDIPUS
Shameless one, who dares to clothe his wily schemes
in words that seem both fair and just!
Why are you trying to trap me again
in the snare which would make me suffer most?
Before, when maddened by misery   765
and all I yearned for was to leave my land forever,
you would not allow it;
later, when I was calmer
and to be in my ancestral home was sweet,
you decreed my exile and drove me out.   770
You did not prate of kinship then—
but now, when you see that this city
and its people welcome me with kindness
you try to lure me away, speaking deceiving words.

Where's the joy in unwanted kindness?   775
It's like being refused when you plead for help—
and then, when things improve
and you have what you wished, the one
you asked decides at last to grant the favor.
What good would that be?   780
And that is what you offer now—
fine words and base actions.
I'll explain exactly what I mean to these men here.
You have come, not to take me back to my home
but to settle me outside your city's borders,   785
so that Thebes will be protected from Athens.
This favor I shall not grant—instead,
my avenging spirit will haunt that place, and
as for my children, their only portion
of my land will be sufficient space to bury them.   790

I know better than you the fate of Thebes,
for I have learned it from truer sources—
from Phoebus Apollo and his father Zeus.
And the lying words from your lips,
which cut like knives, speak   795

more of destruction than deliverance.
But I can tell I do not convince you.
Go away and leave us here! Even now,
we can still enjoy our lives.

CREON
Do you think that what you say hurts me   800
more than it harms yourself?

OEDIPUS
My sweetest pleasure is your failure
to persuade either me or these men.

CREON
Miserable creature—you seem to have learned nothing
in all these years. You bring shame to your grey hairs.   805

OEDIPUS
You are a glib talker—but I have yet to meet
an honest man who always hits the target.

CREON
It is one thing to say much—another, to come to the point.

OEDIPUS
As if you spoke less, or could better convince—

CREON
—not someone with as little sense.   810

OEDIPUS
Off with you—I speak for us all—and do not
spy on me here where I am destined to live.

CREON
Let these men be witnesses to how you answer me.
If ever I got you in my power—!

OEDIPUS
How could that be, when I have such allies?   815

CREON
I'll make you suffer, nonetheless.

OEDIPUS
What action backs this blustering threat?

CREON
Your daughter has been seized and taken away—
and I shall have the other.

OEDIPUS: Ah—woe is me!   820
    CREON: Soon you will have more reason to cry "Woe is me!"

OEDIPUS: You have taken my child?
    CREON: Yes—and I'll take this one here, soon enough, as well.

OEDIPUS
Friends, do something, help me! Will you go back on your word
and not drive this impious man away?

CHORUS
Leave here at once, sir. You have done enough wrong already.

CREON *(to his men)*
It's time to take this girl away—   825
even if she struggles.

ANTIGONE
Oh pity! Where can I hide?
Who will help me, gods or men?

CHORUS
What are you trying to do?

CREON
I won't touch him—   830
but the girl is mine.

OEDIPUS: O lord of this land, I call on you!
    CHORUS: Sir, this is wrong!

CREON: No, it is just.
     CHORUS: How can this be justice?
          CREON: Because I'm taking what belongs to me.

OEDIPUS   Strophe
O city, city!

CHORUS
Let her go—what are you doing, sir?   835
Let her go, I say—or this will end in a fight.

CREON: Keep away—
     CHORUS: Not if you intend to do this.

CREON
You'll have to fight my city if you harm me.

OEDIPUS: It is just what I foretold!
     CHORUS: Take your hands off her, now, at once!
          CREON: Don't tell me what to do if you can't make me.

CHORUS: I'll say it again—set her free!   840
     CREON (to his men): Let's be off—we should get on the road.

CHORUS
Come, come, citizens, people of Athens.
Our city is being attacked.
Come at once!

ANTIGONE
O pity, pity—I am being dragged away. Help me, friends!
(CREON's men drag ANTIGONE away.)

OEDIPUS: Where are you, my child?   845
     ANTIGONE: I am being taken by force.

OEDIPUS: Reach out to me, child—let me grasp your hands.
     ANTIGONE: I'm not strong enough.

CREON *(to his men):* Get on with it—take her away!
    OEDIPUS: Wretched—how wretched I am. Woe is me!
(Exit CREON*'s men with* ANTIGONE *toward Thebes, stage left.)*

CREON
Never again will those two staffs support you.
But since you wish to override
fatherland and friends—in obedience to whose orders   850
I have come here, although I am their king—
then do as you will. In time you'll realize
how little good you do yourself—no more now
than in the past when, ignoring all advice,
you let wild rage destroy you.   855
*(*CREON *starts to leave, but the* CHORUS *blocks his way.)*

CHORUS: Stay where you are, sir!
    CREON: Don't dare to touch me, I say!

CHORUS
Until you give back the girls, you will not be allowed to go.

CREON
Then you will soon pay a greater ransom to my city,
for it won't be only these two I take with me.

CHORUS: What do you intend to do?   860
    CREON: I'll take this man away with me as well.

CHORUS: What you say is dreadful.
    CREON: But it will be done—
unless the ruler of this land himself can stop me.

OEDIPUS
O shameless one—will you dare to touch me?

CREON: Be quiet, I tell you!
    OEDIPUS: Then let these goddesses
not stop me putting such a curse on you now,   865
vile creature that you are, who have torn away
the one who took the place of my poor blinded eyes;
and I call on Helios, the god who sees all things,

to grant my curse the power to make you and your family
suffer all that I have, even until old age.   870

CREON
Do you see what's happening, you people of this land?

OEDIPUS
They see us both, and know that I have only words
to defend myself against your actions.

CREON
I will not control myself longer, but drag him away
by force—even though I'm alone and slowed by age.   875

OEDIPUS
O wretched me!

CHORUS
What mad insolence—to think you can do such things.

CREON
Yet I shall do them.

CHORUS
I can no longer believe that this is my city!

CREON
If his cause is just, even one weak man can triumph.   880

OEDIPUS: Listen to what he says!
    CHORUS: As Zeus is my witness,
he will not achieve his ends.
    CREON: Zeus knows better than you!

CHORUS: What outrageous arrogance!
    CREON: Arrogance perhaps. Yet you must accept it.

CHORUS
O all you people, O nobles of this land,
come quickly, come—these men   885
have gone too far!

(Enter THESEUS *with* ATTENDANTS, *from direction of Athens, stage right.)*

THESEUS

What is this uproar? What is wrong? What has frightened you all
enough to interrupt me as I sacrifice at the altar
of the sea-god who protects Colonus? Tell me everything.
I have hurried here, bruising my feet.   890

OEDIPUS

My friend—I know it is your voice—
this man has done terrible things to me.

THESEUS

What sort of things? What has he done to harm you—tell me—

OEDIPUS

This one you see here, Creon,
has snatched my two dearest children.   895

THESEUS: What did you say?
       OEDIPUS: You heard it right—what I have suffered.

THESEUS

One of you go, my men, as fast as you can
to the altars, and tell everyone there
to leave the sacrifices and hurry on foot or on horseback,
at full gallop, to where those two roads which travelers use   900
run together and meet, to make sure
the girls do not pass and I am not subdued by force
and made to look a fool by this stranger.
Hurry, as I order *(indicating* CREON).
       As for him—
if my wrath would rise to what he deserves   905
he would not escape unscathed.
But by the same rules he invoked
he shall be judged and punished.
(to CREON)
You shall not leave this country until
the girls are brought back and I see them before me.   910
What you have done is an insult to me
and unworthy of your own people and country.

This city believes in justice
and decides nothing without the law—but you,
flouting our land's authority, burst in   915
and snatch who and what you want by force.
Do you think there are no men here, that
this is a city of slaves, and I am nothing?

Yet Thebes did not raise you to be base—
it does not nurture unrighteous men.   920
Nor would you be praised if they knew
how you plunder my goods, and those of the gods,
and drag away by force such wretched suppliants.
I would not come to your country,
even with the best reasons, without   925
the agreement of your ruler, whoever he might be.
I would not plunder nor capture—I would know
how a stranger should behave among the citizens.
You are a disgrace to your own city,
it deserves better. Time has not merely   930
aged you, but also emptied your mind of sense.
I have said it already, and say it again now:
let the maidens be brought here at once—
unless you want to be kept in this land
by force, against your will. What I say   935
comes from my heart as well as my mouth.

CHORUS
Do you see what you've become? Your origins
should make you just, but your actions are evil.

CREON
I do not call Athens a city without men—
and you are wrong, son of Aegeus, to say   940
my deeds were done without thought.
But I could not believe that sympathy for my relatives
would make your people protect them from me.
I was sure they would not accept a man
who killed his father—a man polluted   945
by an unholy marriage and children.
I knew this land had the wise advice
of the Areopagus, which would not allow

such criminals to live in the city,
and confident, I sought and seized my prey—   950
though might not have done so, without
his bitter curses on me and my kin.
It was that which drove me to seek revenge.
Anger does not weaken until it dies—
only the dead feel no distress.   955
So now, do as you wish, since
I am alone and undefended. I know my words
are just—but although enfeebled by age,
I shall try to pay you back.

OEDIPUS
O shameless insolence! Whose old age, mine   960
or yours, are you most insulting
with this talk of murder, incest, and misery
that spews from your mouth—all which I endured
unwillingly. Perhaps it pleased the gods to punish me thus,
because of some ancient grudge against my kin.   965
Try as you will, you cannot find any fault
to reproach me with, nor reason
why I sinned against myself and my own.

Tell me now—if the oracles prophesied to my father
that he would die at the hand of his child,   970
how can I be blamed for this—
being not yet even begotten
nor conceived in my mother's womb?
And once I had been born,
if I came to blows with my father and killed him,   975
ignorant of who he was or what I did,
how can you blame that unwilled, unknowing action?

As to my mother—you should be ashamed, wretched creature,
to make me speak of her marriage, and she your own sister!
But now indeed I shall break my silence   980
since you have forced the issue, with your vile impious mouth.
Yes, she was my mother, alas, the mother who bore me,
and having borne me—both of us unknowing—
she bore my children: her grief and shame.
But what I do know is that you speak of these things   985

concerning her and me with eager relish,
while I reluctantly wed her and reluctantly speak of her now.

But I will not be called evil, neither
for this marriage nor the murder of my father,
for which you bitterly revile me.   990
Answer me one question only—
if someone here and now approached
and tried to kill you—you, such a righteous man!—
would you stop to ask if he was your father, or strike back at once?
I think, as you love your life, you would attack   995
him and not seek the law's permission.
That was the evil plight the gods led me into,
and I am convinced that not even my father's spirit,
should he appear, would speak against me.

Yet you, who are not an honest man, think it is good   1000
to say everything regardless—blurt out the unspeakable,
and make reproaches against me, here in front of these men.
But you cringe and flatter Theseus and Athens his city,
fulsomely tell him how well it is governed and,
in the midst of your praises, don't seem to notice   1005
that if any country knows how to honor the gods,
this one does it best—
this land from which you planned to steal me,
an old man and suppliant, and carry off my girls!
Because of such actions, I beg with fervent prayer   1010
that the goddesses of this holy place
come to my aid and be my allies—then you will learn
the sort of men who guard Athens.

CHORUS
This stranger is a worthy man, my lord. His fate
has been frightful—he deserves our help.   1015

THESEUS
Enough of words—while we stand here talking
the ones who did this evil are in flight.

CREON
What can I do, a helpless man?

THESEUS
Lead the way the others went, and I shall be
your only escort—so that if the girls are still hidden   1020
somewhere in my land, you can take me to them.
But if your men are hurrying them away, no point
in following—others are in pursuit, from whom
those ruffians will never escape to thank their gods.
Come, move on! The hunter has been cornered.   1025
Now fortune makes you the quarry.
What is gained unjustly is soon lost.
And do not think your accomplices will escape.
I know you would not have dared such violence
without other resources and weapons—   1030
there is someone you trusted when you plotted this
and I must discover who it is,
not let my city be weaker than one man.
Are you taking it in, what I say, or are my present words
as pointless as my earlier warnings?   1035

CREON
I understand and must accept all you say—
but when I am back home I will do what is needed.

THESEUS
Threaten as much as you like—but off with you! Oedipus,
you may remain here in peace, and believe
that unless I die first, I will not rest   1040
before you have possession of your children.

OEDIPUS
Bless you, Theseus, for your nobility
and your kindness toward us.
(*Exit* THESEUS *and* ATTENDANTS *with* CREON *toward Thebes, stage left.*)

SECOND *STASIMON*

CHORUS   Strophe A
Oh, to be there—where
the enemy's attacks and shouts   1045
mingle with Ares' brazen cries
along the Pythian or the torch-lit shore,

where the holy goddesses
enact their sacred rites
for mortals silenced
with a golden key   1050
placed on their tongue
by the priestly Eumolpidae.
Here, I know,
Theseus spurs the battle
and soon will be joined   1055
by that pair of virgin sisters
to help the warriors to victory
throughout these lands.

                                                        Antistrophe A

Or soon perhaps they will be west
of the snow-clad peak of Oea,   1060
fleeing on colts
or in swift competing chariots.
The enemy will be vanquished!
The spirit of Ares is fierce
in these people,   1065
and terrible the might
of Theseus' men.
Every bridle flashes
from the bridled cheek-pieces
and every rider races   1070
to honor Athena the goddess
of horses, and the dear son of Rhea,
the earth-girdling sea god.
Are they fighting now, or do they still delay?

                                                           Strophe B
I prophesy   1075
that soon the suffering
of those two girls will cease—
all they have endured from their kinsmen—
and this very day Zeus will bring
victory for our noble struggle.   1080
Oh, to be a dove
as swift as the storm,

to rest on airy clouds
and gaze down at the fray!

                                                    Antistrophe B
Lord of all the gods, all-seeing   1085
Zeus, and your daughter Pallas Athena,
I implore that you grant
this land's defenders
the strength and cunning
to succeed in their ambush.   1090
And may Apollo the hunter
and his sister, who follows
the swift-footed dappled deer,
bring their double protection
to this land and its people.   1095
(CHORUS *turns to* OEDIPUS)
Oh, wandering friend, you cannot say this watcher
was a false prophet—for look, here come
your daughters, brought back to you again.

(*Enter* THESEUS *and* ATTENDANTS *accompanied by* ANTIGONE *and*
ISMENE, *from direction of Thebes, stage left.*)

OEDIPUS: Where—where are they? What do you say?
     ANTIGONE: O father, father,
if only the gods would grant you to see this best   1100
of men who has brought us here to you.

OEDIPUS: O child, child, are you both here?
     ANTIGONE: Yes, it was Theseus
and his men who rescued us.

OEDIPUS
Come to your father, children, and let me
feel your bodies in my arms—it is more that I ever hoped for! 1105

ANTIGONE
Gladly we do this—we too have yearned for your embrace.

OEDIPUS: Where then, where are you?
     ANTIGONE: We are here, father, both of us.

OEDIPUS: O dearest children!
   ANTIGONE: A father loves his children.

OEDIPUS: Supports of my old age!
   ANTIGONE: Ill-fated, all of us!

OEDIPUS
Even should I die I would not be entirely wretched,   1110
now the two of you are here with me. Come closer,
one at each side, both of you cling to your father,
and rest from your desolate wanderings.
Tell me everything that happened—
but with as few words as you can.   1115
Brief speech is most seemly for young women.

ANTIGONE
Here is the one who saved us. It is he who should tell you, father,
what he did. I will say little and leave it to him.

OEDIPUS
Friend, do not be surprised at how
I cannot stop talking to my children, whom   1120
I never thought to see again. I know
this joy I feel has come from you.
It was you, a mortal, who saved them, no one else.
May the gods bless you with every good I wish
for you and your land, because only in you   1125
of all other men have I found reverence
and decency and honest lips.
This is what I know and repay with words of thanks,
for what I now have comes from you alone.

Give me your right hand, my lord,   1130
to let me touch, and kiss your face, if that is permitted.
But what am I saying?—how could someone
cursed from birth think to touch a man
unsmirched by any evil? No, I do not want this,
nor would I allow you to do it. Only the ones   1135
who have lived it can share my pain.
Receive my thanks from where you stand, and for the future,
care for me as well as you have done till now.

THESEUS
I am not surprised that you want to talk
to your children, being so happy to see them,   1140
or if you choose to hear their words before mine.
It does not offend me at all.
Not by words do I wish to give luster
to my life, but by my actions.
And I shall prove it—I did not fail to honor   1145
my pledge to you, old man. Here I am, leading these girls
alive, unharmed by all that threatened them.
As to how the fight was won—no need
to boast when you will hear it from them later.

But I want to ask your opinion   1150
about what I just heard on the way here.
It doesn't sound much, but gives me cause to wonder.
A man should pay attention to everything.

OEDIPUS
Tell me what it is, child of Aegeus,
since I do not know what you ask about.   1155

THESEUS
They say that a man—not a fellow citizen
but one of your own kin—makes supplications
at the altar of Poseidon
where I was sacrificing, before I came here.

OEDIPUS
Where does he come from? What does he ask for?   1160

THESEUS
All I know is that they say
he wants to talk to you—just a few words.

OEDIPUS
What about? To take the seat of supplication is no small matter.

THESEUS
They say he asks only to speak to you,
then to return unharmed from where he came.   1165

OEDIPUS
Who could he be who sits on that seat?

THESEUS
Is there any kinsman of yours from Argos
who might make this request?

OEDIPUS: O dear friend, stay where you are.
    THESEUS: What's the matter?

OEDIPUS: Do not ask me—   1170
    THESEUS: What could it be? Speak.

OEDIPUS
From what I hear you say, I know too well who that suppliant is.

THESEUS
Who is it, then, whom I should object to?

OEDIPUS
My hated son, o lord, whose words
would hurt me more than any other man's.

THESEUS
What—can you not listen, yet not be swayed   1175
against your will? Why should it hurt you to hear him?

OEDIPUS
O lord, his words are most hateful to his father.
Do not compel me to yield in this.

THESEUS
But think—perhaps his suppliant state demands
a duty of respect to the gods.   1180

ANTIGONE
Father, listen to me, though I'm young to give advice.
Let this man here do what he thinks right
and serve the god as he wishes.
Yield to him and to us that our brother comes,
and have no fear that he will force you to act   1185

against your own best judgment.
What harm can come from hearing his words?
Evil deeds are exposed in the telling.
You sired him—and even if he were to wrong you
by the worst crime there is, father,   1190
it would not be right for you to do the same to him.
Let him come. Other men have bad sons
and rage against them—but the good advice of friends
charms and soothes their mood.
Forget these present troubles, but consider   1195
all you suffered through your father and mother,
and when you do, I know you will understand
that evil rage can only lead to further evil.
You have good reason to remember this—
blinded and sightless.   1200
        Yield to us!
Those whose cause is just should not be forced
to wait too long—nor is it right that a man treated well
should not know how to repay that kindness.

OEDIPUS
My child, you win me over with your pleading, although
it pains me. But let it be as you both wish.   1205
Only—if that man comes here, promise me, friend
that he will not get me in his power.

THESEUS
I do not need to hear this more than once,
old man. I do not like to boast—but know that
as long as the gods protect me, you are safe.   1210

(*Exit* THESEUS, *toward Colonus and Athens, stage right.*)

                    THIRD *STASIMON*
CHORUS   Strophe
Whoever wishes
to live beyond
the average span of life
clearly seems a man of folly.
Endless days accumulate   1215
always more pain

always less pleasure
for the man who lives
longer than necessary.
But still the Helper comes   1220
at last to everyone, without
a wedding song or dance or lyre—
the doom of Hades.

                                        Antistrophe

Not to be born is the first choice,
the prize beyond any other.   1225
But once he has seen the light,
the next best is to go back
to that dark place from which he came
as soon as possible.
In thoughtless youth   1230
all seems well at first—
then suffering begins
and every blow strikes home:
envy, factions, war, and murder.
Troubles abound. And afterwards   1235
comes hateful, feeble old age,
crabbed and friendless—
the evils compound.

                    EPODE

And such is what this poor man suffers—
and no one can escape it—   1240
as terrible fate crashes down on his head;
like a north-facing beach
assailed by wind and storm
and battered by waves:
some from the place where the sun sets   1245
some from its rising quarter,
some from the noonday zenith, and some
from the night-shrouded snow-capped mountains.

ANTIGONE
Look father, here is the stranger approaching, alone,
without attendants, and weeping bitter tears   1250
that pour from his eyes as he comes.

OEDIPUS: Who, do you say?

    ANTIGONE: The very one we thought it was, from the
    beginning—it is Polyneices, here.

(Enter POLYNEICES, *from direction of Thebes, stage left.)*

POLYNEICES

Alas, what shall I do first: weep in remorse
for my sins or—tell me, sisters—   1255
for the sorrows of my aged father?
I find him here, in a foreign land
in exile with the two of you
dressed in such filthy rags,
their foul squalor eating into his flesh,   1260
and above his blind eyes, his hair wild and unkempt.
And pitiful as all the rest—the pouch
he carries for whatever food he can beg.
Wretch that I am, to only learn this now—
I am the worst of men to have left you thus   1265
uncared for. I witness against myself.
But sharing his throne with Zeus sits Mercy.
Father, may she stand by you now.
My faults may be remedied—
believe me, they will not increase.   1270
Why are you silent?
Say something, father—do not turn away from me.
Speak. Have you nothing to say to me?
Will you dismiss me with no word, not even tell me why?
Sisters, children of the same father,   1275
try to persuade this stubborn man
to break his implacable silence
and not send me away dishonored—
though a suppliant of the god—without a single word.

ANTIGONE

Speak for yourself, unhappy one—tell him your wish.   1280
If you talk long enough, you may touch his heart,
madden him or arouse his pity—
somehow goad him to speech.

POLYNEICES
Then I shall speak out—you have shown me the way!
and claim the god himself as my helper—for   1285
it was from his altar that the king of this land brought me here
and gave me the right to ask and to listen
and then depart unharmed.
Those are the pledges I hope you will keep,
people of Athens, and my sisters and father.   1290
But first, father, I must tell you why I have come.

I have been banished from my native land
like an exile because, being the eldest,
I thought I had the right to the throne.
But instead, my brother Eteocles, the younger by birth,   1295
drove me away—not having won his case
by argument or trial of arms
but through bribery and persuasion—
which I suspect can be blamed on the Furies
and their curse on our house, or so the prophets say.   1300
So I went to Dorian Argos,
married the daughter of Adrastus,
and made allies of all the noted spearsmen
of the Apian land. Together
we formed seven armies   1305
to march against Thebes, either to die
in a just cause or drive our enemies away.

That is how things stand. You may ask why am I here?
I come to beg you, father, with supplications and prayers
and with those of my allies, who now,   1310
with seven companies behind their seven spears,
are camped on the plain surrounding Thebes.
The first is Amphiaraus, master of spear and lance
and the auguries of birds.
The second is Tydeus, son of Aetolian Oeneus.   1315
The third one Eteoclos, born in Argos.
Hippomedon, the fourth, was sent by his father Talaos,
and the fifth is Capaneus—who brags
that he will burn Thebes to the ground.
Named for his mother, the swift Atalanta,   1320
from her maiden days—the sixth, honest Arcadian

Parthenopaeus, impetuously rushes forward.
And I, the last, am your son—or even if not, but
only born to this evil destiny—that is what I am called,
as I lead the valiant Argive army toward Thebes.   1325
All of us together, I and these noble men implore you,
my father—on your life and the lives of your daughters—
beg you to soften your anger against me
as I go to seek vengeance against the brother
who deprived me of my home and birthright.   1330
For if one can believe what the oracles say,
those you support will be victorious.

Now, by the springs from which we drink
and the gods who protect our race, I beg you to relent.
I am as much a beggar and stranger, as you are—   1335
we both have to please and flatter our host
for a place to call home, we both share the same fate.
And that tyrant who sits on our throne—
I cannot bear to think it!—mocks and disdains us.
If you will take my part   1340
I will need little effort or time to destroy him
and lead you back to you own house.
With you as my ally I can triumph—to say that is no boast.
But without you, I am powerless,
and will not return from Thebes alive.   1345

CHORUS
Because of who sent him here, Oedipus,
answer as you see fit, then set him back on his path.

OEDIPUS
Believe me, you men, guardians of this land,
that if Theseus himself had not sent him,
thinking it right for him to hear my words   1350
I would not even open my mouth to speak.
But as he has been deemed worthy, let him go, after hearing
what I have to say—which will certainly not be pleasant.
(turning to POLYNEICES)
O evil creature—when you had the scepter and throne
which now your brother holds in Thebes,   1355
it was you who drove out your own father

and made him stateless, draped in these rags
which now you claim you weep to see—now
that you have come to the same pass!
No point in tears; this is what I must endure　　　　　1360
for the rest of my life, always remembering that you
are the murderous one who made me live in such hardship.
You drove me out—because of you I became a wanderer
and a beggar. And for all the help you gave—well,
if I had not engendered these daughters　　　　　1365
to care for me, I would not be alive.
These girls saved me, they were my nurses,
they have been like men, not women, in their labor for me.
You two are not my sons, but from some other stock.

The gods watch you now—but not in the way they soon will,　　1370
if those armies start marching against Thebes.
You will never conquer that city.
Before that can happen you will fall, polluted
by fraternal blood—and the same fate awaits your brother.
I curse you again as I did before,　　　　　1375
repeat those curses and call them back to be my allies
to teach you to honor your parents
and not scorn the father who begat you
because he is blind. These girls know better.
My curses are stronger than your supplications,　　　　　1380
stronger than your talk of thrones—if ancient Justice
still sits in the council of law with Zeus.

So go—I spit on you and deny I am your father,
you foulest of beings. Take these curses
I heap upon you: that you will not defeat　　　　　1385
your native land by force of arms nor ever return
to the valley of Argos, but will die by a kindred hand
and slay the one who drove you out.
Thus I curse you—to dwell in the hateful
paternal darkness of Tartarus,　　　　　1390
and I call on the goddesses of this place, and upon Ares,
who inflamed you and your brother both
with this terrible hatred.
Hear—and go—go tell all the Cadmeans,

and all your trusted allies, just what sort of honors   1395
Oedipus has allocated to his own sons.

CHORUS
Polyneices, your past actions gave me little pleasure.
Now leave, as quickly as you can.

POLYNEICES
Alas, for my ill-fated path and hopes,
alas for my comrades. What end is this to the road   1400
we took from Argos. Woe is me—
such an end that I must not speak of it
to them, nor turn them back,
but lead them to our fate in silence.
O sisters, daughters of this man,   1405
you have heard these hard curses of a father.
If they are fulfilled, and somehow
the two of you return to Thebes,
do not, I pray, dishonor me—
but bury me with all due funeral rites.   1410
If so, the praise you win from him
for your caring acts will be increased
by yet more praise for your service to me.

ANTIGONE
Polyneices, I implore you to be persuaded by me.

POLYNEICES
Dearest Antigone, what do you mean? Speak.   1415

ANTIGONE
Lead your army back to Argos as fast as you can,
and do not destroy both yourself and your city.

POLYNEICES
That is impossible. How could I lead them again,
once fear has made me run away?

ANTIGONE
Why should your anger rise again?   1420
What will you gain by ravaging your fatherland?

POLYNEICES
It is shameful for me, the elder,
to run away and be mocked by my brother.

ANTIGONE
Can't you see how this man's prophecies
will be fulfilled—and you two will kill each other.   1425

POLYNEICES
Yes, that is what he wants. But I shall not be deflected.

ANTIGONE
Alas, how unhappy you make me. But who, having heard
these dreadful prophecies, will follow you?

POLYNEICES
I shall not tell them. A good leader
only reports good news, not the bad.   1430

ANTIGONE
It seems that you are truly resolved.

POLYNEICES
Do not try to hold me back. This is my path,
ill-starred and doomed though it be
by our father and his Furies.
But for you two, dear sisters, may Zeus bless you   1435
if you will do what I have asked, when I am dead—
there is nothing else I wish. Embrace me,
and let us say farewell—I shall not see you again while I live.
      ANTIGONE: Oh, what grief!

POLYNEICES: Do not mourn me.
      ANTIGONE: Who could help but mourn for you
as you hurry, foreknowing, toward Hades?   1440

POLYNEICES: If I must, I shall die.
      ANTIGONE: Do not go—let me persuade you.

POLYNEICES: You must not try to do what you should not.
    ANTIGONE: Then woe is me,
if I am to lose you.
    POLYNEICES: The gods order these things,
one way or another. As for you two,
I pray to them that evil will never touch you—   1445
all the world knows you do not deserve to suffer.
(Exit POLYNEICES *toward Thebes, stage left.)*

CHORUS   Strophe
New evils and dooms
coming from somewhere new,
from this blind stranger—
or is this how Fate achieves its goals?   1450
I cannot believe that the gods'
actions are ever without purpose.
Time sees everything, all beings—some
it overthrows, and yet the next day
may raise them high again.   1455
(thunder)
O Zeus, how the thunder rolls!

OEDIPUS
Is there anyone with us, children,
who can go to fetch Theseus?

ANTIGONE
Father, why do you want him here?

OEDIPUS
This winged thunder of Zeus comes   1460
to take me to Hades. Let him be sent for at once.
(a second peal of thunder)

CHORUS   Antistrophe A
See how this fierce blast
crashes down, hurled by Zeus.
Indescribable! Fear
makes my hair stand on end.   1465
My spirit quails. Heavenly lightning
streaks across the sky again.
What does it foretell?

What dread I feel!
Such things always bring disaster.   1470
O terrible sky—O Zeus!

OEDIPUS
Children, this is the prophesied close of my life,
there is no turning back.

ANTIGONE
How do you know? What signs make you sure?

OEDIPUS
I know it well, I am certain. Let someone go at once   1475
to bring the lord of this land to me here.
(*Thunder sounds for the third time.*)

CHORUS   Strophe B
There, hear it again, all around us—
that stupefying clangor of thunder.
Be merciful, O holy one,
be gracious—even if you must   1480
bring ill fortune to our motherland.
May I find you merciful and
not witness a man accursed.
Let me share your favor without loss.
O Zeus my lord, on you I call.   1485

OEDIPUS
Is he near? Will he come, children,
while I am still alive and in my right mind?

ANTIGONE
What is the promise you want to remember?

OEDIPUS
In return for all his kindness,
my wish is to fulfill the pledge I gave.   1490

CHORUS   Antistrophe B
Come, Theseus, beloved king,
come from the depth of the glade

and Poseidon's altar,
where you dedicate the sacrifice.
For this man, who was a stranger   1495
to you and your city
wants to repay your kindness
with his promised favor.
Hurry, come quickly, O lord.

(Enter THESEUS *from direction of Athens, stage right.)*
THESEUS
What is this din I hear above the sounds of the city,   1500
not only from you and the stranger—
is it thunder from Zeus, or the drumming of hailstones?
When the gods send such things,
one dreads the worst.

OEDIPUS
King, your presence gives me pleasure—   1505
one of the gods has blessed your coming.

THESEUS
What is this new state of affairs, O child of Laius?

OEDIPUS
The scales that weigh my life are sinking.
I do not want to die without keeping my word to you and the city.

THESEUS
What proof do you have that your fated end is near?   1510

OEDIPUS
The gods themselves announce it—they are their own heralds—
with all the signs foretold.

THESEUS
What are the signs, old man?

OEDIPUS
These many peals of thunder, and the searing lightning bolts
Zeus casts with mighty arm from his unconquerable hand.   1515

THESEUS
I believe what you say. Your prophecies
have never been false. Tell me what I must do.

OEDIPUS
Son of Aegeus, I shall tell you now
the enduring future of this city.
And then, unaided, I alone shall lead the way   1520
to that place the gods ordained for me to die.
You must never reveal it to any living person,
neither where it is, nor even the region where it lies.
That place will always serve as a better defense
than however many shields or spears of allies.   1525
And the sacred truths you will learn there, alone,
must never be spoken. I myself
would not disclose them to any other person,
not even to my own children, dear though they are to me.
You also must keep those secrets safe forever,   1530
and when you come to the end of your life, tell them only
to your best-loved firstborn son—and let him tell them only to his.
In this way, you will protect your city from the ravages
of those men sprung from dragons' teeth. Many cities,
even if they seem well-governed, act arrogantly.   1535
The gods observe, but can be slow to strike
when men abandon piety for frenzy.
Son of Aegeus, may you never suffer this—
but what I teach you know already!

Let us go to that place now—the god's call   1540
urges me on, we must leave at once!
(OEDIPUS, *daughters,* THESEUS, *and* ATTENDANTS *start to leave the*
stage.)
Children, follow. Now I shall lead you two
just as you once were the leader for your father.
Come, no need to hold my arm,
I shall find the sacred tomb myself, the place   1545
it is my destiny to lie, buried in this land.
This way—come—here. This is where Hermes leads me,
and the goddess of the Underworld.
O sunlight—no light for me, though once I saw it—
my body feels your touch for the last time.   1550

Now the ending of my life will be hidden in Hades.
But, Theseus, dearest of friends,
may you and your people and land
always be fortunate, and in your blessedness remember me,
the dead, as the source of your blessings.   1555
(OEDIPUS *exits stage right, with* ANTIGONE, ISMENE, *and* THESEUS
and his ATTENDANTS.)

FOURTH STASIMON

CHORUS   Strophe
If it is allowed that I pray to the unseen goddess,
and to you, lord of the creatures of night,
Hades—O Aidoneus,
Aidoneus!—I entreat   1560
that with no further pain,
no doom-heavy fate,
the stranger may arrive
at the fields of the dead below
and a resting place by the river Styx.   1565
So many causeless woes he has suffered—
now in justice let the god upraise him.

                                                            Antistrophe
O infernal goddesses of earth
and you, Cerberus, unconquered beast
who sleeps at the gate   1570
where all must pass
and snarl from your cave,
dread hell-hound, untamed guard of Hades.
I beg you, child of Earth and Tartarus,
make Cerberus leave a clear path   1575
for this stranger, our friend,
as he goes toward the fields of the dead.
I call on you, Eternal Sleep,
to let him rest in peace.

(Enter Messenger, stage right.)
MESSENGER
Countrymen—to put it briefly—Oedipus is dead.   1580
But what was done—that cannot be told
briefly, nor what really happened.

CHORUS: The poor man has died?
   MESSENGER: You can be sure
that man has left this life.

CHORUS
How? Was it a blessed and painless death?   1585

MESSENGER
Yes, now we have much to amaze us!
You were there—you saw
how he set off, needing no guide,
he himself leading us all.
And when he had almost reached the sheer edge   1590
of the threshold, where those bronze steps lead below,
he stopped on one of the forked paths
near the hollow basin where the covenant
of Theseus and Peirithous is recorded,
stood between there and the Thorician rock,   1595
then sat down by the hollow pear tree and stone tomb
to free his limbs from the filthy rags that covered them.
Next, he summoned his daughters to bring
fresh water from a flowing stream
to wash his body, and to make libation.   1600
From the green-clad slopes of Demeter's hill
they brought what he needed, tenderly bathed him
and dressed him in the customary linen clothes.
And thus his pleasure was completed,
with nothing left undone.   1605

Then the earth quaked and shuddered like Zeus' thunder.
The girls trembled at the noise
and clutched their father's knees,
weeping and beating their breasts.
When he heard their bitter cries   1610
he took them in his arms to soothe them and said,
"O children, from this day your father ceases to exist.
Everything I was has perished. No longer
need you bear the burden of my care.
I know it was very hard. But one simple word,   1615
I hope, will recompense all your pain and toil.
Never will you be loved

more than I have loved you—of that,
you will indeed be deprived for the rest of your lives."
Clinging to each other, the three of them,   1620
father and daughters, wept. And when they stopped
there was no sound, only silence—until suddenly
came the voice of someone shouting loudly,
and all the hair on their heads bristled with dread.
It was the god who called to him—many times,   1625
over and over, from every part of the grove.
"You there, Oedipus, what is holding us back?
You delay too long. When will you be ready to go?"
When he understood this was the summons from the god,
Oedipus asked Theseus to move closer.   1630
"Dear friend," he said to the king, "give me your hand
in pledge to care for my children—
and you, daughters, give your hands to him.
Promise me never to forsake these two,
but always do the best for them."   1635
Restraining any show of grief, noble Theseus
reassured his friend and swore to keep his pledge.
Having heard this, Oedipus reached out to touch the girls
with his blind hands for one last time, then said,
"Daughters, you must be brave now.   1640
Leave this place, do not turn back
or try to hear and see unlawful things.
Go now, at once—only lord Theseus
may remain, to learn what must be done."

We all heard him say this   1645
and, sobbing as hard as the girls,
we left the place together—and quite soon,
from further away, we looked back but
Oedipus was not there—he had disappeared—
and our lord had his hands raised in front of his eyes   1650
to protect them from some awesome sight
which he could not bear to watch. And then,
without a word he bent low and lifted his arms high
as if to worship at the same time
the gods of the earth and the sky.   1655

How that man perished, no mortal but Theseus can say.
No fiery thunderbolt hurled by the god took him off,

nor did a sudden storm rise from the sea and sweep him away.
Perhaps an escort was sent for him by the god
or the world of the dead beneath his feet   1660
split open to receive him lovingly.
He departed with no lamentations or mourning,
without disease or suffering—a death
beyond any other mortal's to be wondered at.
And whoever thinks my words are foolish or mad—   1665
I shall not try to change their opinion of me.

CHORUS
Where are the daughters and their friends?

MESSENGER
Not far away. Those mourning cries
signal their approach.

(Enter ANTIGONE *and* ISMENE, *stage left.)*
ANTIGONE   Strophe A
Woe, woe. Now it is for the two of us   1670
to lament the inborn curse of our blood,
ill-fated us, that cursed blood from our father,
from whom we took so much pain
and must always bear
a burden beyond reason: 1675
everything we had to see and live.

CHORUS: What happened?
    ANTIGONE: Friends, we can only guess.

CHORUS: Has he really gone?
    ANTIGONE: Just as you might wish—
in the best way possible. Because neither Ares
nor Poseidon rose up against him,   1680
but he was snatched to the fields of the Underworld
to some hidden destiny.
Ah me, poor sister, a night like death
obscures our eyes.
How can we sustain   1685
our hard lives as we wander

the pathless land
or the waves of the sea!

ISMENE
Why ask me? Oh, let murderous Hades
take me now, to join my aged father!   1690
My future is wretched—
a life not worth living.

CHORUS
Best pair of daughters,
you must bravely bear what the god brings,
and not allow this fire of grief to consume you.   1695
No one can blame you for anything.

ANTIGONE   Antistrophe A
I have learned that one can yearn even
for what once seemed dreadful—for then
I could still hold him in my arms.
O dear father, dearest one, now   1700
cloaked in the earth's eternal darkness,
not even there are you unloved—
we shall always love you, she and I.

CHORUS: What he did—
    ANTIGONE: —was what he wished.

CHORUS: What was that?   1705
    ANTIGONE: To die as he wished, in a foreign land,
and to lie in that earth
in a bed below, well shaded forever.
Nor did he go unmourned, unwept—
these eyes, father, weep
my endless tears—nor do I know   1710
how to end this wretched grief
or soothe my sorrow.
You chose to die in this foreign place,
but you died apart from me.

ISMENE

Oh, wretched, wretched! What fate   1715
awaits us both, my dear sister,
deprived now of our father?

*   *   *   *   *
*   *   *   *   *

CHORUS

But his end was blessed—   1720
and so, dear children, cease
your grieving, for no one alive
is beyond the reach of evil.

ANTIGONE: Dear sister, let us hurry back!
    ISMENE: Why—to do what?

ANTIGONE: A longing stirs me—   Strophe B
    ISMENE: What do you long for?   1725

ANTIGONE
To see that dark Underworld home—

ISMENE
Whose home?

ANTIGONE
—of our father. O how wretched it makes me!

ISMENE
But how can we do it—it is not allowed—
don't you understand?   1730
    ANTIGONE: Why do you rebuke me?

ISMENE: But you must remember—
    ANTIGONE: Why repeat it?

ISMENE
—he was not buried, he fell away from us all.

ANTIGONE
Kill me then—take me there and let me die as well!
*   *   *   *   *   *   *   *   *

ISMENE
O misery!   1735
Where then, abandoned and helpless,
shall I live my miserable life?

CHORUS   Antistrophe B
Friends, do not be afraid.

ANTIGONE
Where can I run to hide?

CHORUS: But you are both already safe—   1740
     ANTIGONE: What do you mean?

CHORUS
—safe from anything to harm you.

ANTIGONE: Yes, you are right. So I wonder—
     CHORUS: What do you wonder?

ANTIGONE
How we will get home—
I'm not sure about that.
     CHORUS: Do not think of leaving.

ANTIGONE: We still have many troubles.   1745
     CHORUS: As you did before.

ANTIGONE
If we were helpless then, now it's even worse.

CHORUS
You both have many troubles.

ANTIGONE: We do indeed.
     CHORUS: We must agree.

ANTIGONE
Alas, alas—where can we turn next, O Zeus?
Toward what last hope is fate driving me?   1750

(Enter THESEUS *and* ATTENDANTS, *stage right.)*
THESEUS
Weep no more, my children. It is best not to mourn
those for whom the darkness under the earth
comes as a kindness, or you might anger the gods.

ANTIGONE
O son of Aegeus, we kneel before you in supplication.

THESEUS
What do you wish for, children?   1755

ANTIGONE
To see with our own eyes
our father's tomb.

THESEUS
But that is forbidden.

ANTIGONE
Why is it forbidden, O ruler of Athens?

THESEUS
Your father forbade it. He himself commanded   1760
I should ensure that no one go to that place
nor any mortal voice be raised
near the sacred tomb which holds him.
He told me that if I obeyed his order
my country would forever stay secure and happy.   1765
The Divine Power who took him heard me
swear this—and Zeus, guardian of oaths.

ANTIGONE
If such was his will
we must be content. But send us back
to ancestral Thebes, I beg,   1770

for perhaps we might prevent
our brothers' mutual slaughter.

THESEUS
This I shall do—and whatever else
I can to help you, and to keep my promise
to the newly dead one under the earth.   1775
It is my duty and I shall not fail.

CHORUS
Enough of weeping.
Cease your lamentations.
Nothing will change.
(*All exit toward Athens, stage right.*)

Antigone

Cast of Characters in Order of Appearance

ANTIGONE, daughter and incestuous half-sister of Oedipus

ISMENE, daughter and incestuous half-sister of Oedipus

CHORUS of fifteen Theban elders

CREON, king of Thebes, uncle and guardian of Antigone and Ismene

GUARD

HAEMON, son of Creon, cousin and fiancé of Antigone

TEIRESIAS, a blind prophet

MESSENGER, a servant of Creon

EURYDICE, wife of Creon, mother of Haemon

Nonspeaking Parts

GUARDS and ATTENDANTS

YOUNG BOY who leads Teiresias

S C E N E : *In front of the royal palace of Thebes. Double doors on the stage are the entrance to the palace. One entrance, on the left side of the stage, represents the road to the site of the battle outside the city, and to Polyneices' body. The entrance on the right side of the stage is the direction of the city of Thebes.*

T I M E : *The day after the end of the civil war between Eteocles and Polyneices, Oedipus' two sons. Polyneices had led a foreign force from the city of Argos to attack Thebes. The attackers were defeated, and in the fighting the brothers killed each other.*

(Enter A N T I G O N E, *followed by* I S M E N E, *from the double doors of the palace.)*

A N T I G O N E
Ismene my true sister, born from the same mother,
is there any torment Oedipus suffered
which Zeus will not impose on us?
There is nothing—neither grief nor violence,
shame nor dishonor—no evil   5
you and I have not endured already.
And what is this new edict
the general has decreed to every citizen?
Do you know about it—or haven't you noticed
that the fate of enemies is now to be imposed on our friends?   10

I S M E N E
I have heard nothing about friends, Antigone,
neither good nor bad news since
in one day we two were robbed of two brothers,
both dying together, by each other's hand.
And since the Argive army withdrew—   15
only last night—I do not even know
if my future is fortunate or doomed.

A N T I G O N E
That's what I thought—that's why I brought you
outside the courtyard gates, so no one else will hear.

I S M E N E
Hear what? I can see you are deeply troubled.   20

ANTIGONE

That there will be no tomb—our brothers—
Creon ordains—the thought drives me mad!—
honor for one, dishonor for the other.
Eteocles, so they say, he has treated with justice and customary law,
laid him in earth, to be honored by the dead below.   25
As for the battered corpse of Polyneices—
they say it is proclaimed to all the city—
no one is allowed to mourn or entomb,
but must leave it unburied and unwept, like carrion,
sweet pickings for the birds' pleasure.   30
Rumor says that this is what the noble Creon decrees
even for you and me—even for me!—
and he is coming to make it absolutely clear
to everyone that he does not view
the matter lightly, but for whoever does these things,   35
death by public stoning is the punishment.
This is how it stands, and you soon must show
if you are noble in yourself, or base—though noble born.

ISMENE

What can I do, my poor sister,
to ease the knot of your tormented thoughts?   40

ANTIGONE

Decide if you will share the labor and do it with me.

ISMENE

What labor? What do you plan to do?

ANTIGONE

Will your hands help mine to raise the body?

ISMENE

Is that what you intend—to bury him—even though it is forbidden?

ANTIGONE

Indeed I do—he is still my brother—and yours,   45
whatever you might prefer. I will not betray my duty to him.

ISMENE
O willful one—to go against Creon's command!

ANTIGONE
He has no right to keep me from my own.

ISMENE
No, sister—stop and consider
how our father died hated and despised   50
because of sins he himself exposed,
how he blinded himself, crushing his own eyeballs
and how our mother—his mother/wife, that dreadful double word—
ended her life with a plaited rope;
and thirdly, how our two brothers, in one day   55
slaughtered each other—their wretched fate
to end their lives at each other's hand.
Now we two alone remain—and think
how even worse our fates would be if, in defiance
of law, we disobey the decree of powerful rulers.   60
Do not forget that we are women—
it is not in our nature to oppose men
but to be ruled by their power. We must submit,
whatever they order, no matter how awful.
I shall implore those beneath the earth to understand   65
that I am forced to do these things, and pardon me.
I must obey the reigning power.
It would be mad not to do so.

ANTIGONE
Nor would I try to persuade you—nor welcome
your help later, if you should change your mind.   70
Do what seems best for you. I will bury him.
It will be a noble act, even if it leads to my death.
Loving and loved, I shall lie with him—
a pious criminal. There will be more time
for me to lie among those in the world below   75
than the longest life allows. But do as you please—
though dishonoring what the gods honor.

ISMENE
I do not wish to dishonor him,
but it is against my nature to defy the city's will.

ANTIGONE
Whatever you say,   80
I shall build a tomb for my beloved brother.

ISMENE
You go too far, I fear for you.

ANTIGONE
Don't worry about me—put your own fate right.

ISMENE
At least don't tell anyone what you intend
but keep silent—and I will do the same.   85

ANTIGONE
No—tell everyone. I insist. You will be more hated
for silence than if you shout it from the city walls.

ISMENE
You burn for deeds that chill my blood.

ANTIGONE
I know they will please the ones I most want to please.

ISMENE
If you succeed. But you crave the impossible.   90

ANTIGONE
When I have no more strength, only then I'll stop.

ISMENE
In any case, it is not right to chase the impossible.

ANTIGONE
I'll hate you if you say such things—
and the dead also will hate you, and with justice.
But whatever end comes from my rash act   95

or bad advice, could not be worse for me
than to die without honor.

ISMENE
If that is what you want, then go ahead. And always know,
in spite of your foolishness, that your dearest friends dearly love you.
(*Exit* ANTIGONE *to the left toward the outskirts of the city and*
POLYNEICES' *body.* ISMENE *exits into the palace.*)

(*Enter* CHORUS *of fifteen Theban elders from stage right.*)

PARODOS

CHORUS   Strophe A (100–116)
Sun's first rays, light more beautiful
than ever shone on seven-gated Thebes,
you shine at last,
eye of golden day,
gilding Dirce's lapping stream—
and goading with the sharpest spur
the armored and white-shielded Argive warrior
to frantic retreat.

Maddened by Polyneices'
two-edged arguments, fraternal quarrels,
they attacked our land
like shrieking eagles
with snow-white pinions
weapons fierce as talons
and helmet crested with bristling plumes.

                                              Antistrophe A (117–26)
Over our halls they swooped
with ravening beaks,
over the seven gates, with slashing spears.
But we turned them back
before they were glutted with our blood
or Hephaestus' pine-fed fire could crown our towers.
Such a din of war surged behind—
but they did not conquer the Dragon's seed.

                                              127–33

Zeus hates the blather of a boastful tongue;
seeing them surge forward like a flood

with their arrogance and clanging gold,
he hurled a thunderbolt at one—
already rushing to the highest tower
to give a victory shout—

Strophe B (134–47)

who staggered, almost fell on the hard ground
then righted himself, still clutching the torch,
like a frenzied ecstatic of Bacchus
with a whirlwind's force; but his threats were empty
against our strongest ally and leading trace-horse,
the great War god, who smote them all—
to each a different death.

The seven captains of the seven gates
and their seven matched contenders
offered bronze trophies to Zeus;
but not those two—accursed sons of one father
and one mother, spears set against each other,
javelin heads of equal power;
they fought to the death.

Antistrophe B (148–61)

Now smiling, glorious Victory arrives
to rejoice with all of Thebes,
whose chariots lead the others.
We can forget the war
and celebrate through the night at all the temples,
earth-shaker Bacchus leading our dance.

See, the new king comes,
Creon, son of Menoeceus,
a new king to bring the gods' new fortune.
What plan will he launch,
that he has called
this assembly of elders to hear,
summoning us by general decree?

(*Enter* CREON *from the direction of the battlefield, stage left, with*
ATTENDANTS.)
CREON
Honored men! The gods have put us back on course,
after the great storm that almost wrecked the city.

I have summoned you here,
apart from the others, knowing how loyally   165
you acknowledged the kingship of Laius,
and of Oedipus, when he came to rescue the city
and later, after his death,
stayed faithful to his children.

Now those two are gone in one day—   170
a double doom, killed by each other's polluted hand—
being of the same race and family,
the power and the throne become mine.

It is impossible to know a man,
his character and mind, until   175
he proves himself in action,
through rule and customary law.
I say that whoever governs the city
and does not accept the best advice
but keeps silent through fear   180
will always be unworthy—
and if he favors friends
over his own country, is utterly worthless.

I would never keep silent
if I saw danger approaching the people—
and Zeus, who sees everything, knows this—   185
nor ever make a friend or ally
of any man who threatened
the straight course or the safety
of our ship of state.   190

My laws will make the city great,
and now, in accord with them, I proclaim to every citizen
my edict concerning the children of Oedipus.
Eteocles, though the best of our spearsmen,
perished fighting for his city.   195
Him we shall bury with every ceremony
and libation for the honored dead.
That other of the same blood—I mean Polyneices,
who came out of exile, back to his fatherland
and gods, with a sacrilegious lust to burn   200

the temples and the city down, rooftop to cellar,
slaughter his family and lead the people to slavery—
it has been decreed that no one
may mourn him, nor honor him with burial;
his body must be left exposed, in shame,   205
food for dogs and birds of prey.

Such is my decree—never will I allow
evil men to be honored like the just.
But those who wish the city well,
both living and dead, will be honored by me.   210

CHORUS
This is your desire, Creon, son of Menoeceus,
concerning the enemy and the friend of the city.
We must agree that it is in your power to determine the laws
for the dead as well as for us, the living.

CREON
Make sure my commandments are kept.   215

CHORUS
Younger men could bear the burden better.

CREON
That's not what I mean—the guards for the corpse are already
    assigned.

CHORUS
What then do you want us to do?

CREON
Not to side with those who disobey my orders.

CHORUS
No one is foolish enough to choose to die.   220

CREON
That would be the price of disobedience. But the hope of gain
often leads to destruction.

(Enter GUARD *from direction of battlefield, stage left.)*
GUARD
My lord, I cannot claim to be breathless
from hurrying on my way—
anxious thoughts often made me hesitate,   225
half-turning back. My mind
was divided—one side saying
"Fool, why go where you will only be punished?"
the other: "Wretch, while you dally, someone else
will tell Creon first—then how you'll regret it."   230

Brooding on these things I made slow progress
and a short road became long.
Finally, though, the side that said, "Go forward," won.
Even if my words do me no good, I will speak.
I know that whatever happens,   235
my fate is already ordained.

CREON
What troubles you so much?

GUARD
First, I'll speak for myself:
I did not do the deed, nor see the one who did—
you cannot put the blame on me.   240

CREON
You defend yourself well—
which makes quite clear that what you have to tell will shock.

GUARD
Yes, it's bad—that's why I hesitate.

CREON
Get on with it, speak out—then you can go.

GUARD
Well, here's the story. Someone came   245
and did what's necessary for burial—
sprinkled dry dust on the corpse, and all the proper rites.

CREON
What do you say? What man would dare—?

GUARD
That I do not know. For there was no mark
of spade or pickaxe, no earth thrown up—   250
all undisturbed and dry—nor any sign of wheel-ruts.

Whoever did this left no clues.
And when the first of the day-guard
showed us, we were all amazed and frightened.
We could not see the corpse—although it was not properly
      buried   255
but covered with a layer of dust, as if to avert a curse—
and there was no sign that a wild beast
or a pack of dogs had worried or torn it.

Then the trouble began: angry words,
each guard accusing the others   260
until it almost came to blows—no one there to stop us—
for each could have been the guilty one.
But there was no proof, nothing certain,
even though we were ready to hold red-hot metal
or walk through fire and swear an oath to the gods   265
to show our innocence of the act
and our ignorance of who had done it.

At last there was nothing more we could say,
and the one who pointed this out only made us feel worse
and bow our heads in fearful assent to that truth.   270
We could not argue against him.
We knew that little good would result—
because he said the deed could not be hidden,
that you must be told. And with my usual bad luck
the lot fell on me—so here I am,   275
as unwilling to come as you to receive me,
for no one loves the bearer of bad news.

CHORUS (to CREON)
My lord, I have been wondering if this affair
is driven by the gods.

CREON (to the CHORUS)
Enough—before my fury overwhelms me,   280
and you reveal yourselves as fools as well as doddering ancients.
Intolerable to think, even for a moment,
that the gods would have any concern for this corpse
or honor it like that of a benefactor by decently
covering the body of one who came to burn   285
their pillared temples and sacred shrines,
destroy their land and overturn their laws.
How can you believe the gods accept such evil?
Impossible! It's true, though, that for a long time
there have been factions protesting against me,   290
men meeting in secret, grumbling, reluctant to bow
their necks to the yoke and yield to my rule.

I am convinced it was such men
who bribed the guards to do this deed.
For there is nothing worse for man than money.   295
It is money which destroys cities,
breaks families apart,
corrupts the honest citizen
to shameless, shameful things
and teaches him every act of impiety.   300
Be sure, whoever took the cash to do this deed
in due course will pay it back in pain.
(to the GUARD)
As I still honor Zeus,
I swear and tell you, guard,
that if you do not find the one who did the burial   305
and bring him here before me,
not Hades alone—not mere death—will be sufficient.
Racked and tortured, you'll sing out,
and learn the lesson that when—and if—in future
other bribes are offered, it's better   310
not to snatch them, careless of their source.
More men are ruined by such unlawful gains
than live to have a rich old age.

GUARD
May I speak now, or shall I leave?   315

CREON
Can't you tell that even your voice offends me?

GUARD
Your hearing or your heart?

CREON
You dare define my feelings!

GUARD
I may offend your ears, but the one who did it hurts your heart.

CREON
Clearly, you talk too much!   320

GUARD
Maybe I talk too much—but I did not do the deed.

CREON
You did—and even worse—you sold your soul for silver.

GUARD
How awful—
                that one who is a judge should have so little judgment.

CREON
Judge "judgment" how you please—but if
you will not say who the culprit is,   325
you'll see how your illicit gains bring only woe.
(Exit CREON through the double doors into the palace.)

GUARD
And I pray he'll be found—though whether
he is or not is a question of luck.
But you won't see me again!
Beyond my wildest hopes, I am saved.   330
My luck holds, and I give all thanks to the gods.
(Exit GUARD toward the country, stage left.)

FIRST STASIMON

CHORUS   Strophe A (332–41)

Many things are wonderful, but nothing
more wonderful and awesome than man.
He can travel through surging waves
and high-cresting surf
driven by stormy southern winds
across the grey and dangerous sea.
Year after year, he wears away
the substance of immortal Earth,
tirelessly working the soil
with plough and mule.

                                        Antistrophe A (342–53)

He snares flocks of gaudy birds,
packs of wild beasts,
and whole schools of fish
in the mesh of his nets—
a cunning man indeed.
And he can dominate
every animal that roams the forest
with his skill—
yoke the shaggy troops of horse,
outwit and tame the tireless mountain bull.

                                           Strophe B (354–64)

The art of speech, thought
as swift as the wind, and the need
to create and guard the city
he has learned well—
and how to protect himself
from bitter cold and driving rain.
His genius is endless; ingenious,
he confronts the future, able
to escape the worst sickness.
Only Hades' power—death alone—
he cannot evade.

                                        Antistrophe B (365–83)

Master beyond expectation
of resource and invention,
sometimes his actions are evil,
sometimes good.
Following the laws of man

and swearing to honor the gods',
he and his city prosper. But a citizen
no longer when he rashly disobeys.
He will be unwelcome at my hearth
as in my thoughts—
the man who does such things.

(Enter GUARD *from the direction of the battlefield, stage left, leading*
ANTIGONE. CHORUS *continues.)*
But what do I see—is this a portent?
I cannot deny I know her—
this girl is Antigone,
the unhappy child
of her unhappy father Oedipus.
And what does it mean? Surely you are not brought here
for disobeying what the king decreed,
caught in an act of madness?

GUARD
This is she—the one who did the deed.
We caught her burying him. But where is Creon?   385

CHORUS
Here he comes from the house—and just when we need him.

(Enter CREON *through the double doors from the palace, accompanied by*
ATTENDANTS.)*
CREON
Need me for what? What is happening?

(Enter GUARD *from the plain, stage left.)*
GUARD
My lord, mortals should never say "never";
second thoughts make liars of us all.
I insisted I'd never be back   390
because of your threats—they really upset me!—
but something good and unexpected
gives the greatest pleasure,
and here I am, though I swore not to return,
leading this girl, who was caught red-handed   395
at the burial rites. No need to cast lots

this time—this luck is mine alone!
Now, lord, you can take her, question
and judge and convict her. And grant, I pray,
that I go free from all these evils.   400

CREON
This one you bring here—where and how did you find her?

GUARD
Burying the man; now you know the whole story.

CREON
Are you really sure of what you say?

GUARD
I saw her covering the corpse—
doing what you had forbidden. Is that said clear enough?   405

CREON
How was she seen—and how taken?

GUARD
This is what happened. After we got there,
still brooding on your terrible threats,
and brushed away the dust that cloaked the corpse
to expose the putrefying object,   410
we went to the top of the hill, out of the wind,
to escape the contagion of its stink—
each man taunting those who did not look alert
but seemed to doze or slacken.

And so the time passed,   415
until the round lamp of the sun
with its burning heat stood high above our heads.
Then suddenly, a whirlwind rose
like a curse on the plain, tormenting the forest trees,
and all the air was clogged with dust. We bent low,   420
closed our eyes against this affliction from the gods, and endured.
It took a long time to end—and when it cleared
we saw the girl, bitterly wailing
the sharp cry of a mother bird

who grieves to see the nest empty of her young.   425
That was how she cried when she saw
the bare corpse—grief-stricken lamentation,
and evil curses on the ones who had done this.

At once she sprinkled the body with thirsty dust from the dry ground,
and lifting up a fine bronze pitcher of water,   430
honored the corpse with three libations.
Seeing this, all of us moved forward
to hold her there—which did not seem to surprise her—
and accuse her of this unlawful deed
done now and before, and she denied nothing.   435

In the same moment, I was torn
between joy and grief. It is good to escape
from trouble, but to lead a friend to punishment
is woeful. Yet I must confess that
my own safety is the most important.   440

CREON
And you, with your head bent to the ground,
do you admit or deny what you did?

ANTIGONE
I admit it—I do not deny anything.

CREON *(to the* GUARD*)*
You may go where you will,
no accusation against you.   445
*(*GUARD *exits stage left.)*
(to ANTIGONE*)*
But you—tell me, but briefly—
did you know it had been forbidden?

ANTIGONE
Of course I knew it. Everyone knew.

CREON
Yet you dared ignore those laws?

ANTIGONE
Zeus did not command these things,   450
nor did Justice, who dwells with the gods below,
ordain such laws for men.
Neither do I believe that your decrees,
or those of any other mortal, are strong enough to overrule
the ancient, unwritten, immutable laws of the gods,   455
which are not for the present alone, but have always
been—and no one knows when they began.
I would not risk the punishment of the gods
in fear of any man.

I already knew I was going to die—how could it be otherwise, 460
even if not at your command?
And if I die before my time—to me it seems a gain.
How can a person who lives as I do,
amid so many evils, not welcome death?
I do not fear that fate: it is the common lot, no special woe.   465
But if I should allow the corpse of my brother,
my mother's son, to lie unburied,
that would grieve me; nothing else.
And if it seems to you my acts are foolish,
Well—perhaps it is a fool who thinks so.   470

CHORUS
Like father, like daughter—a wild girl.
She has not learned to bend before the storm.

CREON
Do not forget that the most stubborn
are the first to fail, and sometimes
the iron bar longest-forged in the fire   475
is the one that shatters.
I have seen the bravest, most noble horse
tamed by the smallest curb. A slave
cannot afford proud thoughts when near his master.

She has already shown her arrogance   480
and flouted established law.
And now this second challenge—to do it again
and laughing, boast of her deed.

She will be the man, not I,
if she can go victorious and unpunished!   485
Whether she is my sister's child or even closer kin
than any who worship Zeus at our household altar,
neither she nor her sister will escape
an evil fate. I'm sure that the two of them
plotted this burial together.   490
(to his ATTENDANTS*)*
Go call the other—I saw her just now inside,
raving and out of her mind.
Even before they act, the minds of plotters
are overwhelmed by guilty thoughts!
But I hate even worse the ones who try to glorify   495
their lawless acts when caught.

ANTIGONE
What more do you want, now that you've caught me, than to kill me?

CREON
Nothing more. Because now I have everything.

ANTIGONE
Then what are you waiting for? Nothing you say
pleases me, nor could it ever—   500
no more than my words can please you.
And yet what could bring me more glory and fame
than to bury my own brother?
Everyone would rejoice in this
if fear did not shackle their tongues.   505
But tyranny who has so much of everything
can do and say whatever it wish.

CREON
You are the only Cadmean who takes this view.

ANTIGONE
They all see it as I do—but keep their mouths shut.

CREON
Aren't you ashamed to think differently from all the others?   510

ANTIGONE
There's nothing shameful in honoring one's own flesh and blood.

CREON
Can you deny it was also your own brother who died opposing him?

ANTIGONE
A brother, of the same blood and by the same mother and father.

CREON
Then how can you honor his enemy?

ANTIGONE
He is dead, and will never serve as a witness for your actions.   515

CREON
He will, if you insist on honoring them both equally.

ANTIGONE
It was not a slave who died, but a brother.

CREON
Died attacking this land, while the other defended it.

ANTIGONE
Nevertheless, Hades demands the customary rites.

CREON
But good and bad do not deserve them equally.   520

ANTIGONE
Who knows how these things are judged below?

CREON
An enemy is never a friend, even when dead.

ANTIGONE
My nature is drawn to love; I cannot hate either.

CREON
Well, follow them below if you must, and love them
as much as you please. While I live, no woman will rule me.   525

CHORUS
Look—here by the gate, weeping,
stands Ismene, her fond sister,
with darkened brow,
flushed face,
and tender cheeks glazed by tears.   530

(Enter ISMENE, *led by* ATTENDANTS, *through the double doors of the palace.)*
CREON
You, who slipped unseen into my house
like a snake to drink my blood! Unwittingly,
I nourished two rebels, enemies of my throne.
Tell me, will you admit your part in this burial,
or insist your innocence?   535

ISMENE
I confess to the deed—if she agrees
to let me take my share of the blame.

ANTIGONE
Justice does not grant your claim.
You did not want to help me in my task—nor will I share it.

ISMENE
But now I would be proud to sail with you   540
upon this sea of troubles.

ANTIGONE
Hades, and those below, bear witness to the truth.
I cannot love false friends who only offer words, not acts.

ISMENE
Sister, do not disgrace me—let me die
with you; let us consecrate the dead together.   545

ANTIGONE
No need to die with me—nor claim the credit
for what you did not do. My death will be enough.

ISMENE
But what will my life be worth without you?

ANTIGONE
Ask Creon—it's he you care about.

ISMENE
Why do you torment me? It does not ease you.   550

ANTIGONE
It pains me if you think I mock you.

ISMENE
There must be some way I could help you!

ANTIGONE
Save yourself and flee—I shall not blame you.

ISMENE
Awful—that I cannot share your fate!

ANTIGONE
You chose to live, I chose to die.   555

ISMENE
At least I tried to dissuade you.

ANTIGONE
Your choice seemed right to some—others agreed with mine.

ISMENE
Yet we are equally wrong.

ANTIGONE
Be brave. You will live—but my life already
ended long ago, in service to the dead.   560

CREON
I must say that one of these girls has just shown how foolish she is;
the other has been that way since her birth.

ISMENE
It's true, my lord—whatever sense I once had,
my misery has taken away.

CREON
It went when you allied yourself with evil people.   565

ISMENE
But what would life be worth for me, alone without her?

CREON
Don't even mention her. She no longer exists.

ISMENE
But will you kill your own son's future bride?

CREON
There are other fields for him to plough.

ISMENE
But not so well-matched as she to him.   570

CREON
I forbid my sons to marry evil brides.

ISMENE
Dearest Haemon, how your father demeans you!

CREON
And how you madden me—with this talk of marriage.

ISMENE
Will you really deny this girl to your own son?

CREON
It is Death who will stop the marriage.   575

ISMENE
So it is already decided that she has to die?

CREON
Yes—decided for you, decided by me.
No more delays. Servants, take them both inside.
From now on they must behave like women,
not roaming free. Even the bravest try to run away   580
when they feel that Hades is near.
(*Exit* ATTENDANTS, *with* ANTIGONE *and* ISMENE, *through the
double doors into the palace.* CREON *remains.*)

SECOND *STASIMON*

CHORUS   Strophe A (582–92)
How fortunate, those who do not know
the bitter taste of evil,
whose house was never shaken by the gods
nor their whole family doomed—
assailed as by an earthquake,
a landslide, a tidal wave
leaving everything in ruins,
a wild Thracian wind
scooping black sand from the ocean's depths
to batter the rocky shore
which groans under its onslaught.

Antistrophe A (593–603)

Ancient and present woes
oppress the house of Labdacus.
From one generation to the next
there is no escape from the gods' curse.
Even now, these last shoots
from the stock of Oedipus
which promised light and hope
are smothered in bloody dust
by the gods of the Underworld;
by wild words and Furies in the mind.

Strophe B (604–14)

Great god Zeus, even the most
arrogant act of man cannot restrain your power.
All-conquering Sleep cannot overcome you
nor the wheeling months of Heaven.

You reign, ageless master of time,
from the marble brilliance of Olympus.
In the present and the future,
as in the past, the same law prevails:
that man who thinks himself
the most blessed and fortunate
will fall the furthest.

                                        Antistrophe B (615–25)

Hope ranges the world
and cheers most men at times,
but can also deceive
with fool's gold and lustful fantasies,
until the dreamer stumbles into what seems cold ash
and burns his feet in fire.
It was a wise man who told
how evil shows the fairest face
to those whom the gods will destroy.
They soon meet their doom—
live but a short time before disaster.   625
(*Enter Haemon from the city, stage right. The* CHORUS *continues.*)
Here is Haemon, your youngest and last-born.
Does he come grieving
for the fate of Antigone
and because he will be cheated
of his marriage bed and bride?   630

CREON
We'll know soon enough—with no need for seers.
Tell me, child, now you've heard my final judgment on her,
have you come in anger against your father,
or will you accept my decision, and still love me?

HAEMON
Father, I am your son, and what you say is good.   635
Your advice will keep me on the right path
and I shall heed it. No marriage
could be more important than your guidance.

CREON
Yes, son, it is best that you want
to follow your father in everything.   640

This is what men pray for: to have a household
of obedient, loyal children
who will defend their father against all enemies
and respect his friends.
The man who begets worthless children—what can you say   645
except that he has made a stick for his own back,
become a laughing stock to all the world?

And never, my boy, be deceived by the pleasure
a woman can give; that fire
soon dies down, and nothing is worse   650
than sharing your bed with someone who hates you.
A false lover is worse than a festering sore.
Spit her out like an enemy, like a piece of rotten food—
let this girl find her true husband in Hades.
I caught her openly disobeying—   655
the only person in the city who dared to do so—
and shall not go back on my word to the people.
I will execute her. Let her implore Zeus, the god of kinship,
as much as she likes; if I allow my own family
to flout my orders, everyone would do the same.   660

The man who rules his household justly
will also be a righteous citizen.
But the one who tries to overstep the rule of law
or impose his will on the leaders,
gets no applause from me.   665
It is essential to obey in both small and great matters
the man the city appoints, whether his demands are just,
or quite the opposite. I am confident
that he would command or serve equally well,
would stand his ground in the front line,   670
brave comrade and defender.
There is no greater evil than anarchy,
which destroys cities, ruins houses,
breaks ranks, and leads to rout and retreat.
In the final analysis,   675
it is obedience which saves most men,
and thus we must preserve the proper order of things.
And there is no way we can allow a woman to triumph.

Better to be defeated by any sort of man
than seen as weaker than a woman.   680

CHORUS
Unless old age has robbed us of our wits,
it seems to us that what you say makes sense.

HAEMON
Father, it is the gods who give to men
the highest gift, the power of reason.
I do not know how—and find it hard—to say   685
that you are not always right, and
there might be other ways to understand this matter.
It is my duty to observe and listen
to what the people talk about and blame you for.
Dread of your icy glance stops every citizen   690
from any comment which might displease you.
But in the darkness, I hear them, their murmurings,
the city weeping with pity for her—
the girl who least deserves to perish
for such a glorious deed—she,   695
who when her own brother fell in bloody battle
would not leave him lie unburied, to the mercies
of feral dogs and carrion birds.
Is she not worthy of honor, and a crown of gold?
Such are the muffled rumors that spread.   700

For me, father, there is nothing
more precious than your prosperity.
What greater glory for children than their father's renown,
or what for a father than the fame of his children?
But, father—do not maintain one fixed opinion,   705
insisting that it and no other is right;
for whoever believes that he knows best
and no one else can equal him in word or deed,
such men are exposed as empty vessels.
It is no shame for a wise man   710
to be flexible and learn from others.

You've seen how trees on the banks of a stream
swollen with winter rain, which bend to its force, survive,

but those that fight the storm die uprooted.
It's the same if the captain does not adjust his sails   715
to a sudden wind—his ship is overturned,
his decks are swamped, and his keel goes upwards.
You too, should calm your anger and consider.
I know I am only young, but
let me give my opinion. Of course   720
it would be wonderful if men were born wise—
but that's not what usually happens.
The best thing is to listen to good advice.

CHORUS
It is right, Lord, if his words seem just, that you should learn from him
as much as he from you. What you both say makes sense.   725

CREON (to CHORUS)
Is someone of our age to be taught about
the laws of human nature by such a stripling?

HAEMON
I do not speak of anything unrighteous. And though I am young,
judge me, please, by my actions, not my years.

CREON
Such as honoring those who cause disruption?   730

HAEMON
I do not say you should honor anyone evil.

CREON
But is she not infected by that sickness?

HAEMON
Her fellow citizens of Thebes deny it.

CREON
Is the city to tell me how to govern?

HAEMON
Now you sound like someone even younger than me!   735

CREON
Am I to rule this land as I wish or according to others?

HAEMON
The city does not belong to one man alone.

CREON
Does not the city belong to he who rules?

HAEMON
You would be the perfect ruler for an empty desert.

CREON *(to the* CHORUS*)*
He might be fighting as a woman's ally!   740

HAEMON
Are you a woman?—because it's your side I'm on.

CREON
How? By attacking your father? You are vicious!

HAEMON
I see it's not just matters of law that you're wrong about.

CREON
Wrong—to protect my god-given authority?

HAEMON
You do not protect it when you flout the gods' laws.   745

CREON
O vile creature—even lower than a woman!

HAEMON
You will not catch me sinking to shameful actions.

CREON
But everything you say is in defense of her.

HAEMON
—and in defense of you, and me, and the gods below.

CREON
Do not think that while she lives you'll marry her.   750

HAEMON
Her death will lead to another.

CREON
Are you arrogant enough to threaten me?

HAEMON
How can I make threats against such empty nonsense?

CREON
Your empty so-called wisdom will end in tears.

HAEMON
If you were not my father, I'd say you can't think straight.   755

CREON
What arrogance, you woman's lackey!

HAEMON
You want to speak, but will not listen.

CREON
Is that so? Listen, I swear by the gods of Olympus
that you'll gain nothing by reviling and opposing me.
(to his ATTENDANTS)
Bring her out, that hateful wretch—and let her die   760
here, before her bridegroom's eyes, at once.
(ATTENDANTS exit through the double doors into the palace.)

HAEMON
Don't think you can do it in my presence
or that you'll have the pleasure of seeing me watch it—
nor ever see me again. Do what you want
with your mad friends—if you have any friends left.   765

(He rushes off toward the plain, stage left.)

CHORUS
He's gone. Young men's anger is swift and fierce,
and their grief almost too heavy to bear.

CREON
Let him go. He can do—or dream—the act of a brave man,
but nothing will save the two girls from their fate.

CHORUS
Surely you will not kill them both?   770

CREON
No, you're right. Not the one who did nothing.

CHORUS
And what fate do you intend for the other?

CREON
I will lead her on desolate paths
into a hidden rocky cave and leave her there alive
with the least food the law requires,   775
so that the city can escape pollution.
And there, praying to Hades, the god of the Underworld,
the only god she honors, perhaps
she'll manage to survive—or else will finally learn
how futile it was to put her trust in Hades.   780

THIRD STASIMON

CHORUS   Strophe A (781–90)
Eros, invincible in battle,
Eros, consumer of riches,
who slumbers through the night
on a maiden's soft cheeks,
ranges the furthest seas and visits   785
lonely huts on the high pastures.
No one escapes—neither immortal gods
nor men whose lives are short as those
of mayflies that live for only a day—
the one you touch is driven mad.   790

Antistrophe A (791–800)

Even just men's thoughts you warp to crime,
stirring conflict between kindred—
between father and son.
But triumphant desire
that shines from the eyes   795
of the newly married bride
is stronger than the greatest laws.
Unconquerable Aphrodite
sits among the gods
and plays her games of power.   800

KOMMOS

(ANTIGONE *is brought from the palace through the double doors by*
guards.)
And now I too am overcome
and carried beyond the realm of loyalty and law,
no longer able to hold back my tears
when I see Antigone being led toward
the bridal chamber where she will sleep with Death.   805

ANTIGONE   Strophe B (806–22)
Behold me, fellow citizens
of my ancestral land,
walking the last mile, the last road,
seeing the sun's light
which I shall never see again   810
for the last time.
Hades, the god of death,
who puts us all to sleep,
leads me living to the banks of Acheron.
No wedding songs are sung for me   815
as I become his bride.

CHORUS
What glory and praise you deserve
as you depart for the cavern of death—
not struck by fatal disease nor
slaughtered in war, but still alive   820
and of your own free will—you alone
of all mortals will enter Hades.

ANTIGONE   Antistrophe B (823–38)
Like that story I heard of our Phrygian guest,
the daughter of Tantalus—of how,
on the peak of Sipylus, she was enclosed   825
and hedged about, as ivy clings to a wall,
by a stony accretion; and how,
they say, the rain and snow that fall
on the mountain top erode her form,
and the ceaseless tears   830
that pour from beneath her brows
become streams down the hills. Like her,
in a rocky cave, the gods lull me to sleep.

CHORUS
But she was a goddess, born of gods
and we are mortal, of mortal stock.   835
Yet it is a great thing to have it said,
when you die, that your destiny
was equal to that of a god.

ANTIGONE   Strophe C (839–56)
By the gods of my father I ask:
why do you mock me—   840
not even waiting until I have gone,
but still here before your eyes?
O city! city!—
you propertied men of the city!
But fountains of Dirce,   845
and holy groves of Thebes with its many chariots,
you at least can testify how no one laments me,
and by what an aberration of justice
I go to the heaped stones of my prison and unnatural tomb.
What a wretched creature I am—   850
with nowhere to dwell, neither
among mortals or corpses,
not the living nor the dead.

CHORUS
Boldly you pressed to the furthest limit,
my child, until you stumbled against   855
the awesome throne of Justice—as if doomed
to pay the price of your father's sins.

ANTIGONE   Strophe C (858–75)
Ah! now you touch
on the worst thing of all—
that tripled pity, pain, and anguish I feel   860
at the thought of my father,
the dreadful fate
of the noble house of Labdacus,
and the tainted madness of that marriage bed
where my poor accursed mother slept   865
incestuously with my father, her own son.
Those were my parents—
already at birth I was doomed
to join them, unmarried, in death.
Brother, your ill-fated wedding   870
killed us both—though I am yet alive.

CHORUS
Your piety is admirable. But
the man who holds the power
must also be acknowledged.
Stubborn willfulness destroyed you.

EPODE (876–82)

ANTIGONE
No funeral hymns, no marriage songs; unloved,
unwept and wretched, I am led along the ordained path.
Never again shall I, miserable one,
raise my eyes toward the sacred eye
and light of the sun—   880
no dear friend is here to mourn me
nor weep for my harsh fate.

CREON
And who indeed do you think would not lament
and groan before their death, if there were any point in it?
(to GUARDS)
Take her away at once—lead her   885
to the covered tomb we prepared, as I ordered,
and leave her there alone. She can decide
whether she wants to die, or bury herself alive.
There will be no bloodguilt for us—and
she will lose her place on the face of the earth.   890

ANTIGONE
Tomb, bridal chamber, deep-dug final home,
where I go to find my own—
my kinsmen who have died,
whom the great Persephassa accepts among the dead.
I, the last one left, and the most wretched,   895
descend before my life has reached its natural end.
When I am there, how fervently I hope
that my father will greet me lovingly,
as will you, dear mother, and Eteocles my brother,
for with my own hands I washed your bodies,   900
adorned you, and made all
the funerary libations. And now, Polyneices,
it is for tending your body that I am rewarded thus.
And yet, to those who understand such things, I did well.

Believe me—not even if my own children   905
or husband lay dead and rotting
would I have done this thing and defied the city.
What law do I invoke by speaking thus?
If my husband died, I could find another.
Another man could give me another child.   910
But with my mother and father buried in Hades
no brother could ever come into being from them.

This is the law I obey, honoring you above anything else,
though Creon believed I was wrong
to dare that terrible act, dear brother.   915
And now he leads me away, his cruel grasp
depriving me of my rightful future—

a marriage bed and the rearing of children.
Thus I am cursed, deserted by my friends,
and must go, alive, to the deep-dug house of the dead.   920

I do not know what holy law I have transgressed
nor who will be my ally
if I cannot turn to the gods for help
and my piety is called irreverence. If I have erred,
and my punishment seems good to the gods   925
I must accept it, and forgive them.
But if my judges are wrong, then let them suffer
even worse evils than they impose on me.

CHORUS
Still the same storm, the same fierce winds,
batter her soul.   930

CREON
Let them take her quickly away—
or they'll regret their slowness.

ANTIGONE
These words
are my sentence of death.

CREON
I give you no encouragement to hope   935
that it will not be fulfilled.

ANTIGONE
City of my fathers, land of Thebes,
you ancestral gods and Theban lords:
look well upon me
as I am led away, unhesitating;   940
I who am the last of your royal family.
See what I suffer—and from what sort of men—
for my obedience to the laws of piety.
(ANTIGONE *is led out by* GUARDS, *stage left.*)

FOURTH *STASIMON*

CHORUS   Strophe A (944–54)
Even lovely Danaë was forced to exchange
the light of heaven for that sealed bronze room
where she was hidden, guarded, and tamed.
Yet though of a family as honored as yours,
dear child, it was her fate
to be the vessel of Zeus' golden seed.
The power of destiny
is a fearsome thing—neither wealth
nor Ares and the force of arms,
nor towering walls nor a dark ship
on a wild ocean will help you escape.

                                          Antistrophe A (956–65)
And the short-tempered son of Dryas,
king of the Edonians, as punishment
for his mocking taunts was tamed by Dionysus
and penned into a rocky prison
where the surging strength of his madness ebbed   960
as he learned the power of the god he had provoked.
He thought he could halt those troupes of maenads—
Bacchic women with their pitchy torches,
calling *Eoui!*—but brought the wrath
of the flute-playing Muses down on his head.   965
                                          Strophe B (966–76)
And by the dark rocks
where two seas clash,
on the shores of Bosphorus
and at Thracian Salmydessus,
Ares witnessed the savage attack   970
on the sons of Phineus by his new wife,
saw how viciously—
weaving comb and spindle
like daggers in her blood-stained hands—
she pierced their eyeballs   975
and blinded them both.

                                          Antistrophe B (977–87)
The doomed boys wept for their wretched state,
their birth from that unhappy marriage,
and for their mother, banished to a stony place.
In her own right she had been born   980

queen of the Erechthids
and nurtured in windy caves
in a land of mountains and horses
half-way around the world,
a daughter of the wind-god Boreas.   985
Yet even on her, my child,
the ageless Fates turned their malevolence.

(*Enter the blind prophet,* TEIRESIAS, *led by a* BOY, *from the direction of
the city, stage right.*)
TEIRESIAS
Lords of Thebes, we have shared the road,
two finding the way with the eyes of one—
this is how the blind must travel, with a guide.   990

CREON
What news do you bring, ancient Teiresias?

TEIRESIAS
I will tell you—and you must trust the prophet and obey.

CREON
I have not disobeyed your will in the past.

TEIRESIAS
And that is why you steered the city on the right course.

CREON
I know it, and can testify to your help.   995

TEIRESIAS
But know now that you are walking on the razor's edge.

CREON
What is it? I tremble at your words.

TEIRESIAS
You will learn, when you hear what my art reveals.
For as I sat on my ancient seat of augury
where all the birds come,   1000
I heard something strange,

an evil screeching I could not understand,
from birds who tore at each other with murderous claws.
The rush of their wings beat a strong message.
At once, fearful, I tried to make a burnt offering   1005
on the altar. But from the sacrificial victim
Hephaestus accepted nothing—
the fire would not kindle. A noxious liquid
trickled onto the embers, smoke rose,
flesh spattered, the gallbladder exploded   1010
and the fat melted away, leaving the thighbones bare.
Such was the failure of my attempt at prophecy, as this child
      explained—
for he is my guide, as I am a guide for others.
And it is your fault; the city is sick because of your will.   1015
All the altars and hearths of the city
are tainted by birds and dogs with carrion
from the ill-fated body of Oedipus' son.
That is why the gods will not accept our sacrificial prayers
nor our burnt offerings,   1020
and why the birds do not call out good omens clearly—
their voices are clogged with the blood and fat of a slain man.

Consider this, my child.
Every man can make mistakes.
But though he errs, he   1025
can leave behind his folly and misfortune
and heal the wrong he did, if he is not self-willed—
stubbornness is always stupidity.
Yield to the dead, do not keep killing
the one already dead. Where is the valor in that?   1030
I wish you well—my words are well meant—
to learn from a good adviser is to your advantage.

CREON
Old man, you all aim your arrows at me
like archers at a target. Even from your plots
I am not safe—all you fortune-tellers work against me,   1035
for years I have been bought and sold like merchandise.
Profit from me as much as you wish—barter
the white-gold electrum from Sardis, and Indian gold.
But you will never cover that man with a tomb—

not even to hide his corpse from the eagles of Zeus,   1040
who would tear at the rotten flesh and carry those gobbets up
to gorge at the foot of his holy throne.
Not even in dread of such pollution
will I allow that man to be buried.
No human act can ever defile the gods, as I know well.   1045
And even the cleverest mortals fail shamefully, old man Teiresias,
when they exaggerate the worth of shameful things for profit's sake.

TEIRESIAS
Alas, is there a man who knows or understands—

CREON
What? What grand statement are you making?

TEIRESIAS
—understands how far the power of reason is our best
    possession.   1050

CREON
As far, I guess, as to know that thoughtlessness is the greatest ill.

TEIRESIAS
And yet you are infected with that same sickness.

CREON
I do not wish to insult the seer!

TEIRESIAS
But that is what you do, when you say my prophecies are false.

CREON
All seers are too fond of money.   1055

TEIRESIAS
And all tyrants are greedy, and only love gain.

CREON
Do you not know that you are speaking of your ruler?

TEIRESIAS

I know it very well. You rule because through me you saved the city.

CREON

You may be wise, seer, but you love to make trouble.

TEIRESIAS

You will goad me to say what's best left in my thoughts.   1060

CREON

Speak if you must, as long as you don't ask payment.

TEIRESIAS

Is that what you think is my motive?

CREON

Know well that you cannot bend me to your purposes.

TEIRESIAS

And you should know as well, that you will not live
through many more swift circuits of the sun   1065
before you yourself will give, in exchange for corpses,
a child of your loins, a corpse of your own flesh and blood.
For you have thrust below one who belongs above,
blasphemously entombed a living person,
and at the same time have kept above ground   1070
a corpse belonging to the chthonic gods—
unburied, unmourned, unholy.

Neither you nor the heavenly powers should have a part in this,
but your violence has forced it. Now, sent by those gods,
the foul avenging Furies, hunters of Hell,   1075
lie in wait to inflict the same evils on you.
Do you still think I have been bribed to say these things?
Believe me—not much time will pass before
your home will resound with the wailing of women and men.
The cities are seething with hatred against you   1080
as the torn flesh of their dead sons
with its unholy carrion stench
is brought by savage dogs and raptor birds back to their hearths.
How you provoke me! until, like an archer,

wrathful, I loose these arrows into your heart— 1085
deadly arrows whose fiery sting you cannot escape.
(to the BOY, *guiding him)*
Child, lead me back to my own house, let this man
vent his anger on younger men;
and may he learn to speak more wisely,
and think better thoughts, than he does now. 1090
(Exit TEIRESIAS *and* BOY *toward the city, stage right.)*

CHORUS
Lord, the man has gone, but has prophesied dreadful things.
And we know—since the time our hair was glossy-black
until today when we're all white-haired—
that in what he foretells for the city, he is never wrong.

CREON
I know this too, and it troubles me greatly. 1095
It is terrible to yield—but stubbornly to resist
and bring ruin upon yourself—that also is terrible.

CHORUS
Child of Menoeceus, you must seek good advice.

CREON
What should I do? You tell me, and I will obey you.

CHORUS
Go—go, release the girl from her closed chamber 1100
and build a tomb for the one lying exposed.

CREON
This is what you think I should do—give in, surrender?

CHORUS
Be as quick as you can, my lord, for the gods' avengers,
the swift-footed Harms, come to cut down the sinner.

CREON
It is very hard to change my mind—but I shall try. 1105
Necessity cannot be fought against.

CHORUS
Go now, at once—and do it yourself, do not leave it to others!

CREON
Immediately—I'm going, just as I am! And you servants—
go, go—every one of you. Take axes, hurry,
rush to that place—you can see it from here.   1110
And now, my thoughts have cleared, I know
that it is I who must free her, being the one who bound her.
The best way to live, I admit it at last,
is in obedience to the customary laws.
(*Exit* CREON *and his* ATTENDANTS *toward the plain, stage left.*)

FIFTH *STASIMON*

CHORUS   Strophe A (1115–25)
You have many names—
you who were the glorious child
of Cadmus' daughter
and loud-thundering Zeus;
you who keep watch on far-famed Italy,
who on the bosomy hills of Demeter's Eleusis   1120
are worshipped by many—
O Bacchus,
god of the mother-city of Bacchic Thebes
on the banks of the swift stream Ismenus,
where the wild dragons' teeth were scattered—   1125
                                          Antistrophe A (1126–36)
Beyond the double-crested rock,
with their smoky torches
they follow you, the Corycian nymphs,
your Bacchants;
and by the Castalian spring,   1130
on the ivy-hidden slopes
of Nysa's hills, and the green
vine-covered headlands
they follow; and all through the streets
of Thebes you can hear ring out   1135
their ecstatic voices and cries of *Euoi!*

                                          Strophe B (1137–45)
Thebes, which you honor
more than any other city—

as your mother did,
she who was destroyed by a thunderbolt—   1140
now that its citizens are gripped by plague,
stride on your healing feet
across the slopes of Parnassus
and the groaning strait,
to cleanse and to save us.   1145

Antistrophe B (1146–54)

O chorus leader of the stars
whose breath streams fire,
guardian of the night's voices,
son begotten of Zeus—
Lord, manifest, appear to us   1150
with your troupe of Thyiads,
frenzied and raving,
who dance through the night
for the giver of all, the great god Iacchus.

(Enter MESSENGER *from the direction of the plain, stage left.*)
MESSENGER
Neighbors of Cadmus and the house of Amphion,   1155
there is no rank or style of human life
I would choose to praise or criticize.
A man's bad luck or good fortune
will change from day to day—
not even a seer can prophesy what might happen.   1160
Take Creon—whom I once thought deserved to be envied,
who saved the Cadmean land from enemies
and was proclaimed its monarch,
set everything to rights and gloried in his children—
now he has thrown it all away.   1165
It seems to me that when a man loses his joy in life,
his reason to live, he becomes a breathing corpse.
No matter how great the treasure and power he achieves,
I cannot think they would have more worth
than a puff of smoke, once his joy in life has gone.   1170

CHORUS
What new grief for our king do you come to report?

MESSENGER
Dead—they are dead. And the living are to blame for their deaths.

CHORUS
Who lies dead? And who killed them?

MESSENGER
Haemon is dead—
his blood spilled by a kindred hand.   1175

CHORUS
His father's hand? Or someone else?

MESSENGER
It was his own act—in fury at his father for the murder.

CHORUS
O seer, your prophecy was true, and is accomplished!

MESSENGER
That is what happened; now you must consider what should be done.

CHORUS
Yes, and look—here comes poor Eurydice,   1180
Creon's wife. Either she heard us from the house,
talking of her child, or she arrives by chance.

(Enter EURYDICE through the double doors from the palace.)
EURYDICE
All of you here, citizens—I heard your words
as I came to the door, on my way
to offer prayers to the goddess Pallas—   1185
and as I lifted the bar of the gate,
about to open it, a cry of evil tidings
to my household assailed my ears. I fell back
into the arms of my women, fainting.
Whatever it was I thought I heard, say it again   1190
and I will listen. I am used to bad news.

MESSENGER
Dear mistress, I was there, and will describe
what I saw, leaving nothing out.
Why should I soothe you with words
later proved false? It is always better to tell the truth.   1195

As his guide, I went with your husband
up to the furthest part of the plain, where still
unmourned, the body of Polyneices lay, ravaged by dogs.
We entreated Pluto, and the goddess of the crossroads,
to hold back their anger and show mercy.   1200
We laved the remains with purifying water,
broke off branches to burn what was left
and heaped a high mound of his native earth
for a tomb. Then we turned toward the maiden's
stone-paved prison, the chamber of Hades' bride.   1205

Already, from afar, one of us had heard
a wailing voice from that accursed place
and came to tell our master Creon.
The garbled anguished sounds grew louder
the nearer we approached. He also groaned   1210
and loudly cried: "How wretched I am!
How could I foretell I was about to tread
the most unhappy path of all I've walked?
It is my son's voice that greets me! Servants,
hurry, closer, look—go to the tomb   1215
where the stones that sealed its mouth were pulled away
and tell me if I am right to recognize that voice as Haemon's—
or if the gods deceive me."

Obeying our master's desperate commands
we went deeper into the tomb   1220
and there beheld the girl—hung by the neck
in a noose of her linen veil—
and he, pressed close, clutching around her waist,
moaning and wailing the loss of his bride to the Underworld,
the deeds of his father, and his doomed marriage.   1225
When Creon saw him, a horrid cry burst from his lips
and he moved toward him, calling,
"Poor unhappy boy, what have you done?

What passed through your mind?
You have gone mad and destroyed yourself.   1230
Come out, my child, I beg you."
But the boy glared at him wildly
and kept silent—then spat in his face
and drew his double-edged sword. When his father
ran to escape, the blow missed.   1235
The doomed boy, furious with himself, curved
his body forward and thrust the sword deep into his own side.
Half-conscious, he lifted his weakened arms to embrace the girl
and choking, coughed a stream of blood onto her white cheek.
His corpse enfolding hers,   1240
their marriage rites at last achieved in Hades—
a sight to demonstrate how lack of wisdom
is mankind's greatest curse.
(*Exit* Eurydice *through the double doors into the palace.*)

CHORUS
What do you think of that?
She went back inside without a word, neither good nor bad.   1245

MESSENGER
I am as surprised as you. But I hope,
though having heard such awful news of her child,
she will not cry her lamentations throughout the city,
but stay at home and grieve with her maidservants.
Her judgment is good enough not to make that mistake.   1250

CHORUS
I am not convinced. To me, both heavy silence
and too loud a show of grief seem equally ominous.

MESSENGER
Soon we'll know if she is holding back
some secret plan in her angry heart;
I'll go inside the house to see—you're right,   1255
such strange silence is troubling.
(*Exit* MESSENGER *through the double doors into the palace.*)

CREON *and* ATTENDANTS *enter carrying the body of* HAEMON *from
the plain, stage left.*)

CHORUS
And here indeed comes the lord himself,
bearing in his arms the undeniable token
of the madness—if I am allowed to say this—
and the error which is his alone, no one else's.   1260

CREON   Strophe A (1261–83)
Alas, the blunders of deluded minds,
stubborn and deadly!
Behold us, closest kinsmen—
yet killer and killed.
Alas for all my misdirected and ill-fated plans.   1265
O my child, you died too young.
Ah, such grief!
A life cut short
through my stupidity, not yours.

CHORUS
At last you learn what justice is—but too late.   1270

CREON
Alas, the wretched man I am,
the bitter lesson learned at last:
as if a god had struck a mighty blow to my head
that forced me down a wild road,
stupefied, to overturn and trample my joys.   1275
Ah, such misery,
the weary burden of mortals!

(Enter Messenger through the double doors of the palace.)
MESSENGER
My master, you come with laden arms already,
I can see that (indicating HAEMON's body)—but you will soon find
even worse things, there in the house.   1280

CREON
What could be worse than the pain I now feel?

MESSENGER
The queen your wife is dead, the mother of this corpse—
true mother, poor lady; her death wounds fresh.

CREON   Antistrophe A (1284–1305)
O harbor of Hades,
clogged with the dead, impossible to purify—   1285
why have you chosen me to destroy?
(to the MESSENGER*)*
Herald of grief, what is your new message?
Why attack again a man already defeated?
—What is it you say, boy?
What new thing do you tell me?   1290
Ah—there is a new victim—the death of my wife—
calamity upon calamity, ruined heaped upon ruin.

(Doors of the palace open and the body of EURYDICE *is visible.)*

CHORUS
Look, you can see her—she is no longer hidden inside.

CREON
O agony.
What else must I endure?   1295
Just now my child was in my arms,
now, wretch that I am,
I look upon another corpse.
Alas, poor tragic mother,
alas, tormented son.   1300

MESSENGER
It was at the altar, with a sharp-edged sword,
that she struck until her eyes saw only darkness—
having wept first for the fate of her son Megareus
and then for Haemon her youngest, and with her final breath
called down evil on you—child killer, slayer of sons.   1305

CREON   Strophe B (1306–27)
No, no more, I shudder with dread.
Will no one release me—
stab me full in the chest
with a two-edged sword?
How wretched I am.   1310
What anguish I suffer!

MESSENGER
Yes—because you have been blamed for both sons' deaths—
denounced by your dead wife before she died.

CREON
What did she do, how did she kill herself?

MESSENGER
With her own hand she struck into her heart   1315
when she heard the bitter cries mourning her child.

CREON
Only to me the guilt belongs, these acts
can never be blamed on another mortal.
It was I who killed you,
I, the most wretched—I admit it.   1320
Servants, lead me away now,
as swiftly as can be done,
lead me out of here—I
who have ceased to exist,
who have become less than nothing.   1325

CHORUS
What you say is good—if any good can come from such evil.
Get away as soon as you can, when evil is underfoot.

CREON   Antistrophe B (1328–53)
Come, let it come,
let the highest one,
he who grants the best death,   1330
come for me, bring my last day.
Come, let it come, the finest fate—
that I may never see another day.

CHORUS
What happens will happen. Now, you must do
what is needed for the present. The future lies in the hands of
    others.   1335

CREON
But I have prayed so hard for that wish to be fulfilled.

CHORUS
Do not pray for anything.
Mortals have no deliverance from fated misfortune.

CREON
Lead me—a vain and worthless man,
away from here. Oh, my son!   1340
Unknowing, unwilling, I killed you,
and you as well, my poor wife.
Oh, the agony!
To whom can I turn, where can I look?
All that I touch goes warped and askew   1345
and once again, cruel fate
has leapt onto my back, come down on my head.
(*Exit* CREON *and his* ATTENDANTS *into the palace.*)

CHORUS
Reason is the greatest part of happiness,
and knowing not to sin against the gods,
but to honor and revere them.   1350
The mighty boasts of haughty men
bring down the punishment of mighty blows—
from which at last, in old age, wisdom comes.

Notes

Oedipus the King

In the choruses there is not a one-to-one correlation between the Greek lines and our translation. When there is a note on a line in the chorus and there is a discrepancy or an ambiguity, we bracket the line number [ ] and give the original Greek line. The Greek text has some missing lines, which we have indicated with asterisks. Many of these lines have not been assigned line numbers in the historical numbering of the text, which we follow.

1: Cadmus was the founder of Thebes and great-great-grandfather of Oedipus; see House of Thebes, p. xxviii.

3: Suppliants carried wreaths of olive or laurel, entwined with wool, which they laid on the altar.

5: Paeans are hymns of supplication to Apollo as a god of healing. The word also is used as a title of Apollo in his role as god of healing.

17: Zeus is the king of the gods who rules from Mount Olympus.

19: Thebes had two marketplaces.

20: The double shrines are the two temples of Thebes, one on the west side of the city and the other, the temple of Athena Cadmeia. The goddess Athena is also called "Pallas," "Pallas Athena," or "Athena."

21: A reference to the temple of Apollo Ismenus, where divination was practiced using burnt offerings. Ismenus, a river that runs through Thebes, was named after the son of Amphion and Niobe in Theban myth.

27: The Greek has *pyrphoros,* "fire bringing." The Greek physician Hippocrates uses the word to mean "fever bringing." An epithet applied to Zeus, Prometheus, and Apollo, here it probably refers to Apollo, who is associated with causing plagues, as in Book 1 of the *Iliad.*

30: Hades is the god of the Underworld and the dead. It can also mean the place, the Underworld.

36: The Sphinx is a mythical creature, having the body of a lion and a female human head, often with a serpent's tail and an eagle's wings. In Greek myth the Sphinx is usually winged and female. Aeschylus mentions a wingless Sphinx, but Sophocles and Euripides both give it wings. The Sphinx is called the singer because she gave her riddles in verse. The "tribute" was the life of the person who failed to answer the riddle correctly.

69: Creon is both the brother-in-law of Oedipus and a distant patrilineal cousin; see House of Thebes, p. xxviii.

71: The city of Delphi was a main Panhellenic center for the worship of Apollo. Apollo is the archer-god, god of music and prophecy. Presiding over the Temple of Apollo was the priestess, called the Pythia, who, perhaps enraptured by volcanic fumes, delivered oracles. Delphi was also called Pytho. The names *Pytho* and *Pythia* derive from the serpent *(pytho)* that Apollo killed there. Apollo, also called Phoebus, which means "bright" or "pure," was identified with Helios, the god of the sun.

83: Bay, or laurel, leaves were sacred to Apollo.

124: Creon says "robbers" in the plural, but Oedipus says "robber" in the singular. This suggests that Oedipus already suspects, perhaps unconsciously, that he is Laius' murderer.

131: Throughout the play there are ironic references to foot and feet. *Oedipus* means "swollen foot."

151–215: The *parados* is here a liturgical prayer in form and content.

151: Apollo obtained his powers from Zeus, who ultimately, as king of the gods, decides all things. The voice of Zeus is sweet because it is anticipated that the oracle will solve the problem of the plague.

[154]: A reference to Apollo, who was born on the island of Delos, where there was a major sanctuary of Apollo.

[157]: The child of Hope is the voice of the oracle, because Apollo is the hope for Thebes.

159: The Greek does not have "your" but just "sister Artemis." Artemis is the sister of Apollo and in this passage the epithet "sister" means sister of Apollo, not sister of Athena. Technically, however, Athena and Artemis were half-sisters, since Zeus was their father. Since Apollo is associated with medicine and healing, and Artemis with childbirth, these two gods would help against the symptoms of the plague. Athena had the role of general protector of the city.

[174]: The fertility of the land and people was paramount for the survival of any premodern agricultural society.

178: The west is where the sun sets. Hence, it was thought of as the realm of darkness and the dead.

181: The lack of proper burial and burial rites caused a physical and moral pollution on the land.

[187]: Athena is the golden daughter of Zeus.

[190]: Ares is the god of war, the son of Zeus and Hera.

[195]: Amphitrite is the wife of Poseidon, god of the sea. Her chamber is in the Atlantic. Amphitrite's chamber and Thrace are the two opposite ends of the world.

197: The phrase "beyond the Hellespont" is not in the Greek.

203: Apollo here and in line 919 is called *Lukeian.* A frequent epithet of Apollo, its meaning is uncertain. It may derive from a word meaning "light" or perhaps "wolf."

[208]: Lycia is a region in Asia Minor, usually associated with Apollo and Artemis. It has no connection to the epithet *Lukeian.*

[211]: Bacchus is another name for Dionysus, the god of wine.

[212]: A maenad is a female follower of Dionysus, usually depicted wearing a faunskin and carrying a rod known as a *thyrsus.* Maenads followed in the entourage of Dionysus and frequently shouted *"Euoi."*

219: The Greek word for stranger also means "foreigner."

228: A line is missing.

235: Oedipus calls down this punishment on himself. This curse is thus full of irony. On another level, Oedipus already suspects that he has killed Laius. Calling down this curse is a means of proving to himself that he is not the killer.

242: Such a penalty would cut off the polluted individual from all religious rites and from membership in the kinship group. This was a much more severe penalty in premodern times, when people depended on their kinship groups to survive.

255: That is, by Apollo.

267–68: This is the genealogy of Oedipus; see House of Thebes, p. xxviii, and Glossary of Names.

284: Teiresias, the blind seer, first appears in Homer's *Odyssey*. Three different reasons are given in Greek myth for his blindness: for revealing the secrets of the gods, for seeing Athena naked, or for saying to Hera that women enjoy sex nine times more than men (Apollodorus *Bibliotheca* 3.6.7).

301: Zeus and many of the other gods resided on Mount Olympus and hence were called Olympian.

304: The phalanx, the fighting unit of Greek armies in the time of Sophocles, consisted of a number of rows of heavily armed infantry, advancing in unison.

362: At this point in the play the audience knows that Oedipus is the murderer of Laius. Oedipus, the man of knowledge, is the last to know—or at least the last to admit it.

378: The rule of a king was often threatened. Oedipus is not wrong to suspect Creon of trying to take power. Ultimately, Creon does manage to become ruler of Thebes. However, at this point in the story Creon is innocent of plotting against Oedipus.

391: The singer is the Sphinx. She is called dog-haunched because she was the daughter of the Chimaera and Orthos. The Chimaera was part lion, part snake, and part goat. Orthos was a dog of monstrous size.

397: Oedipus has the intelligence to answer the riddle of the Sphinx but not the self-knowledge to know who he is. There is a pun in these lines, since Oedipus calls himself ignorant, and yet his name, *Oede*, sounds like the word *oeda*, "to know."

410: Loxias is another epithet of Apollo. The word may mean "oblique" and refer to Apollo's ambiguous oracles. More likely, it derives from a word that means "light," *luk* or *lux*.

420: Cithaeron is the mountain near Thebes where Oedipus had been exposed as a baby.

442: The Greek reads *tyche*, "fortune."

463: Delphi is situated in rocky mountains, two thousand feet above sea level.

[469]: "Apollo" is not in the Greek.

[471]: Keres, the daughters of Night, are the spirits of death and vengeance. They are sometimes identified with the Furies. Apollo is seen as having sent the plague because of the death of Laius, and his oracle has prophesied that the expiation of bloodguilt is necessary to thwart the plague. Hence, he is accompanied by the avenging Keres.

[474]: Mount Parnassus stands just above Delphi and is used to stand for Delphi itself.

[479]: The mountain bull with crippled foot can be identified with Oedipus, whose name means "swollen foot."

[481]: Delphi was considered the center of the earth; hence, the omphalos, or navel of the earth, could be found there. It was located in the main shrine to Apollo. This omphalos is supposedly the stone that the goddess Rhea substituted for Zeus when his father Cronos was swallowing his children. A Greek omphalos of uncertain date can still be seen today at Delphi.

[491]: Polybus is King of Corinth and the adoptive father of Oedipus.

[506]: The word "Sphinx" is not in the Greek.

514: Oedipus' reaction to Teiresias' accusation is to shift his investigation from the murder of Laius to that of a plot against him by Teiresias and Creon.

534: Oedipus means that it is Creon's intention to murder him.

551–52: These lines are ironic, since it is Oedipus, not Creon, who has harmed a kinsman.

623–24: Because these lines do not make much sense in the context, editors suggest that two or more lines are missing.

644–45: Athenian law recognized an oath by the accused as evidence of innocence.

661: Helios is the god of the sun. It was common to invoke the sun in oaths.

679: "Oedipus" is not in the Greek.

716: The Greek traveler Pausanias in the second century AD visited this spot and described it: "Further along the road you come to the split as they call it; on this road Oedipus murdered his father . . . the memorial of Laius and his servant is on the midmost of three roads, under a mound of uncut stones (*Description of Greece* 10.5.2).

719: Infant exposure is a frequent motif: consider Moses, Romulus and Remus, Sargon, Cyrus, Perseus, and Telephus. Infanticide was practiced in Greece with the exposure of deformed and handicapped children. In this case, the curse was a form of handicap. The Greek audience would have found such exposure of an infant to be normal.

733: Phocis is a pastoral region, east of Delphi.

734: Also spelled *Daulia*. Daulis is a city in the region of Phocis, east of Delphi.

763: This is the same servant whom Creon mentions in line 118. There appears to be a slight inconsistency in the story. The servant came back to Thebes, but if Oedipus had already been king, he would have had to come to Thebes, defeat the Sphinx, and marry Jocasta, all before the servant returned.

774: Corinth, a wealthy city-state northwest of Athens, rivaled Athens and Thebes in power.

775: Dorian denotes one of the three main divisions of the Greek people. Dorians were mostly centered in the Peloponnesus, whose major city was Sparta.

776: He was the first of citizens because he was heir to the throne.

820: These would be the normal punishments for someone who had bloodguilt.

847: The Greek does not contain the word "justice." The Greeks saw fate as weighed in scales, as in the *Iliad* (22.209–213), where Zeus balances scales to determine who will win a fight and who will die. In Greek art Themis, the goddess of justice, is depicted as holding two scales.

[867]: Olympus is the highest mountain in Greece, where Zeus and his fellow gods and goddesses dwell. Olympus here stands for Zeus. The chorus is saying that these laws come from the gods.

[871]: The god referred to is the divine virtue inherent in the laws.

[873]: The Greek reads *hubris*, which we translate as "pride." Here, Sophocles personifies *hubris*, an undesirable trait, which means "excessive pride," "arrogance," "excessive egotism." *Hubris*, especially toward the gods, often caused the gods to become angry and punish the offender. Tyrants were often guilty of *hubris* in their behavior to their people and to the gods. Creon, in *Antigone*, is a prime example of this.

[900]: Abae, in the district of Phocis, was the location of a major oracular shrine of Apollo, while Olympia, in the district of Elis in the Peloponnesus, had a major oracular shrine of Zeus.

923–1070: Aristotle (*Poetics* ch. 11) discusses the dramatic irony of this scene. The Corinthian Messenger comes to bring good news to Oedipus, that with the death of Polybus he will soon become king of Corinth. The effect is just the opposite, since his arrival reveals Oedipus' real identity, bringing destruction.

965: The Greek has "hearth of Pytho," which we have rendered "the shrine of the Pythian seer."

970: Oracles were often fulfilled in an unusual way, especially since they were often given in an ambiguous way. If Polybus had died out of longing for Oedipus, it would have fulfilled the oracle, and without bloodguilt. An example of an ambiguous oracle can be seen in the case of the Lydian ruler Croesus. He was told by the Delphic Oracle that if he crossed the Halys River to fight the Persians, a mighty empire would fall. When he crossed the river, he was defeated. He complained to the Oracle at Delphi, who retorted that Croesus had destroyed a mighty empire, his own (Herodotus, *Histories* 1.91.4).

982: The Greeks saw dreams as omens foretelling the future. Freud saw them as manifestations of the unconscious.

987: We have translated the Greek phrase "great eye" as "cause to rejoice." Since the eye was connected with light, the expression means "light of comfort."

999: "Eyes" repeats one of the main themes of the play, the relationship of sight, knowledge, and blindness.

1024: Childlessness is a frequent motif in Greek myth, such as the case of Aegeus, father of Theseus, and Acrisius, the grandfather of Perseus.

1035: The Greek reads "dreadful cause of shame" and "swaddling clothes."

1036: The Greek reads literally, "From that occurrence you were named as you are."

1037: There is some ambiguity in the Greek. Oedipus seems to say, "Did my father or mother do this [i.e. name me]?" The Corinthian Messenger takes Oedipus to mean, "Did my father or mother do this deed?"

1051: This is the same shepherd that Oedipus sent for in line 860. This coincidence, that the survivor of the attack on Laius is also the man who gave the baby Oedipus to the Corinthian Messenger, is the sort of improbability that Aristotle criticized in *Poetics* ch. 25.

1056–57: At this point Jocasta realizes that Oedipus is her son and the murderer of Laius. She tries to prevent him from inquiring further and from discovering the truth of who he is.

1062–63: Jocasta refers to her pollution from incest, but Oedipus thinks she is distressed by finding out he might not be of high birth. Among the Greek aristocrats, it would have been disgraceful to be born from peasants or servants.

1068: This line reinforces the central theme of the play, Oedipus' search for self-knowledge.

1079: Again, Oedipus, the man of knowledge, refuses to see the solution clearly before him. Since he wants to know, but does not want to know, he is the last to realize who he is.

1080: The Greeks considered Fortune to be particularly fickle. The months are Oedipus' brothers because they represent the passing of time, which has brought him changing fortune.

[1089]: A reference to the Athenian festival, the Pandia, which followed immediately after the Great Dionysia. This festival was conducted at night under the full moon.

[1099]: Nymphs were long-lived, but not deathless, like the gods.

[1100]: Pan, half man and half goat, was the protector of shepherds. He is connected with sex and fertility and often seduces maidens. He is also associated with music, maenads, and Dionysus.

[1104]: The Lord of Cyllene is Hermes, whose mother, Maia, lived in a cave in Mount Cyllene, in the district of northeastern Arcadia. Bacchus (Dionysus) was often associated with mountains and orgiastic rites with maenads. He was the god most associated with the city of Thebes.

1109: Mount Helicon in Boeotia was the home of the Muses. We have chosen to follow the reading of all the extant manuscripts, "Helicon." Many other translations follow a nineteenth-century emended text.

1120: This line reflects the motif of seeing and knowing.

1123: A slave reared in the house would have higher status than a bought slave.

1136: Some editors suggest a line is missing in the Greek text. Since there is disagreement, this possible missing line is not assigned a line number.

1137: Arcturus is the brightest star of the constellation Boötes, and the third brightest star in the sky. It was usually visible with its heliacal rising in mid September. During the hot dry summers, shepherds would pasture flocks in the mountains, where forage was readily available.

1153: Athenian courts required that a slave give testimony only under torture, since it would be presumed that he would lie otherwise. The Shepherd, although sent off to retire, was still a slave.

1162: Oedipus is still pursuing the idea that he was the son of some servant, rather than the obvious, the son of Laius and Jocasta.

1186–96: These lines introduce the theme "count no man happy until he dies," which is taken up as the final words of the chorus at the end of the play.

1207: A reference both to nautical harbors and to Jocasta's womb. The philosopher Empedocles equated harbor and womb in his writings. This echoes lines 420–23, where Cithaeron is called the harbor.

1223ff.: The final scene of a Greek tragedy after the last *stasimon* is called the *exodus* or *exode* (Aristotle *Poetics* ch. 12). Violent action, such as murder and suicide, always takes place off stage, so the device of a messenger is often used to report those actions.

1226: Greek society was based on kinship. Hence, in a Greek city-state of the classical period, all citizens would be kinsmen who belonged to interrelated kinship groups. Oedipus would be a kinsman of members of the chorus.

1227: The Phasis River, in the region the Greeks called Colchis, meets the Black Sea at the eastern shore, and would therefore be at the end of the world. It was to this area that Jason and the Argonauts had sailed. The Ister is the Danube, which extends from Germany until it, too, empties into the Black Sea.

1268: The usual clothing of a Greek woman would be a peplos, which consisted of a large rectangular piece of wool, placed around the body and fastened at both shoulders with a pin or brooch. The brooches, which had to be fairly heavy and large to hold the heavy wool garment, were about six inches long and often in the shape of modern safety pins. Some have been excavated from the fifth century BC that were decorated with the heads of Sphinxes.

1276–79: Oedipus now knows who he is, but cannot bear to know. Hence, he blinds himself in an ultimate act of repression. This mirrors Teiresias' speech in lines 408–28, where he says Oedipus has eyes but cannot see.

1291: Oedipus had earlier put a curse on Laius' murderer. The normal way of dealing with bloodguilt and the pollution resulting from it would have been to exile the polluted party.

1297: We are uncertain how Oedipus' blindness was depicted on stage. One possibility is that he changed to a new mask. Another is that some indication of blindness and gore was put on his existing mask, such as ribbons or red paint.

1300–1302: The Greeks believed that no rational man would harm himself. Hence, self-mutilation must come from the gods.

[1318]: Reminiscent of the goad used by Laius (line 809).

1414: In fact, Oedipus is polluted because of the murder and incest, and everyone would avoid his presence and touch.

1445: By delaying a decision on exile until Creon could consult Apollo, Sophocles created an ambiguous ending. The epic tradition and other tragedies had various endings. Euripides in *Phoenician Women* and Aeschylus in his Oedipus trilogy had Oedipus remain in Thebes to be cared for by his sons.

1447: The obligation for burial in Greek religion fell on the next of kin. Even if Oedipus were not blind, Creon would be under this obligation.

1460–61: Euripides (*Phoenician Women* 63) portrays them still as children at the time of Oedipus' blinding.

1515: Some scholars (e.g., R. D. Dawe) have suggested that everything from this line on might be spurious.

1520: This answer could mean either that Creon agrees to Oedipus' request or that he refuses it. We interpret the answer to mean that Creon agrees to exile only if he consults Apollo and receives an answer to that effect.

1521: The Greek literally says "Lead me from here." Scholars disagree about Oedipus' final exit. There are four possibilities: he can exit to the left, which would mean he was going into exile; he could exit through the double doors into the palace; he can exit to the right, toward the city. The fourth possibility is that he could simply not exit, but stand alone on the stage. We have chosen to have him exit into the palace, since we interpret Creon's answer to Oedipus in line 1520 to indicate that he is firm in his position about consulting the gods before making a decision. Also, in lines 1515–16, Creon tells Oedipus to go into the house, and Oedipus agrees.

1528–30: Some scholars argue that these last lines are spurious, noting that the first two lines are almost identical to Euripides *Phoenician Women* 1757–58 and similar to lines 1687–89, as well as Euripides *Andromache* 100–102. We do know that actors in antiquity regularly interpolated lines into Sophocles' plays, and that may be the case here. However, it was normal for Sophocles to end a play with a short choral speech. If this section is not genuine, another, similar song must have been here. Since Sophocles knew Herodotus and the sentiment of these lines is also reflected in the story of Croesus, as told in Herodotus *Histories* 1.32, this might be another indication that the lines are genuine.

Oedipus at Colonus

In the choruses there is not a one-to-one correlation between the Greek lines and our translation. When there is a note on a line in the chorus and there is a discrepancy or an ambiguity, we bracket the line number [ ] and give the original Greek line. The Greek text has some missing lines, which we have indicated with asterisks. In the traditional numbering of the Greek text, in some cases, several of these missing lines have not been assigned line numbers.

1–8: At the end of *Oedipus the King*, it is implied that Oedipus surrenders the throne in favor of Creon as regent, since his sons, Eteocles and Polyneices, are still too young to rule. Oedipus begged for exile, but Creon insists on consulting the Oracle at Delphi to see what Apollo decides. We can reconstruct from remarks in *Oedipus at Colonus* what happened subsequently. There is no reference to the oracle having been consulted. Apparently, Oedipus remained at Thebes. After some time the people decided to expel Oedipus because he was a defilement. His two sons did not try to prevent his exile. However, his two daughters remained loyal. Antigone went into exile with him and shared his tribulations. Ismene remained in Thebes to watch the events and look after Oedipus' interests.

15: Antigone is seeing the Acropolis of Athens in the distance. The audience of the first production of this play sat in the Theater of Dionysus, the god of wine, on the slopes of the Acropolis and could see the temples on it. The Acropolis, or "high city," was the high hill where the city had originally been settled. In time of war, the population could retreat into it. By Sophocles' time it had become the religious center of the city and housed the temples of Athena and Poseidon: the Parthenon, the Athena Nike temple, and the Erechthium.

40: Earth (Gaia) is the mother goddess who gave birth to the gods. Darkness is one of the first gods.

42–43: The Eumenides (Kindly Ones) were also know as the Erinyes, or Furies. They were spirits of vengeance, the Underworld goddesses who guarded bloodguilt. Aeschylus, in *Eumenides,* describes how the Furies were brought to Athens to be guardians of bloodguilt, but they were subservient to the law courts, especially the Areopagus.

54: Poseidon was the god of the sea and of earthquakes. Athens, like most Greek cities, was intimately connected with the sea. Poseidon was one of Athens' most important gods, worshipped on the Acropolis. He also had a major temple at Cape Sounion, visible to Athenian sailors when they left behind the territory of Athens by sea and when they first returned. Poseidon was also worshipped at Colonus, where he had an altar.

55: The Titans were the gods who ruled in the generation before Zeus; they battled Zeus for supremacy and lost. Prometheus, son of the Titan Iapetus, was the god who gave fire to man, for which he was punished by Zeus.

57–58: The Bronze-mouthed Threshold was called the Threshold of Hades. It was a chasm that was thought to lead to the Underworld (see lines 1590–98). The name suggests that the mouth of the chasm had brazen steps. It may have been called the "mainstay" of Athens because, as the center of religious worship, it would protect the city.

59: Colonus was a hero of the region. He was called "horseman" because here men first learned to use horses, given to them by Poseidon.

69: Theseus, the son of Aegeus, was one of the first kings of Athens. He was said to have united Attica, the region around Athens. He slew the Minotaur, half-man and half-bull, in the Labyrinth of Crete. He also fought against the Amazons and wed an Amazon, Hippolyta. Aegeus gave his name to the Aegean Sea when he threw himself off a cliff into the sea, thinking that Theseus had been killed by the Minotaur.

86: Phoebus is a another name of Apollo, the son of Zeus and Leto. The god of prophecy, music, and medicine, he is often associated with Helios, the sun, and hence bears the name *Phoebus* (shining). In *Oedipus the King* Apollo's oracles foretold that Oedipus would kill his father and marry his mother.

95: Zeus is king of the gods and rules from Mount Olympus. A sky god, he throws the thunderbolt and lightning and moves the clouds.

100–101: The Goddesses are the Eumenides, to whom wine offerings were never made.

107: Athena was the patron goddess of Athens. Pallas is another name for Athena.

127: The chorus here refers to the Furies, but out of dread and awe they do not pronounce the name (see note on lines 42–43).

184: Various scholars have argued that one line for Oedipus, two lines for Antigone, and then one for Oedipus have been lost. These possible lost lines are not assigned line numbers in the standard Greek text.

220–21: Laius was the father of Oedipus, and Labdacus his paternal grandfather. see House of Thebes, p. xxviii.

228: Fate *(Moira)* is man's share in the world, not his predetermined destiny.

265–74: In this passage, as well as lines 521–49 and 962–99, Oedipus defends himself on the grounds that he was a victim of the gods, ignorant of whom he killed and whom he married. In addition, he killed in self-defense.

313: Aetna was in Sicily and was known for its horses. A "Thessalian hat" was a wide-brimmed hat used to shade the sun. The type was developed in Thessaly and became a regular hat of travelers. The horse would not have been seen by the audience, and Ismene enters on foot.

330: There is a deliberate ambiguity here. Antigone and Ismene are both his daughters and his sisters, since they share the same mother.

337–60: Sophocles may have gotten this comparison from Herodotus *(Histories* 2.35). This passage sees a world turned upside down; fathers wander as beggars, the care owed by sons is given by daughters.

354: Cadmus was the founder of Thebes. Hence "Cadmean" is used as another name for Theban.

367: Creon is the brother of Jocasta and brother-in-law of Oedipus. Initially, he served as regent for Oedipus' two sons, who now want the throne for themselves.

375: The younger brother is Eteocles.

378–79: Polyneices married Argeia, the daughter of Adrastus of Argos.

389: "Thebes" is not in the Greek.

405–7: Whoever has possession of the tomb controls the sacrifices and prayers. Offerings at a grave could make the spirit of the dead propitious to the one making them. If the Thebans controlled the tomb, they could use the power of the dead Oedipus to protect them against their enemies. The pollution caused by the bloodguilt over the death of Laius prevented Oedipus from being buried in the territory of Thebes. If his body were buried in Thebes, pollution would result, and the Furies would attack the land again.

413: The Oracle of Apollo at Delphi provides advice and direction for the characters in this play as well as in *Oedipus the King* and *Antigone.*

444–49: Ordinarily it would be the sons who would support and look after the father. Here, Oedipus curses his sons for their disloyalty and contrasts them with his loyal daughters.

457: The Eumenides here are called by another of their names, the Semnai, which means "holy" and "awful." We have translated Semnai as "Awesome."

466–67: The Grove of the Eumenides is sacred. By entering it Oedipus has caused pollution, which must be cured.

481: For the absence of wine, see line 101 and note.

546–48: Oedipus might be innocent of homicide before a court, but nonetheless he committed an act of pollution by any killing, and doubly so because he slew his father, who was related by blood. Spilling of blood would require purification.

562–64: Theseus was born in Troizen to Aethra, daughter of King Pittheus, and an unknown father, Aegeus. When he reached manhood, he found a sword and sandals, left under a rock by Aegeus. With these, he journeyed to find his father. Like Oedipus, along the way he encountered monsters and slew them. Having gone through these trials, he came to Athens and was accepted by his father.

679: The god Dionysus is the son of Semele, the granddaughter of Cadmus, and Zeus. Thus Dionysus is a distant cousin of Oedipus.

[683]: The two goddesses are Demeter, the goddess of grain, and her daughter, Persephone, wife of Hades and the queen of the Underworld.

[687]: Cephisus is a river god who gave his name to a river near Colonus.

692: The Muses were the goddesses of the poetic arts, the daughters of Zeus and Mnemosyne (memory).

693: Aphrodite is the goddess of love. The "golden reins" may refer to her chariot.

694–706: The chorus now praises the olive, one of the three fundamental crops of the Greek world, and particularly Athens. The island of Pelops is the Peloponnesus, in southern Greece. It is a peninsula, not an island. "Dorians" were the branch of Greek tribes that inhabited that area.

[698]: The "self-renewing" olive refers to the olive tree on the Acropolis, sacred to Athena. This olive tree was burned by the Persians when they sacked the Acropolis during the Persian Wars, in the early fifth century. Supposedly, it managed to survive and come back to life. The Athenian audience would have been familiar with this legend.

[705]: The epithet "Morios" means "all-seeing," since Zeus acts as a guardian of the olive.

[706]: As well as being the patron goddess of Athens, Athena is the goddess of the olive.

713: Cronos was the father of Zeus, Poseidon, and Hades, as well as Demeter, Hera, and Hestia.

719: The Nereids are sea nymphs, daughters of the sea god Nereus.

790: Although Oedipus is talking about his sons, Antigone also meets her death and is buried in Thebes.

791–99: Oedipus' intense anger arises because Creon and Thebes have been content to let him wander as a beggar, and only when they need him for their own gain do they try to bring him back.

834: The Greek reads "O city."

864: The goddesses are the Eumenides.

868: Helios is the god of the sun.

870: Creon ultimately suffers the suicide of his son, Haemon, and his wife Eurydice, as portrayed in *Antigone*.

895: Oedipus no longer considers Polyneices and Eteocles to be his children because they did not aid him in his exile.

948: The Areopagus had the responsibility to judge homicide cases and the re-sulting issues of bloodguilt. The Athenian audience would have known that the Are-opagus could well give sanctuary to someone who had committed bloodguilt else-where, as was true of Orestes when he came to Athens for judgment, as depicted in Aeschylus' *Eumenides*.

996: Although Athenian law might take into account self-defense, in all cases bloodguilt would arise. According to Plato (*Laws* 869) there was no defense for killing a parent: "To this one killer, no law will allow the plea of self-defense; no law will permit him to kill his father or mother, who brought him into the world."

1046: Ares is the god of war. The brazen cries of Ares refer to the clash of bronze weapons in war.

[1047–53]: Pythian is another name for Apollo. The "Pythian shore" refers to an Ionic temple of Apollo in Daphne, about six miles from Colonus, near the bay of Eleusis. The "torch-lit shore" refers to Eleusis itself, the center of the Eleusinian Mysteries, a cult dedicated to the worship of Demeter and Persephone, as well as Dionysus, where torch-light processions took place. The "holy goddesses" are Deme-ter and Persephone. The Eumolpidae were the family from which the chief priests were drawn. The golden key alludes to the oath of secrecy taken by all initiates into the cult of the Eleusinian Mysteries. Anyone who revealed the secrets, knowingly or unknowingly, would be put to death.

1060: Oea borders on Mount Aegaleus, near Daphne, in the vicinity of Eleusis.

[1073]: Poseidon is the son of Rhea and Cronos.

1092: The sister of Apollo is Artemis.

1132–36: Although Oedipus earlier argued his innocence (lines 265–74), here he sees himself as polluted. Innocence alone would not resolve pollution; purification by the Eumenides is necessary.

1167: Polyneices, his son, had gone to Argos to raise troops to attack Thebes.

1211–23: Beginning with Homer, the earliest Greek poet, Greeks complained bitterly about the woes of old age. When he wrote these lines, Sophocles was ninety.

1220: The Helper is death.

[1221]: Hades is the god of the Underworld. The name can also refer to the Underworld itself.

1228: "That dark place" is the earth or the Underworld. In Greek myth, man was created out of the earth by Prometheus.

1267: Mercy was a goddess who helped Zeus dispense justice. There was an altar to Mercy in Athens.

1299: Only here and in line 1434 are the Eumenides called Furies (*Erinyes* in Greek), by which name they are avenging spirits. Elsewhere in the play they are called Eumenides.

1302: Adrastus was the king of Argos.

1304: Apis was a mythical king of the Peloponnesus who rid the land of monsters.

1316: Eteoclos should not be confused with Eteocles, the brother of Polyneices.

1319: Because of his arrogance towards the gods, Zeus blasted him with a thun-derbolt when he scaled the walls of Thebes.

1388: The audience would have known that Polyneices and Eteocles would slay one another in the battle for the throne of Thebes.

1390: Tartarus is that portion of the Underworld where the gods cast the most wicked sinners to receive punishment without end.

1410: The audience would know the myth that Antigone was condemned to death for burying Polyneices. Sophocles had told the story almost forty years earlier, in *Antigone*.

1534: The "men sprung from dragons' teeth" are the Thebans. When Cadmus founded Thebes, he populated the land by sowing dragons' teeth, which turned into men. Although Athens had defeated Thebes at various times before Sophocles wrote this play, when the play was finally performed, in 401 BC, it was clear that the prophecy had no efficacy. Thebes had joined with Sparta to beat Athens in the Peloponnesian Wars, which ended in 404.

1547–48: Hermes was the messenger god. He had the task of leading the souls of the departed to the Underworld. The "goddess of the Underworld" is Persephone.

1556: The "unseen goddess" is Persephone.

1559: Aidoneus is another name for Hades.

1565: Styx is the river that surrounds Hades, and must be crossed to enter.

1568: The Eumenides (Furies).

1569: Cerberus is the three-headed dog who guards the entrance to Hades. *Cerberus* is not present in the Greek text in this line or in line 1575; the Greek simply has "beast."

1576: This is probably Death.

1591: See notes to lines 57–58.

1594: Theseus and Peirithous, the king of Thessaly, went to the Underworld to kidnap Persephone. They were caught by Hades. Later the hero Heracles rescued Theseus.

1595: We do not know the significance of "Thorician rock." There is an Attic town and deme (area subdivision) known as Thoricus, called after a hero of the same name, known for its silver mining, but it is unknown what that would have to do with Colonus.

1600: These are the normal preparations for burial of the dead in Greek culture.

1625: It is uncertain who this god is. It could be Hermes, who escorts the dead to Hades, or possibly Persephone (see lines 1547–49).

1718–19: Two lines of Ismene's speech are missing.

1734: Some scholars suggest that a line is missing here, with Ismene speaking in the first half of the line and Antigone in the second half. This missing line is not assigned a line number.

Antigone

In the choruses there is not a one-to-one correlation between the Greek lines and our translation. When there is a note on a line in the chorus and there is a discrepancy or an ambiguity, we bracket the line number [ ] and give the original Greek line.

1: Antigone and Ismene are full sisters. Both are the incestuous children of Oedipus and Jocasta. Oedipus is the son of Jocasta and Laius. Their mother, Jocasta, committed suicide on learning of the incest. Oedipus blinded himself and subsequently died as an exile in Colonus, in Athens. See *Oedipus at Colonus*.

3: Zeus is king of the gods and rules from Mount Olympus.

8: Creon assumed the throne on the death of Eteocles and Polyneices. As king, he would also be commander-in-chief of the military.

10: "Friends" especially includes Polyneices, her brother. The enemies are the defeated Argive invaders. Although Polyneices led the Argives against the city, she considers him a Theban whose body should receive proper reverence.

15: Argive refers to Argos, a city-state in the Peloponnesus where Polyneices raised the troops to invade Thebes.

23: Burial was of utmost importance in Greek religion and culture, and both her brothers had to be buried according to law and custom, regardless of any crime or guilt; see Introduction, pp. liii–liv.

24: The issue of god's law versus man's law is the major theme of this play.

32: The next of kin had the primary obligation to bury the dead.

36: Public stoning was rare in the Greek world. However, it is often threatened in Greek tragedy, so it probably represents the idea of a method of execution in preclassical times.

38: It is a religious and moral requirement of Greek society to bury one's kin. Antigone is saying that aristocrats bury their kin and that failure to do so would make even an aristocrat base and ignoble.

49–52: These lines suggest that Oedipus died in Thebes, unhonored. In *Oedipus at Colonus* he dies at Athens, honored by the gods. *Antigone* was written ten to fifteen years before *Oedipus the King* and almost forty years before *Oedipus at Colonus*. Sophocles was not consistent in his treatment of the myth.

54: Jocasta hanged herself *(Oedipus the King* 1263–64).

65: The gods of the Underworld demand that the dead be buried; they inflict punishment on those who neglect this duty.

72: Antigone is willing to disobey man's law to uphold the law of the gods that demand burial for one's kin, but she acknowledges that she is bound by man's law and may be executed.

100: It is customary to invoke the sun in a hymn of victory and celebration.

[104]: Dirce and Ismenus are Thebes' two rivers.

[106]: "Argive warrior" stands for the entire Argive army.

[119]: Thebes had seven gates. The attacking Argive army had seven main leaders, including Polyneices, each of whom attacked one gate.

[123]: Hephaestus is the god of the forge and the volcano and is thus also associated with fire.

[126]: The "Dragon's seed" are the men of Thebes who were born from dragon's teeth sown by Cadmus, the founder of Thebes; see Introduction, p. xxvi.

[128]: This boastful attacker was named Capaneus, who swore that even Zeus himself would not keep him from sacking Thebes (Aeschylus *Seven against Thebes* 424). Because of his *hubris*, Zeus struck him dead with a lightning bolt when he tried to breach the walls of Thebes (Euripides *Phoenician Women* 1172–86).

[136]: Bacchus is another name of Dionysus, the god of wine, son of Semele, the daughter of Cadmus, founder of Thebes, and Zeus.

[139]: The "War god" is Ares.

[143]: To commemorate a victory, it was customary to dedicate captured weapons to a god.

[144]: The "accursed sons" are Eteocles and Polyneices.

148: Victory was a goddess, often associated with Athena, called Athena Nike. Her temple was on the Acropolis at Athens.

[163]: The "great storm" is a ship metaphor. The ship of state is a frequent motif in Greek literature.

171: Eteocles and Polyneices are polluted because they shed kindred blood.

197: It was customary to pour libations of water, wine, honey, or olive oil on the dead.

206: This line is reminiscent of the beginning of Homer's *Iliad* (1.1–6), where the wrath of Achilles causes the bodies of the Achaeans to be a feast for the dogs and a banquet for the birds. This fate is the ultimate in dishonor for a Greek.

256: The curse is the pollution that comes from an unburied body.

307: Hades refers either to the ruler of the Underworld or to the Underworld itself. Here it stands for death.

332–41: This "Ode to Man" glorifies the nature of man and his intelligence, but emphasizes that for a city to prosper, man must honor the gods.

[365–75]: The one "Following the laws of man" may refer to Creon, who obeys man's laws, contrasted with Antigone, who disobeys them. Creon links the justice of the gods with the laws of man, but fails to obey gods' laws. The relationship of man's laws to gods' laws is the crux of Sophocles' drama and the struggle between Creon and Antigone: man must live under laws, but those laws must respect the gods.

396: Burial rites included washing the body, libations and rites, and burial.

450–70: In this speech Antigone puts forth the eternal struggle between the laws of the gods—what Aristotle calls natural law—and the laws of man and raises the issue of whether the state can override the laws of the gods. Aristotle comments on this passage in *Rhetoric* 1.13.1: "For there really is, as every one to some extent divines, a natural justice and injustice that is binding on all men, even on those who have no association or covenant with each other. It is this that Sophocles' *Antigone* clearly means when she says that the burial of Polyneices was a just act in spite of the prohibitions: she means that it was just by nature."

459: While Antigone argues that Creon's edict violates the laws of the gods, nonetheless she admits that she is subject to the law. Likewise, Gandhi, in the twentieth century, preached civil disobedience and passive resistance to laws but admitted that everyone was subject to the law.

487: Each household held an altar to Zeus, a symbol of the solidarity of the house. Creon has power over Antigone not only because he is king but also because he is her closest male kinsman. She doubly defies him as ruler of the state and the male kinsman who holds power over her.

508: Cadmus was the founder of Thebes. Hence, Thebans are also called "Cadmeans" in the play.

519: The crux of Antigone's argument is that the gods of the Underworld demand burial of kinsmen, no matter what the circumstances.

525: Men held all the power in Greek society. It would have been shameful and would have destroyed a man's honor if he were ruled by a woman.

530: The chorus is commenting on Ismene's expression, which would not show under the mask. Alternately, she might have changed masks.

557: "Others" are the gods of the Underworld and Polyneices.

568: The most common marriage among Greeks was to a patrilineal first cousin. Haemon and Antigone are matrilineal first cousins. By having his son marry a child of Oedipus and grandchild of Laius, Creon would solidify the legitimacy of his rule and his son's. If Haemon and Antigone had a son, that child would be the grandson of Oedipus, and there would be no question of the continuity of the ancient descent lines of the family of Laius.

572: The manuscripts ascribe this line to Ismene, but some scholars give the line to Antigone.

[594]: Labdacus was the paternal grandfather of Oedipus. For the curse on the house, see Introduction, p. xxvi.

601: The "bloody dust" is the dust that Antigone put over her brother's corpse. It is bloody because the burial of Polyneices is causing Antigone's death.

603: The Furies were goddesses of the Underworld who pursued and punished those polluted by bloodguilt, which could be incurred by such things as killing or leaving a body unburied.

606: Sleep is the brother of Death.

609: Mount Olympus is the home of Zeus and the gods.

626: Creon had a daughter, Megara, who wedded Heracles, and a son Megareus (sometimes called Menoeceus), who sacrificed his life to save Thebes in the recent attack by Polyneices.

675–77: Creon's defense of the rule of law, necessary for any state to survive.

717: The ship of state image again.

737: Athens was a democracy when this play was written. Tyranny had existed in many Greek cities, as well as Athens, in the sixth century, but by the fifth century it had been eliminated from most of Greece.

776: Creon's original edict (lines 35–36) called for stoning. However, since Antigone is a blood relative, actively taking her life might cause bloodguilt and a pollution. By walling her up in a cave and giving her some food, she would eventually die of starvation, causing no bloodguilt. For the same reason, weak or deformed infants were exposed in the wild rather than simply killed by the parent. Sophocles used this vehicle to show how much Creon distorted gods' laws, since he buries the living and leaves the dead unburied.

780: Some commentators make Creon exit here. However, it is more likely that he remains on stage, since he has sent his attendants to bring Antigone in at lines 760–61, and he addresses her in line 883.

781: Eros is the adolescent attendant of Aphrodite, the goddess of love. He brings intense physical desire, often at the behest of Aphrodite. He is often depicted as a small boy with wings.

805: "Death" is not in the Greek.

814: Acheron, "River of Pain," is a river of the Underworld. Here it is synonymous with Hades.

823: "Phrygian guest" refers to Niobe, the daughter of Tantalus who came from Phrygia in Asia Minor to Thebes. She married Amphion, the king of Thebes. Niobe boasted that she had more children than Leto, the mother of Apollo and Artemis, and that her children were more beautiful. In revenge, Apollo and Artemis killed her children. Niobe wept inconsolably, until she was turned into stone on Mount Sipylus, in Phrygia. Tantalus was a son of Zeus, who stole food from the gods. Because he had eaten the food, he became immortal. Hence, he was punished for all time in the Underworld, where he is always hungry and thirsty. He stands in water up to his chin and when he tries to drink, the water recedes. When he tries to eat from overhanging trees, the wind blows the fruit away.

835: Niobe was a granddaughter of Zeus.

854–57: The chorus seems to be saying that Antigone is paying the penalty for disobeying Creon's decree. Another interpretation is that she is dying because she relied on the justice of the unwritten laws. All this is part of the curse of the house of Laius, as her subsequent speech reveals.

870: This probably refers to the wedding of Polyneices to Argeia, daughter of Adrastus. That wedding allowed Polyneices to gain Argive allies with which to attack Thebes.

889: See comments on line 776.

894: Persephassa is another name for Persephone, queen of the Dead and wife of Hades

899: "Eteocles" is not in the Greek.

905–20: (904–20 in the Greek text) Some editors have rejected these lines as spurious, because they do not see Antigone's sentiment as consistent with her position on burial. Goethe said that he wished Sophocles had never written these lines. However, the sentiment finds some parallels with Herodotus 3.119. Aristotle (*Rhetoric* 3.16.1417, 132–33) discusses this passage as belonging to Sophocles, so it must be genuine. The problem of the editors who reject these lines is that they do not fully understand the nature of the obligation to bury kin. The obligation goes to the nearest patrilineal relative and could possibly extend to matrilineal relatives to the degree of second cousin. The obligation to bury a husband would fall on the husband's blood relatives, not on his wife. Ordinarily, the duty would not fall on a woman at all. If there were no close male blood relatives available, the obligation would fall on the kinship group, the phratry, and then on the tribe. Part of Antigone's argument is that she can always get another husband or child, but not another brother. Since a wife passed into the kinship group of her children, she would not be a real parent of that child. Hence, her kinship obligation of burial would be to her parents and brothers, not her husband and children. In this speech Antigone is reasserting her obligation to bury her brother as paramount. Aeschylus sums up the position of the woman in this kinship structure in a speech by Apollo in the *Eumenides* (657–61): "I will explain this, too, and see how correctly I will speak. The mother of what is called her child is not the parent, but the nurse of the newly-sown embryo. The one who mounts is the parent, whereas she, as a stranger for a stranger, preserves the young plant, if the god does not harm it."

944: Danaë was the daughter of Acrisius. He had received an oracle that Danaë's son would kill him. To avoid the oracle, he imprisoned Danaë in a cavern. However, Zeus, in a shower of gold, came into the cave and impregnated her. She gave birth to Perseus, who later fulfilled the oracle. The parallel is not exact, since Danaë was imprisoned, not to kill her, but to prevent her from becoming pregnant. An additional result of Antigone's entombment would be that she would die childless.

956: The son of Dryas was Lycurgus, king of the Edonians in southern Thrace. He resisted Dionysus bringing his worship into Thrace. As a punishment he was either blinded or imprisoned in a cave in Mount Pangaion and then pulled apart by horses. In another version he was driven mad and killed by his son.

958: See line 135 and note to that line.

[963]: "Bacchic" is not in the Greek. These female followers of Bacchus are also known as maenads.

[965]: The Muses are the goddesses of the arts, including music and poetry.

[968–69]: The Bosphorus is a strait between the Asian and European parts of Turkey. It leads from the Mediterranean to the Black Sea. Salmydessus is in Thrace, on the west coast of the Black Sea.

[970–76]: Phineus married Cleopatra, daughter of Boreas (the North Wind). She bore him two children. Phineus imprisoned Cleopatra and then married Eidothea, who blinded her two stepsons, using a shuttle, a stick used in weaving. To punish Phineus, Zeus offered him blindness or death, and Phineus chose blindness.

[982]: The Erechthids were the ancient royalty of Athens. Cleopatra was a granddaughter of Erechtheus. Her mother, Oreithyia, the daughter of Erechtheus, had been taken as a wife by Boreas.

987: The Fates—Clotho, Atropos, and Lachesis—spun out the fate of gods and men. Even the gods could not overturn the decision of the Fates.

1007: Hephaestus here stands for fire.

1011: In a Greek sacrifice fat would be wrapped around the thighbones and burned for the gods, who would enjoy the smoke that resulted. Here, the fat melts but does not catch fire. Consequently, there is no smoke to please the god, nor any fire from which to make prophecies.

1018: An unburied body causes a miasma, a pollution on the land; see 1043–44.

1038: Sardis was the major city of Lydia in Asia Minor. In the sixth century, its fabulously wealthy king, Croesus, was one of the earliest to mint coins. At the beginning of his reign (ca. 561 BC) he minted coins of electrum, a mixture of gold and silver.

1064–72: Teiresias summarizes a major theme of the play in these lines: Creon has confused the natural order of the universe by leaving the dead unburied and burying the living.

1080–83: These lines refer to part of the myth that Sophocles had not previously mentioned in the play but that would have been known to all the Athenian audiences. Creon refused burial to the Argive dead who attacked Thebes. Theseus, king of Athens, intervened and forced Creon to bury the Argive dead. The further continuation of the myth relates that the children of the Seven against Thebes, the *Epigonoi,* return and later capture Thebes.

1104: The Harms are personifications of the forces of vengeance.

1115: Cadmus' daughter is Semele, the mother of Dionysus (Bacchus).

1119: The Greeks had settled in southern Italy and Sicily in great numbers since the eighth century BC. With their colonies they brought the vine and the worship of Dionysus to Italy. In the fifth century southern Italy became known for its wine production and cults of Dionysus.

1120: Demeter was the goddess of grain, whose central worship in Athens was at Eleusis, about six miles from the center of the city, through a cult known as the Eleusinian Mysteries. Dionysus was also worshipped as part of this cult.

1122: Bacchus was associated with Delphi and healing, as well as with Thebes.

1125: Cadmus founded Thebes by sowing a dragon's teeth; see note to line 126.

1128: The Corycian Cave is in the mountains near Delphi. It was inhabited by nymphs.

1130: Castalia is a stream flowing above Delphi, which comes out in cataracts near Mount Parnassus.

1132: Nysa is often called the home of Dionysus. The name is applied to more than a dozen places, and it is uncertain which place is referred to. Here it may refer to Nysa in Euboea, which was famous for wine.

1140: This refers to Semele, who died of fright when Zeus appeared to her in his true form, accompanied by peals of thunder and flashes of lightning.

1143: Parnassus is the mountain near Delphi.

1144: If Nysa is in Euboea, "strait" refers to the waters between the island of Euboea and the mainland.

1151: Thyiads is another name for Bacchants, or maenads, who accompany Dionysus.

1154: Iacchus is another name for Dionysus.

1155: Amphion was a king of Thebes who built the walls of the city.

1175: The Greek is ambiguous. It could mean "by his own hand" or "by a kinsman's hand." The chorus takes it to mean "by a kinsman's hand," but the true meaning is made clear by the Messenger's answer.

1185: Pallas is another name for Athena.

1191: Her son, Megareus, had already died in the fighting around Thebes just before the play began.

1199: The goddess of the crossroads is Hecate, an Underworld goddess to whom offerings were made at crossroads.

1222: The Greek says "a piece of linen." We have translated "veil" to capture the image of a bridal chamber of death.

1301: This line is corrupt in the Greek, and line 1302 is missing, but the context must be close to what we have.

Glossary of Terms from Greek Tragedy

agon: A musical or gymnastic contest.

anagnoresis: A recognition of events.

anapests: In poetry, a metrical foot consisting of two short syllables and one long syllable.

antistrophe: A choral song sung by the chorus as it moved or danced from right to left. *See also* strophe; epode.

auletes: A person who played an *aulos,* a double flute, usually in the orchestra.

aulos: The double flute, which accompanied lyric passages.

chorus: A group of singers that usually represented some group, such as the elders of a city. Sophocles used a chorus of fifteen singers. They often comment on the action and sometimes can be seen as the voice of the poet.

coryphaeus: The chorus leader.

deuteragonist: The second actor. The first actor was the protagonist; the third, the tritagonist.

dithyramb: A choral song, sung by a chorus of fifty to honor Dionysus. There were dithyramb competitions at the Great Dionysia.

dochmiac: A meter used to indicate intense emotion, consisting of one short syllable, followed by two long syllables and a short syllable.

eccyclema: A wheeled device used to display an interior scene in ancient tragedy.

episode: A part of the drama between choral songs.

epode: A choral song sometime added to the strophe and antistrophe in a different meter, and recited by the chorus standing still.

exode (exodus): A scene not followed by choral song.

iambic trimeter: The basic meter of Greek tragedy, consisting of three feet, containing a short syllable followed by a long syllable.

kommos: A lyric song between actors and chorus.

machina: A crane to lower and raise an actor playing a god onto the stage.

meter: The rhythm of Greek tragedy, consisting of metrical units called feet, made up of short and long syllables.

monody: A lyric song, sung by one actor, usually a lament.

orchestra: The round semicircle of the theater in front of the stage. The word means "place for dancing."

parode: The first song of the chorus.

parodos (parodoi): A side ramp for entrances and exits.

peripeteia: A reversal of fortune.

prologue: The first part of the tragedy, before the chorus enters.

protagonist: The first, or main, actor.

satyr play: The fourth play presented by an author. It was short and satiric.

skene: A stage building at the rear of the orchestra. It had a door from which actors could enter and exit, and it could represent a location, such as a palace.

stasimon: A song sung after the chorus has entered the orchestra.

stichomythia: A rapid dialogue between two actors, often consisting of half lines or single lines.

strophe: A choral song sung by the chorus as it moved or danced from left to right. *See also* antistrophe; epode.

tetralogy: A set of four plays, consisting of three plays, called a trilogy, and a fourth play, the satyr play, presented at the Great Dionysia.

theatron: The seats in which the audience sat to view the tragedy.

theologeion: A raised device from where the god might speak.

trochaic trimeter: A meter, accompanied by the *aulos,* consisting of a long syllable followed by a short syllable.

Glossary of Names

Abae: Site of a major oracular shrine to Apollo in the district of Phocis.

Acheron: "River of Pain," a river of the Underworld, mentioned in *Antigone* 814.

Acropolis: The "high city." The center of Greek cities was usually placed on a high hill. The Acropolis, which was the center of Athens, contained temples to Athena and Poseidon.

Adrastus: King of Argos and father-in-law of Polyneices.

Aegeus: King of Athens, father of Theseus.

Aetna: A region in Sicily containing a volcano of that name.

Agenor: King of Phoenicia and father of Europa and Cadmus, who founded Thebes.

Aidoneus: Another name of Hades.

Amphiaraus: One of the Seven against Thebes.

Amphion: A king of Thebes who built the city walls.

Amphitrite: Wife of Poseidon, god of the sea.

Antigone: Daughter of Oedipus and Jocasta and sister of Ismene, Eteocles, and Polyneices.

Aphrodite: Goddess of love and sex.

Apis: A mythical king of the Peloponnesus.

Apollo (Phoebus Apollo): God of archery and light, associated with prophecy, especially through his oracle at Delphi.

Arcturus: The brightest star of the constellation Boötes, which had its helical rising in September.

Areopagus: The court where murder was tried.

Ares: God of war, son of Zeus and Hera, and father of Harmonia by Aphrodite.

Argeia: Daughter of Adrastus, king of Argos, and wife of Polyneices.

Argos: A city-state in the Peloponnesus.

Artemis: Virgin goddess, sister of Apollo, goddess of the hunt and of animals.

Atalanta: Mother of Parthenopaeus, one of the Seven against Thebes. Noted for her swiftness, she defeated her suitors in the footraces.

Athena (Pallas Athena): A virgin goddess, associated with the olive; the patron goddess of Athens.

Athens: A city of the region of Attica, home of Sophocles.

Attica: The territory of which Athens was the center.

Bacchants (maenads): Female followers of Dionysus.

Bacchus (Dionysus): *See* Dionysus.

Boreas: The North Wind.

Bosphorus: The strait from the Mediterranean to the Black Sea.

Cadmus: Founder of Thebes.

Capaneus: One of the Seven against Thebes.

Castalian spring: A stream above Mount Parnassus, near Delphi, sacred to Apollo and the Muses, where the Pythia was accustomed to bathe. Pilgrims to the shrine of Apollo purified themselves by washing in it. The spring later became associated with the poetic inspiration of the Muses.

Cephisus: A river in Attica, as well as the name of the river god.

Cerberus: The three-headed dog who guards the entrance to Hades.

Choregos: A wealthy citizen who bore the cost of a play production, especially the Chorus for a play, as a form of taxation.

Chrysippus: Son of Pelops, raped by Laius.

Cithaeron: The mountain near Thebes where Oedipus was exposed as a baby.

Colonus: Suburb of Athens; also the name of the hero after whom Colonus was named.

Corinth: A wealthy city-state, northwest of Athens, that rivaled Athens and Thebes in power.

Corycian cave: A cave in the mountains near Delphi.

Creon: Brother of Jocasta, king of Thebes in *Antigone*.

Cronos: Father of Zeus, Poseidon, Hades, Demeter, Hera, and Hestia; son of Uranus and Gaia.

Cyllene: A mountain in Arcadia, associated with the god Hermes.

Danaë: Daughter of Acrisius and mother of Perseus by Zeus.

Darkness: One of the first gods.

Daulis (Daulia): A city in the region of Phocis.

Death (Thanatos): God of Death and brother of Sleep.

Delphi: The city in central Greece where the Temple of Apollo and Apollo's priestess, the Pythia, was located.

Demeter: Goddess of grain, sister of Zeus, and mother of Persephone by Zeus.

Dionysus (Bacchus): God of wine, born in Thebes from the union of Semele and Zeus.

Dirce: A river of Thebes.

Dorian: One of the three main divisions of the Greek people.

Dryas: Father of Lycurgus, king of the Edonians in Thrace.

Earth (Gaia): Mother Earth, the progenitor of all life.

Eleusinian Mysteries: The cult of the worship of Demeter and Dionysus.

Eleusis: Site of the cult of the worship of Demeter and Persephone.

Erechthids: Ancient royalty of Athens.

Erinyes: *See* Furies.

Eros: Adolescent attendant of Aphrodite who brings carnal lust.

Eteocles: Son of Oedipus and Jocasta, brother of Polyneices and Antigone.

Eteoclos: From Argos, one of the Seven against Thebes.

Euboea: Island east of the Greek mainland.

Eumenides: *See* Furies.

Eumolpus: Founder of the family that provided priests to the cult of the Eleusinian Mysteries.

Eurydice: Wife of Creon, mother of Haemon and Megareus.

Fates: Three goddesses, Clotho, Atropos, and Lachesis, who determine the destiny of gods and men.

Furies (Erinyes or Eumenides): Goddesses of the Underworld who avenge bloodguilt.

Great Dionysia: A state religious festival in Athens, taking place in late March or early April, in honor of the god Dionysus, at which Greek tragedies were performed.

Hades: God of the Underworld and the Dead; brother of Zeus and husband of Persephone. "Hades" can also refer to the place, the Underworld itself.

Haemon: Son of Creon and Eurydice.

Hecate: Goddess of the crossroads.

Helicon: A mountain in Boeotia, the home of the Muses.

Helios: God of the sun.

Hephaestus: God of the forge and the volcano, son of Hera.

Hera: Queen of the gods; wife and sister of Zeus.

Heracles: Son of Zeus and Alcmene, a hero who rids the world of monsters.

Hermes: Messenger god, who leads the departed to the Underworld.

Hippomedon: Son of Talaos, one of the Seven against Thebes.

Iacchus: Another name for Dionysus.

Ismeme: Daughter of Oedipus and Jocasta and

sister of Antigone, Polyneices, and Eteocles.

Ismenus: A river of Thebes.

Jocasta: Wife and mother of Oedipus, sister of Creon, and widow of Laius.

Justice: An earth goddess, daughter of Zeus and Themis (law).

Keres: Spirits of death and vengeance. Daughters of Night, they are sometimes identified with the Furies.

Labdacus: Father of Laius and grandfather of Oedipus.

Laius: Father of Oedipus and husband of Jocasta; king of Thebes.

Leto: Mother of Apollo and Artemis by Zeus.

Loxias: An epithet of Apollo, perhaps meaning "light."

Lycia: A region in Asia Minor associated with Apollo and Artemis.

Lycurgus: King of the Edonians in southern Thrace.

Maenads: See Bacchants.

Megareus (Menoeceus): Elder son of Creon and Eurydice, killed in attack on Thebes.

Menoeceus: Father of Creon; also son of Creon.

Merope: Wife of Polybus and adoptive mother of Oedipus.

Muses: Daughters of Zeus and Mnemosyne; goddesses of arts, including music and poetry.

Nereids: Sea nymphs, daughters of Nereus.

Nike: Goddess of victory; also Athena Nike, Athena who brings victory.

Niobe: Daughter of Tantalus, wife of King Amphion of Thebes. Her children were killed by Apollo and Artemis.

Nysa: A home of Dionysus.

Oea: A mountain near Eleusis.

Oedipus: King of Thebes, son of Laius and Jocasta, husband of Jocasta, and father of Antigone, Ismene, Polyneices, and Eteocles.

Olympia: Site of a major oracular shrine of Zeus in Elis, in the Peloponnesus.

Olympus: The highest mountain in Greece, where Zeus and his fellow gods and goddesses dwelt.

Paean: Hymn of supplication or praise to a god.

Painted Stoa (Stoa Poikile): A building in the agora, or marketplace, of Athens, which contained paintings of Athenian military victories and various spoils.

Pallas: See Athena.

Pan: Half man and half goat, he protects shepherds. He is connected with sex and fertility, often seducing maidens, and is also associated with music, maenads, and Dionysus.

Parnassus: A mountain above Delphi, home to Apollo and the Muses.

Parthenopaeus: Son of Atalanta, one of the Seven against Thebes.

Pelops: Son of Tantalus and grandfather of Agamemnon and Menelaus.

Perithous: A companion of Theseus in his descent to the Underworld in a plot to kidnap Persephone.

Persephassa: Another name for Persephone.

Persephone: Daughter of Demeter and Zeus, wife of Hades, and queen of the Underworld.

Phasis: A river in Colchis, on the Black Sea.

Phineus: King of Thrace, whose wife blinded his two sons from a former marriage.

Phocis: A pastoral region east of Delphi.

Phoebus: Another name for Apollo, meaning "shining" or "bright."

Phrygia: A region in Asia Minor.

Polybus: King of Corinth and adoptive father of Oedipus.

Polydorus: Son of Cadmus and Harmonia; second king of Thebes.

Polyneices: Son of Oedipus and Jocasta and brother of Antigone, Ismene, and Eteocles.

Poseidon: Brother of Zeus and Hades and son of Cronos and Rhea; god of the sea and earthquakes.

Prometheus: Son of Iapetus, one of the Titans. He stole fire from Zeus to give it to man. His name means "Foresight."

Pythia: The priestess of Apollo at Delphi who delivers his oracles.

Pytho: Another name for Delphi. It also is the name of the Pytho or Python, the serpent killed by Apollo at Delphi.

Salmydessus: A Thracian city on the southern shore of the Black Sea.

Sardis: Capital of Lydia in Asia Minor, where early coinage was developed.

Semele: Mother of Dionysus by Zeus and daughter of Cadmus, founder of Thebes.

Seven against Thebes: The seven who attacked Thebes with an Argive army, trying to put Polyneices on the throne. Besides Polyneices, they were Amphiaraus; Tydeus, son of Oeneus; Eteoclos of Argos; Hippomedon, son of Talaos; Capaneus; and Parthenopaeus, son of Atalanta.

Sipylus: A mountain in the region of Phrygia in Asia Minor. Niobe is turned into this mountain by her weeping.

Sleep (Hypnos): God of Sleep, child of Night, and brother of Death.

Sphinx: A mythical creature having the body of a lion and a female human head, often with a serpent's tail and an eagle's wings.

Styx: A river that runs through the Underworld.

Tantalus: Son of Zeus and father of Niobe. He was punished for eternity by the gods for stealing some of their food.

Tartarus: The deepest part of the Underworld, where sinners are punished.

Teiresias: Blind Theban prophet.

Thebes: City of Boeotia in Greece.

Theseus: Son of Aegeus and king of Athens. He killed the Minotaur in the labyrinth in Crete.

Thrace: An area of northeastern Greece, bordering on the Black Sea.

Thyiads: Another name for Bacchants.

Titans: The gods who ruled before Zeus and battled him for supremacy.

Tydeus: Son of Oeneus, one of the Seven against Thebes.

Underworld (Hades): Realm of the dead, ruled by Hades and his wife, Persephone.

Victory: *See* Nike.

Zeus: King of the gods, who rules from Mount Olympus. The son of Cronos and Rhea, he married his sister, Hera.

Suggestions for Further Reading

General Books

Eastering, P. E., ed. *The Cambridge Companion to Greek Tragedy*. Cambridge: Cambridge University Press, 1997.

Foley, Helene P. *Female Acts in Greek Tragedy*. Princeton: Princeton University Press, 2001.

Goldhill, Simon. *Reading Greek Tragedy*. Cambridge: Cambridge University Press, 1986.

Goldhill, Simon. "The Great Dionysia and Civic Ideology." In Winkler and Zeitlin, *Nothing to Do with Dionysis*, 97–129.

Goldhill, Simon. *Love, Sex, and Tragedy: How the Ancients Shaped Our Lives*. Chicago: University of Chicago Press, 2005.

Heath, Malcolm. *The Poetics of Greek Tragedy*. Stanford: Stanford University Press, 1987.

Hegel, Wilhelm. *Hegel on Tragedy*. Edited by Anne and Henry Paolucci. Westport, CT: Greenwood Press, 1978.

Irigaray, Luce. "The Bodily Encounter with the Mother." In *The Irigaray Reader: Luce Irigaray*, edited by Margaret Whitford, 34–36. Oxford: Blackwell, 1991.

Jones, John. *On Aristotle and Greek Tragedy*. Cambridge: Cambridge University Press, 1986.

Kitto, H. D. F. *Form and Meaning in Drama*. London: Methuen, 1956.

Kraus, Chris, Simon Goldhill, Helene P. Foley, and Jaś Elsner. *Visualizing the Tragic: Drama, Myth, and Ritual in Greek Art and Literature*. Oxford: Oxford University Press, 2007.

Lecoq, Jacques. *The Moving Body*. Translated by David Bradby. New York: Routledge, 2001.

Lefkowitz, Mary. *Lives of the Greek Poets*. London: Duckworth, 1981.

Lesky, Albin. *Greek Tragic Poetry*. New Haven, CT: Yale University Press, 1983.

Lloyd-Jones, Hugh. *The Justice of Zeus*. Berkeley: University of California Press, 1971.

Nietzsche, Friedrich. *The Birth of Tragedy*. Translated by Walter. Kaufmann. New York: Random House, 1967.

Parker, Robert. *Miasma: Pollution and Purification in Greek Religion*. Oxford: Oxford University Press, 1983.

Parker, Robert. *Athenian Religion: A History*. Oxford: Oxford University Press, 1996.

Pedrick, Victoria, and Steven M. Oberhelman, eds. *The Soul of Tragedy*. Chicago: University of Chicago Press, 2005.

Rehm, Rush. *Greek Tragic Theatre*. London: Routledge, 1992.

Reinhardt, Karl. *Sophocles*. Translated by H. Harvey and D. Harvey. Oxford: Blackwell, 1979.

Segal, Charles. *Interpreting Greek Tragedy: Myth, Poetry, Text*. Ithaca, NY: Cornell University Press, 1986.

Sourvinou-Inwood, Christine. *Tragedy and Athenian Religion*. Oxford: Lexington Books, 2003.

Taplin, Oliver. *Greek Tragedy in Action*. London: Routledge, 1978.

Vernant, Jean-Pierre, and Pierre Vidal-Naquet. *Myth and Tragedy in Ancient Greece*. Translated by Janet Lloyd. New York: Zone Books, 1988.

Vickers, Brian. *Towards Greek Tragedy*. London: Longman. 1973.

Wiles, David. *Tragedy in Athens*. Cambridge: Cambridge University Press, 1997.

Wiles, David. *Greek Theatre Performance: An Introduction*. Cambridge: Cambridge University Press, 2000.

Winkler, John J., and Froma I. Zeitlin, eds. *Nothing to Do with Dionysus?* Princeton: Princeton University Press, 1990.

Zeitlin, Froma I. *Playing the Other: Gender and Society in Classical Greek Literature*. Chicago: University of Chicago Press, 1995.

Zimmermann, Bernhard. *Greek Tragedy: An Introduction*. Translated by Thomas Marier. Baltimore: Johns Hopkins University Press, 1991.

Origins of Greek Drama

Burkert, Walter. "Greek Tragedy and Sacrificial Ritual." *Greek, Roman, and Byzantine Studies* 7 (1966): 87–121.

Carpenter, Thomas H., and Christopher Faraone, eds. *Masks of Dionysus*. Ithaca, NY: Cornell University Press, 1993.

Cole, Susan Guettel. "Procession and Celebration at the Dionysia." In *Theater and Society in the Classical World*, edited by Ruth Scodel, 25–38. Ann Arbor: University of Michigan Press, 1993.

Green, Richard, and Eric Handley. *Images of the Greek Theater*. Austin: University of Texas Press, 1995.

Pickard-Cambridge, Arthur W. *Dithyramb, Tragedy, and Comedy*. Edited by T. B. L. Webster. 2nd ed. Oxford: Oxford University Press, 1962.

Pickard-Cambridge, Arthur W., John Gould, and D. M. Lewis. *The Dramatic Festivals of Athens*. 2nd ed. Oxford: Oxford University Press, 1989.

Sophocles

Blundell, Mary W. *Helping Friends and Harming Enemies: A Study in Sophocles and Greek Ethics*. Cambridge: Cambridge University Press, 1989.

Bowra, Maurice. *Sophoclean Tragedy*. Oxford: Oxford University Press, 1944.

Burton, Reginald W. B. *The Chorus in Sophocles' Tragedies*. Oxford: Oxford University Press, 1980.

Edmunds, Lowell. *Oedipus: The Ancient Legend and Its Later Analogues*. Baltimore: Johns Hopkins University Press, 1985.

Ehrenberg, Victor. *Sophocles and Pericles*, Oxford: Blackwell, 1954.

Gardiner, Cynthia P. *The Sophoclean Chorus*. Iowa City: University of Iowa Press, 1987.

Gellie, George H. *Sophocles: A Reading*. Melbourne: Melbourne University Press, 1972.

Griffith, Mark. "The Subject of Desire in Sophocles' Antigone." In *The Soul of Tragedy*, edited by Victoria Pedrick and Steven M. Oberhelman, 91–135. Chicago: University of Chicago Press, 2005.

Hogan, James C. *A Commentary on the Plays of Sophocles*. Carbondale: Southern Illinois University Press, 1991.

Jameson, M. H. "Sophocles and the Four Hundred." *Historia* 20 (1971): 541–68.

Knox, Bernard. *The Heroic Temper: Studies in Sophoclean Tragedy*. Berkeley: University of California Press, 1964.

Scodel, Ruth. *Sophocles*. Boston: Twayne Publishers, 1984.

Seale, David. *Vision and Stagecraft in Sophocles*. Chicago: University of Chicago Press, 1982.

Segal, Charles. *Tragedy and Civilization: An Interpretation of Sophocles*. Cambridge, MA: Harvard University Press, 1981.

Segal, Charles. *Sophocles' Tragic World*. Cambridge, MA: Harvard University Press, 1995.

Whitman, Cedric. *Sophocles*. Cambridge, MA: Harvard University Press, 1951.

Winnington-Ingram, R. P. *Sophocles: An Interpretation*. Cambridge: Cambridge University Press, 1980.

Zeitlin, Froma I. "Thebes, Theater of Self, and Society in Athenian Drama." In *Greek Tragedy and Political Theory*, edited by J. Peter Euben, 101–41. Berkeley: University of California Press, 1986.

Oedipus the King

Ahl, Frederick. *Sophocles' Oedipus: Evidence and Self-Contradiction*. Ithaca, NY: Cornell University Press, 1991.

Bloom, Harold, ed. *Modern Critical Interpretations: "Oedipus Rex."* New York: Chelsea House, 1988.

Burkert, Walter. *Oedipus, Oracles, and Meaning: From Sophocles to Umberto Eco*. Toronto: University College, 1991.

Cameron, Alister. *The Identity of Oedipus the King*. New York: New York University Press, 1968.

Edmunds, Lowell. *Oedipus: The Ancient Legend and Its Later Analogues*. Baltimore: Johns Hopkins University Press, 1985.

Edmunds, Lowell, and A. Dundes, eds. *Oedipus: A Folklore Casebook*. New York: Garland Publishers, 1983.

Freud, Sigmund. *The Interpretation of Dreams*. 3rd ed. Translated by James Strachey. New York: Basic Books, 1955.

Griffith, R. Drew. *The Theatre of Apollo: Divine Justice and Sophocles' "Oedipus the King."* Montreal: McGill University Press, 1996.

Knox, Bernard. *Oedipus at Thebes: Sophocles' Tragic Hero and His Time*. New Haven, CT: Yale University Press, 1957.

Littman, Robert J. "The Plague of Athens: Current Analytic Techniques." *Amphora* 5, no. 1 (2006): 10–12.

Mullahy, Patrick. *Oedipus: Myth and Complex—A Review of Psychoanalytic Theory*. New York: Grove Press, 1992.

O'Brien, Michael J., ed. *Twentieth-Century Interpretations of "Oedipus Rex."* Englewood Cliffs, NJ: Prentice-Hall, 1968.

Pucci, Pietro. *Oedipus and the Fabrication of the Father: Oedipus Tyrannus in Modern Criticism and Philosophy*. Baltimore: Johns Hopkins University Press, 1992.

Segal, Charles. *Sophocles' "Oedipus Tyrannus": Tragic Heroism and the Limits of Knowledge*. 2nd ed. Oxford: Oxford University Press, 2001.

Oedipus at Colonus

Edmunds, Lowell. *Theatrical Space and Historical Place in Sophocles' "Oedipus at Colonus."* Lanham, MD: Rowman and Littlefield, 1996.

Travis, Robert. *Allegory and the Tragic Chorus in Sophocles' "Oedipus at Colonus."* Lanham, MD: Rowman and Littlefield, 1999.

Vidal-Naquet, Pierre. "Oedipus between Two Cities: An Essay on *Oedipus at Colonus.*" In *Myth and Tragedy in Ancient Greece,* edited by Jean-Pierre Vernant and Pierre Vidal-Naquet. Translated by Janet Lloyd, 329–59. New York: Zone Books, 1990.

Wilson, Joseph P. *The Hero and the City: An Interpretation of Sophocles' "Oedipus at Colonus."* Ann Arbor: University of Michigan Press, 1997.

Antigone

Butler, Judith P. *Antigone's Claim: Kinship between Life and Death.* New York: Columbia University Press, 2000.

Gibbons, Reginald, and Charles Segal. *Antigone.* Oxford: Oxford University Press, 2003.

Goheen, Robert. *The Imagery of Sophocles' "Antigone": A Study of Poetic Language and Structure.* Princeton: Princeton University Press, 1987.

Johnson, Patricia J. "Woman's Third Face: A Psycho-Social Reconsideration of Sophocles' *Antigone," Arethusa* 30 (1997): 369–98.

Lewis, R. G. "An Alternative Date for Sophocles' *Antigone." Greek, Roman, and Byzantine Studies* 29 (1988): 35–50.

Loraux, Nicole. *Tragic Ways of Killing a Woman.* Translated by Anthony Forster. Cambridge MA: Harvard University Press, 1987.

Nussbaum, Martha C. *The Fragility of Goodness: Luck and Ethics in Greek Tragedy and Philosophy.* 2nd ed. Cambridge: Cambridge Universtiy Press, 2001.

Steiner, George. *Antigones: How the Antigone Legend Has Endured in Western Literature, Art, and Thought.* Oxford: Oxford University Press, 1984.

Theodorakis, Mikis. "On Antigone" *http://www.mikis-theodorakis.net/mikant-e.html*

Tyrrell, Wm. Blake, and Larry J. Bennett. *Recapturing Sophocles' "Antigone."* Lanham, MD: Rowman and Littlefield, 1998.

Greek Texts and Commentaries on Greek Texts

Dawe, R. D. *Studies in the Text of Sophocles.* Leiden: Brill, 1978.

Dawe, R. D. *Sophocles' "Oedipus Rex."* Cambridge: Cambridge University Press, 1982.

Griffith, Mark. *Sophocles' "Antigone."* Cambridge: Cambridge University Press, 1999.

Jebb, Richard C. *Sophocles: The Plays and Fragments, with Critical Notes, Commentary, and Translation.* Part 1, *The Oedipus Tyrannus,* 2nd ed., 1887; Part 2, *The Oedipus Coloneus,* 1889; Part 3, *The Antigone,* 3rd ed., 1900. Reprint, Bristol: Bristol Classical Press, 2003–4.

Kamerbeek, J.C. *The Plays of Sophocles: The Antigone.* Leiden: Brill, 1978.

Kamerbeek, J. C. *The Plays of Sophocles: Oedipus Coloneus.* Leiden: Brill, 1984.

Kamerbeek, J. C. *The Plays of Sophocles: The Oedipus Tyrannus.* Leiden: Brill, 1997.

Lloyd-Jones, H., and N. G. Wilson, eds. *Sophoclis Fabulae.* Oxford: Oxford University Press, 1990.

Aeschylus

Goldhill, Simon. *Language, Sexuality, Narrative: The Oresteia.* Cambridge: Cambridge University Press, 1984.

Lebeck, Anne. *The Oresteia: A Study of Language and Structure.* Cambridge, MA: Harvard University Press, 1971.

Rosenmeyer, Thomas G. *The Art of Aeschylus.* Berkeley: University of California Press, 1982.

Taplin, Oliver. *The Stagecraft of Aeschylus.* Oxford: Oxford University Press, 1977.

Winnington-Ingram, R. P. *Studies in Aeschylus.* Cambridge: Cambridge University Press, 1983.

Euripides

Burian, Peter, ed. *Directions in Euripidean Criticism.* Durham, NC: Duke University Press, 1985.

Foley, Helene. *Ritual Irony: Poetry and Sacrifice in Euripides*: Ithaca, NY: Cornell University Press, 1985.

Halleran, Michael. *Stagecraft in Euripides.* London: Croom Helm, 1985.

Michelini, Ann Norris. *Euripides and the Tragic Tradition.* Madison: University of Wisconsin Press, 1987.

Segal, Charles. *Dionysiac Poetics and Euripides' Bacchae.* Princeton: Princeton University Press, 1982.

Segal, Erich, ed. *Euripides: A Collection of Critical Essays.* Englewood Cliffs, NJ: Prentice-Hall, 1968.

Vellacott, Philip. *Ironic Drama: A Study of Euripides.* Cambridge: Cambridge University Press, 1975.